FEMINIZING THE UNIONS

Feminizing the Unions

Challenging the culture of masculinity

SHEILA CUNNISON
JANE STAGEMAN

Avebury

Aldershot · Brookfield USA · Hong Kong · Singapore · Sydney

© Sheila Cunnison and Jane Stageman 1995

All rights reserved. No part of this publication may be reproduced, stored in a retrieval system, or transmitted in any form or by any means, electronic, mechanical, photocopying, recording or otherwise without the prior permission of the publisher.

Published by
Avebury
Ashgate Publishing Limited
Gower House
Croft Road
Aldershot
Hants GU11 3HR
England

Ashgate Publishing Company
Old Post Road
Brookfield
Vermont 05036
USA

First published in hardback 1993 by Avebury. ISBN 1 85628 635 5

British Library Cataloguing in Publication Data
Cunnison, Sheila
    Feminizing the Unions: Challenging
    the Culture of Masculinity
    I. Title II. Stageman, Jane
    331.88082

ISBN 1-85972-100-1

Printed and bound in Great Britain by
Hartnolls Limited, Bodmin, Cornwall

Contents

Acknowledgements		vii
Introduction		
i	Themes and perspectives	3
ii	Historical overview	20

Part One: Branch and Workplace
1	Male control at the branch - Case 1	35
2	Collective bargaining at the grass-roots - Case 2	47
3	Changing consciousness and political ideology - Case 3	56
4	Male power, industrial action and changing consciousness - Cases 4 and 5	68
5	Taking over from the men - Cases 6 and 7	81
6	Grass-roots women speak to the movement	101
7	A pattern for the future? - Case 8	119

Part Two: Union Policies towards Women
8	Attraction, encouragement and education	131
9	Union democracy and empowerment	149

Part Three: Negotiation, Masculinity and Femininity
10	The trade union as a negotiator - Case 9	171
11	Challenging masculinity through negotiation	183
12	A culture of femininity: attending to diversity	201
13	Feminizing negotiation	219

Conclusion
14	Feminization: new priorities, old themes	237

Appendices
1   1979 TUC Charter for Equality for Women within Trade Unions   247
2   Summary of cases and action referred to in text   249
3   Numbers and proportion of women in the movement in 1985 and 1990   252
4   Postal questionnaires 1990   254
5   Abbreviations   255

References   259

Index   275

Acknowledgements

We would like to acknowledge all those who have assisted us in producing this book. In relation to Part 1 we thank COHSE, NUPE and NUT for granting access to branch and association meetings; individual trade unionists from COHSE, GMBU, NUPE, NUT and TGWU for discussions and interviews; and the school meals workers for their help and friendliness (Chapter 2). In relation to Parts 2 and 3 we thank all who helped but especially the women trade unionists who gave their time to complete questionnaires, or to discuss problems and to reply to queries. Friends and colleagues made useful contributions. We thank especially Anne Hunt for reading and commenting on our first draft, Tanya Baker, Kathleen Lennon, Frances O'Grady, Dilys Page, Joy Marshall and Lena Milosevic for various helpful suggestions, and the last two, additionally, for childcare support. We are grateful to the University of Humberside for use of library, office and other facilities. The book was jointly planned and we take joint responsibility for the present text. Financial support for the research reported in Chapters 1 - 6 was provided by the SSRC.

INTRODUCTION

1 Themes and perspectives

Key themes

This book explores three interrelated themes crucial for understanding and changing the position of women in the trade union movement. The first is the struggle of women to get their voices heard and their concerns addressed. This is analysed in context of the culture of masculinity, which constitutes the second theme. It examines ways in which masculine culture pervades the union movement and supports structures of male power and dominance, suppressing women's voices and subordinating their concerns. It draws attention to the challenges women make to the culture of masculinity and their attempts to operate through their own culture of femininity, a femininity redefined and reclaimed from stereotypical definitions of men and the media. This culture of femininity is the third theme. Trade union culture is seen as currently in process of change and enrichment through its gradual incorporation of feminine cultural values and practices. Our title, 'Feminizing the Unions', refers to this process of change.

The book is written with students of women's and gender studies courses in mind. It has an explicit sociological perspective and is grounded in empirical and observational research. The first part uses original research material about women at the grass-roots of the movement to draw out arguments about the processes and mechanisms of male control and to identify processes which underlie women's challenge to that control. The second and third parts look more widely at policies to empower women and increase their participation within the movement.

The book has a clear relevance for feminist inquiry and debate. It raises questions about male power in the union movement and women's challenges to it; and about the relation between gender, democracy and union representation. Its focus on women at the grass-roots points up the relation between male power and sex-related occupational segregation. It confirms the crucial importance of the difference between women's and men's lives, especially in respect of responsibility for domestic and caring work and the organization of time. It draws attention to dilemmas confronting feminists, including coping with the differences between women arising from race, class, sexuality and disability. It suggests that the differences between the shape of women's and men's lives can empower rather than disempower women, so that their energies and distinctive voice become accessible to the trade union movement, bringing to it new resources and strengths.

Our approach is analytical rather than prescriptive, but our commitment to feminism and our sympathy with the trade union movement (cf. Redclift and Sinclair, 1991) make it difficult to avoid prescription altogether. Where we have been prescriptive we have tried to state clearly and explicitly the evidence and arguments on which our views are based.

Sociological perspectives

The major forces which shape industrial society are those of capitalism and gender. These provide the context within which we analyse women's struggles, using the sociological notions of social structure, culture and values.

Gender and patriarchy

Gender refers to social rather than biological differences between women and men. Throughout we work on the assumption that the main behavioural differences between women and men are socially constructed, elaborated on basic biological differences. We select two characteristics of gender of particular relevance to our analysis of women and trade unions. The first is its 'systemic' nature (Cockburn, 1991:6). It pervades all areas of social life and is strategically involved in structural relations of male dominance and female subordination. This power structure is underpinned by a cultural system which privileges men, valuing men's work more highly than women's, associating men with power and authority, objectifying women and associating them with domestic and sexual rather than productive roles. This systemic structural and cultural domination by men can be described by the term patriarchy.

The domination and subordination which characterises patriarchy is not between the powerful and the powerless, but rather between the more and the less powerful. Women within western industrial patriarchy do have resources of power with which to resist and to challenge men. This process of challenge is the underlying theme of the book.

An important characteristic of gender is its role in structuring the work which is performed in society. This work is of two kinds, reproductive and productive. Reproductive work is about the physical reproduction of the next generation and the unpaid tasks of daily servicing which reproduce the current and future labour force. Productive work is the production of goods and services for exchange in the market. The unpaid work of reproduction is mainly performed by women and takes up a great deal of their time, considerably more at some stages of their life cycle than others.

It can be argued that most women have three fairly distinct working lives, structured by the system of reproduction (Cunnison, 1987). During the first life, from leaving school until the birth of children, women's concerns revolve largely around romantic and domestic relationships. During the second life, until children reach their mid-teens, women tend to be preoccupied with servicing and caring for the family. Women reach their third working life when the pressure of caring for children is lifted (though it may be replaced by caring for elderly parents). In the first life paid employment is perceived as secondary in importance to establishing domestic relations, often as a temporary prelude to home and children (Pollert, 1981; Westwood, 1984). In consequence, interest in unionism tends to be low. In the second, preoccupations with domestic responsibilities limit most women to part-time work, and they have little time or energy for trade unionism. In the third, relationships at work may become more important to them. They have more time to think about their situation though, by then, they are often trapped in low-status jobs. Time and energy no longer present practical barriers to trade union activity, and more women show interest.

Men's role in productive work is larger than women's and a much more significant part of their lives, but in reproductive work their role is marginal. Two important consequences flow from this. First, women's responsibility for domestic work handicaps them in the labour market, forming the basis of systematic occupational segregation by sex, whereby they are assigned to low-paid, low-status and often part-time jobs. Second, the different involvement of women and men in reproductive and productive work leads them to develop different social identities. Women may be thought of as having a 'double identity' derived from significant participation in both reproductive and productive work; in contrast, men's identity tends to be more one-dimensional, heavily invested in productive relations. Attached to these identities are different sets of cultural values, relating to femininity and masculinity - what it means to be a woman or a man. Men are the dominant voice in society and male self-definitions of masculinity accord fairly closely with society-wide definitions. But for women, whose voice is muted or suppressed (Ardener, 1975), self-definitions of femininity differ in content and emphasis from the male-controlled societal definitions.

Capitalism and wage labour

To understand the position of women in trade unions we must next consider how the capitalist system of production orders people's lives. Like gender, it is highly influential and pervasive. Furthermore, it is intimately bound up with the system of patriarchy in the structuring of occupational segregation and of women's domestic labour. We comment further on the connection between patriarchy and capitalism later.

The trade union movement itself is a direct response to the way in which the capitalist system operates but its particular shape and character is influenced by the fact that it exists in a gender-ordered society. The capitalist system divides people according to whether or not they own or control significant blocks of capital, whether they are employed as managers or as workers, whether they work in manufacturing, service or extractive industries, whether they are in lightly or heavily capitalised industries, whether they are employed or unemployed, and so on.

The basic divide, however, is between the masses of weekly and monthly paid workers who make up the bulk of the industrial workforce, and the employers and top managers who control the various industries. The structure of capitalist accounting where wages constitute a cost - sometimes the major cost - of production, and the operation of the market, result in a constant pressure by employers to limit the wage bill. Workers have created a trade union movement to fight for their interests in what is a ceaseless struggle to redress inequalities of power and material reward between them and their employers. Employers continually attempt to prevent wages rising. In periods of recession they often attempt to reduce the wage bill by cutting hours or jobs. Additionally the pursuit of profit entails continuous technical change which redefines the position of workers, both in relation to one another and to capital. Technical change downgrades the skill of some jobs and renders others obsolete. Although new jobs are created, a small proportion only are skilled; the general tendency is towards deskilling (Braverman, 1974).

The divide between weekly and monthly paid workers and top managers and employers marks a great disparity in power and resources. An individual worker's need for employment and for wages is far more pressing than an employer's need for that particular worker; employers can find alternative workers or alternative ways of getting goods produced far more easily than workers can find alternative employment. In the face of these inherently more powerful and concentrated interests, the trade unions act to defend workers' interests, their wage levels, their right to jobs and their need for benefits.

Alongside their defensive role trade unions, from their inception, have developed broader aims with a more positive, cutting edge, directed towards establishing a fairer, more equal society. Trade unions are constantly called on to exercise their defensive role; the nature of capitalist relations makes this inevitable. Attempts to move to a differently ordered and fairer society are less evident.

Ethnic identity, diversity and oppression

Relationships of oppression and subordination are central defining features of both patriarchy and capitalism. However, there are other systematic forms of social oppression in western society, related to perceived social, physical and mental differences between people and the identities associated with them. They are mainly connected with skin colour, physical and mental disability, age and sexual orientation. Though endemic, such forms of oppression are not so significant structurally as gender.

The differences and the identities associated with them are constructed and maintained by a complex interplay between self-defining factors and factors impinging from outside. Most significant in employment is discrimination relating to ethnic and cultural difference, widely known as racism. Racism is used by employers to divide workers who are then more easily controlled and more efficiently exploited. A circular process comes into being: exploitation serves to strengthen ethnic and cultural identity and divisions between groups which are then open to further exploitation. This situation is compounded by discrimination, coming from workers of the ethnic and cultural majority.

The most insidious and widespread form of racial discrimination is based on skin colour. This has led to a stratified workforce where black people are largely relegated to low-paid low-status jobs, to shift-working and unsocial hours, and where they suffer higher than average levels of unemployment. Discrimination against immigrant and refugee workers is also increasing. Racism has been publicly acknowledged and condemned.

Attempts have been made to control it through legislation (Race Relations Act 1976), the Commission for Racial Equality, and equal opportunity policies.

Discrimination by employers on account of sexual orientation is less common, perhaps because sexual orientation is more often kept private. Capitalist employers, however, benefit through privileging heterosexuality with its association between women's financial dependence and their cheap labour. Discrimination against disabled people arises in other ways. They may have different and additional needs (in the form of technological and other equipment) which appear to employers as costs. By not employing disabled people employers avoid such costs.

Differences in the social construction of gender roles means that although women and men may be discriminated against on the same basis, for example skin colour, the form and content of that discrimination differs for women and men. Thus in an ethnically stratified workforce where black people are clustered on the lower grades, it is black women rather than black men who invariably come out at the very bottom. Each group which has a distinctive place in the labour market has distinctive needs and interests which arise from it. Within trade unions such groups have, like women, begun to assert their right to a distinctive voice.

Acknowledging the existence of different needs among different groups of women does not mean abandoning either the notion of women as a meaningful social category or the idea of a culture of femininity. The overarching presence of patriarchy means that, in spite of difference, nearly all women live their lives under the shared constraints of caring and domestic responsibilities and of systematic subordination to men within the labour market. It is these common constraints that construct women as a meaningful social category and which lay the basis for a common culture of femininity, but it must be recognised that the category and the culture of femininity both embody important elements of diversity.

Feminist perspectives

Patriarchy and capitalism

Feminism's focus on patriarchal relations has stimulated a theoretical debate on the relationship between capitalism and patriarchy. The main contention is whether patriarchy and capitalism can be considered as independent systems and, if not, what is the nature of their interdependency.

Walby notes that patriarchal relations are persistent through time and place, but always exist in articulation with other social systems such as capitalism (Walby, 1986:50). Some writers argue that in the case of capitalism, the relationships are so intertwined that the two must be regarded as forming a single social system (Eisenstein, 1979; McDonough and Harrison, 1978; see also *Sociology*, 1989). Walby however sees the two as analytically independent and proposes a 'dualist' analysis, a synthesis of Marxist and radical-feminist theory (Hartmann, 1981; Walby, 1986). She acknowledges that there are problems to such an approach but suggests they are not insuperable.

Another point of disagreement is the importance to be attached to structural factors as opposed to cultural practices. Walby gives pre-eminence to structural factors (Walby, 1990). Our view differs. We consider that cultural practices, specifically the culture of masculinity, play a key part in maintaining patriarchal relations within trade unionism and we present evidence in support of this view.

On a more substantive level, there are different opinions as to whether women's position in the labour market is determined by their position in the family - the conventional opinion - or vice versa. Walby holds the unconventional opinion. Our view differs: it seems to us that women's domestic lives, their family position and aspirations have an existence and importance which, although closely linked to labour market relations, is partially independent of them.

Patriarchy and power

Recent studies about the nature and distribution of male power (Cockburn, 1991; Connell, 1987) have raised several issues of relevance to our enquiry. The first is the terms under which men hold power, in particular the complicity of women in accepting men's power. Second is the complexity and variability of the distribution of power. Within public life although most power is held by men, many of them hold very little; and while most women hold little or no power, a small number do become powerful. A third issue is that power need not be used to dominate but can be used, as 'capacity', to enable and empower (Cockburn, 1991:241; Haraway, 1988).

Sameness and difference

One of the longest debates within feminism is about sameness and difference. Are the differences between women and men due to their different biology? And if so, are they wholly biologically determined, 'essential' differences? Or can women be considered basically the same as men, and different only because of their social conditioning? Or are differences partly or largely social constructions, elaborated on the basis of biological difference? This debate is not to be confused with that about differences among women, which we refer to later, using the term diversity (Barrett, 1987).

Divisions in feminism in the 1930s were closely related to the debate about sameness and difference. The main division then was between 'equal rights' feminism - concerned with equal pay and other issues of paid employment, and 'welfare feminism' - concerned with the problems of working class women in the community (Banks, 1981). With the second wave of feminism the debate sharpened. In the late seventies there was a split between socialist feminists who held gender to be primarily socially constructed and radical feminists who included elements of both biological determinism and social construction. These two strands had different priorities in relation to trade unionism. Socialist feminists sought to put women on an equal labour-market footing with men and supported abortion rights, maternity and paternity leave, childcare provision and communal care. Radical feminists saw male-female relations as the source of women's subordination. Their trade union agenda reached out to women in the community, prioritizing issues such as male violence, motherhood and women's and children's health.

Although we consider social construction to be more influential, we admit that some differences may be determined biologically. Until women and men have equal opportunities to develop, the range and influence of such differences cannot be known. However, regardless of whether society or biology lies at their root, the fact of difference remains. Women and men, as currently constituted, differ not only in their access to power but also in their social identities, lifestyle and values, which constitute what we have termed the different cultures of femininity and masculinity.

Invisibility and inaudibility

The second wave of the feminist movement drew attention to the social invisibility and inaudibility of women, the fact that their contributions to social life were consistently ignored (Olsen, 1980; Oakley, 1974; Spender, 1982). Anthropologists, sociologists and others drew attention to the way in which women's voices were often muted or silenced, and to the exclusion of women from various arenas of public debate (Ardener, 1975; Cunnison, 1983b; Pateman, 1975).

The trade union movement is par excellence a man's world where women, often in spite of efforts to the contrary, are little seen and seldom heard. Our book is part of the general feminist endeavour towards making the activities of women in the movement more visible, of acknowledging their past and present contributions and looking to their future role. We bring the experiences of women members into sharp relief, looking at their hopes and aspirations and their struggles to gain greater access to the movement. We question male stereotypes of passive and acquiescent women (cf. Purcell, 1979). We present evidence of trade union women who have confronted and challenged their subordination. We look mainly at women in public service employment, a large and predominantly female sector of the labour force, undervalued both by the society they serve and the unions which represent them.

Diversity of voice

Second wave feminism began with an emphasis on sisterhood and on the worldwide existence of women's subordination to men. Fairly early, however, this was challenged by working class women who saw the movement as dominated by white middle class women. The movement's basic unit of organization was the consciousness raising group, used initially to express the commonality of women's oppression. Later it served to express the identity and oppressions of diverse groups, black and disabled women and lesbians (Bryan et al., 1985; Griffin, 1982; Morris, 1991). The notion of a uniform sisterhood was replaced by that of an alliance between diverse groups of women with different identities but common elements of oppression (Anthias and Yuval-Davis, 1983; Amos and Parmar, 1984; Barrett and McIntosh, 1985). Both the notion of women's social invisibility and that of diversity of voice raise questions about the current status of democracy within the union movement.

The emergence of different voices within feminism was part of a wider social movement in which oppressed groups asserted their identity. Group identities were based both on old forms of belonging - different national, ethnic or cultural groups, and on new - people with disabilities, lesbians and gays, old and young people. A common theme was to affirm positive aspects of group identity and to confront discrimination by an asserting pride (Morris, 1991). The terminology used in referring to oppressed groups is a sensitive issue and one in which opinions are both changing and divided (see Note at end of this section; see also TUC, 1991c: Appendix 2).

Feminism and equal opportunities

The 1975 Sex Discrimination and 1976 Race Relations Acts opened new possibilities for the pursuit of equal opportunities by women and other oppressed groups. Support was given by the Equal Opportunities Commission (EOC), National Council for Civil Liberties (NCCL now Liberty), by some trade unions and newly-founded law centres. Equal opportunity policies were introduced in employment, education, housing, sport and leisure. Gender and race were most frequently addressed, disability and sexuality less so. Similar legislation was passed and equal opportunity movements emerged in North America, Europe and Australasia.

Insights into women's work

Feminists interested in women and work have developed conceptual tools and analyses which have clarified the position of women in the labour market. Some men have also contributed to these analyses. Foremost was the conceptualization of women's reproductive labour and its relation to that of the total economy of societies, industrialized and non-industrialized (Coulson et al., 1975; Edholm et al., 1977; Gardiner, 1975; James, 1976; Seccombe, 1974). Sociologists also drew attention to social conventions which defined care for the sick and old as the responsibility of women and examined how this limited their participation in the labour market (Finch and Groves, 1980). They have also considered the connection between women's reproductive role, employment patterns and low trade union activity (Martin and Roberts, 1984). They have pointed to the relation between women's domestic responsibilities and their trade union involvement.

In the late seventies and early eighties, feminists rediscovered the family wage. This concept emerged as an aspect of male trade unionists' struggle in the nineteenth century; Rathbone challenged it in the 1930s in connection with the family endowment movement, and the challenge was repeated in the seventies with Land's attacks on the 'myth of the male breadwinner' (Land, 1975:82). Humphries, however, drew attention to its positive role in maintaining the working-class family as a bulwark against the social fragmentation wrought by capitalism (Humphries, 1977). In the eighties feminists finally placed it firmly at the centre of the debate about women's pay (Barrett and McIntosh, 1982).

Perhaps the most significant insight was the introduction of gender into definitions of work and skill. Feminists drew attention to the time, effort and skill involved in housework and caring. They pointed out that, though unpaid, these activities were of crucial economic importance (Gardiner, 1975; Oakley, 1974). Saying that housework was not 'proper work' was revealed as yet another way of making women's work invisible.

In conventional usage skill refers to abilities (technical, mental or organizational) attaching to jobs or to people. Ability is one element entering into traditional definitions of skill; far more important has been power, the power to define a job as skilled regardless of the abilities required and on this basis to argue for higher pay. Feminists argued that the difference in skill attributed to women's and men's work is largely socially constructed in this way. Under the old journeyman/apprenticeship system, skill was a matter partly of seniority - of being gradually allowed to perform increasingly complex tasks. Partly it was a matter of greater ability gained through years of experience. But since the factory system became established, claims to skill have been won by powerful groups - invariably men - through negotiation between employers and male-dominated trade unions (Phillips and Taylor, 1980; Walby, 1986). Women's claims have not been presented by the unions and as a consequence the jobs they typically perform are regarded as lacking in skill.

Feminists have also explored the way certain jobs are constructed around stereotypical female aptitudes, for example jobs involving sexual and emotional work (Cunnison, 1986; Davies and Rosser, 1986; Filby, 1991; Pringle, 1988; Wouters, 1989), or around the times in which women are 'free' to participate in the labour market (Allen and Wolkowitz, 1987; Beechey and Perkins, 1987). Cockburn has analysed the factors behind the mystique connecting technology and machinery to the male sex and linked them with the exclusionary practices of male trade unionists (Cockburn, 1981, 1983, 1985).

Recognition that skill is socially constructed through the exercise of men's power provides the basis for challenging systems of job grading which consistently maintain men's privilege. This gives a secure base from which to argue for radical change. Union women's demands include: a re-evaluation of grading hierarchies; a recognition of the importance of 'tacit' skills learned by women in the course of care and service work in the home; and an attempt to eliminate gendered job segregation.

Trade union culture and masculinity

The influence of masculinity on trade union culture runs as a central theme throughout this book. There appear to be certain very firmly entrenched core features to masculinity. According to Kimmel (1987:26-8) its main characteristic is the urge to dominate, to exert power over women - and over other men. There are three other main strands. It is associated with anti-femininity, with a repudiation of stereotypically feminine or 'sissy' behaviour such as the free expression of emotion. It is strongly associated with paid work and it is directed to the achievement of status and independence (Tolson, 1977). Finally, it places a positive value on mental and physical toughness, competition, aggression and, in certain circumstances, violence.

This culture presents problems for women trade unionists, barriers to their participation and hence to their representation in the trade union movement. Trade union activity at the grass-roots is organized around a model of a male worker whose identity is largely located in paid work. Historically the dominant image has been the man in the cloth cap - miner, docker or shipyard worker - engaged in hard physical full-time labour, or the skilled craftsman. His pattern of life consists of stints of paid work which alternate with periods of leisure in which he is more or less free to do as he chooses. He is usually seen as the provider of a family, a breadwinner entitled to a family wage. This is a far cry from the model woman worker whose identity is bound up with unpaid family service, who is not thought of as a serious worker, and for whom domestic work often replaces leisure.

In the hierarchy of the union bureaucracy the image of the paid officer is a hardworking, hard-nosed, thrusting, aggressive and competitive man, willing to work very long and irregular hours, to frequent pubs and clubs, as the need arises. At the top of the movement are the trade union 'barons', leaders of the biggest unions, men concerned with issues of power and position and usually tied to punishing work schedules which take priority over day-to-day family concerns. It is a culture which does not formally exclude women but which makes very few concessions to the existence of any different set of values and patterns of behaviour. It is a culture where few women feel at ease and where most find difficulty in expressing their views.

This depiction of masculinity within the union movement is oversimplified, perhaps a caricature, but there is an essential truth behind it: at each level of union organization, women find values and behaviour that do not fit with their experience. This is a complaint which surfaces repeatedly in studies of women unionists (Cameron, 1989; CLCLC, 1985/6; Cockburn, 1981, 1985, 1991; Cunnison, 1983a, 1986; LRD, 1991; Rees, 1990; Roundtable, 1988; Stageman, 1980; USDAW, 1990).

Masculinity and femininity are complementary gender identities defined in relation to one another. There is not one simple model for the masculine or feminine gender identity but variations according to social class, ethnic group, age and geographical area, and over time. It is more correct to speak of masculinities and femininities in the plural (Connell, 1987). Gender identities change only slowly, in response to broad social and economic changes in society. Some researchers have suggested that, although masculinity is the dominant identity the engine of change lies with femininity, that ideas about masculinity change in response to changes in the feminine identity (Kimmel, 1987:15; Segal, 1990). This holds out hope for women's efforts to change trade union culture.

The culture of femininity

The sociologist Segal has written about the difference between the feminine and the masculine:

> One thing is certain: although, individually, women and men can and do exhibit every combination of active and passive, gentle and aggressive, dependent and assertive thoughts and behaviour, our attachments to the ideas and discourses constructing polarised gender images live on. At the heart of the matter, the equations of the 'feminine' and 'love', the 'masculine' and 'power', endure, bound up with the institutionalised continuities of past and present - of women's central engagement with childrearing and personal life, men's with economic and social power (Segal, 1990:295).

However, there is less agreement about how these differences are constructed and their range and nature.

Men's control over the mass media and over financial resources means that it is their perceptions which prevail in the public consciousness and which are deeply implanted in women's minds. Men's definitions prevail also in academic discourse. Freud and other psychoanalysts after him, most of whom have been men, spent much effort in trying to understand the feminine identity, asking the question 'What is it that women really want?' (Segal, 1990:60). Academic men have had a big influence on notions of femininity - which until recently tended to be seen as the obverse of masculinity, rather than examined in its own right - though there have been some challenges to this view, notably from the female psychoanalyst Karen Horney.

The second wave of the feminist movement produced a new interest in the concept of femininity, its construction and the part it plays in processes of social change (Chodorow, 1978; Dinnerstein, 1978; Gilligan, 1982; Grimshaw, 1989; Mitchell, 1974). This focus on the feminine has in turn produced renewed interest in masculinity, on the part of women as well as men (Cockburn, 1981, 1988; Hearn, 1987; Hearn and Morgan, 1990; Kimmel, 1987; Segal, 1990; Tolson, 1977).

Feminist sociologists and philosophers argue that women develop a specific gender identity and a specific set of values different from those of men. Three elements have been identified as particularly significant in the construction of women's gender identity: patterns of childrearing, patterns of care and service, and the experience of subordination. First, childrearing. Both girls and boys are brought up by women, usually within a family unit. In the transition to adulthood, boys have to break from their mothers and look towards a male world. Girls, however, continue to identify with and build on relationships with their mothers and the caring and nurturing models provided by them. As a consequence girls tend to perceive the world in terms of relationships, to invest them with considerable importance, and to judge the rightness and wrongness of their actions according to the effects on other people. Boys tend to develop a greater sense of autonomy than do girls; in contrast to girls, they tend to judge wrongness and rightness according to learned rules of behaviour, paying far less attention to the effects of their actions on others (Chodorow, 1978; Gilligan, 1982; Grimshaw, 1986). Second, most women are put under an obligation, by the societies of which they are a part, to care for and to serve others, both in an out of employment. Men, by and large, do not share such obligations. The third element in constructing women's gender identity is their experience of subordination or oppression.

Broadly speaking, women are subordinated to men both in domestic life and paid employment. The experience of subordination has been noted by both Grimshaw and Cockburn as a critical factor leading women to develop their own specific set of values. Grimshaw writes that women's concerns and ethical priorities 'are a response to the material circumstances of life and a resource developed in the face of deprivation and oppression rather than just as a result of the development of the self in infancy and early childhood' (Grimshaw, 1989:252). Cockburn writes of 'an alternative gender-specific set of values' which arises out of women's pervasive experience of oppression (Cockburn, 1988:309, 326). Moreover as Grimshaw points out, women's responsibility for childrearing, their obligation to care and their subordination are widespread over time and place and thus the basic gender identity and gender-specific values which arise from them are likely to have considerable stability (Grimshaw, 1986:225).

Other feminists, for example the philosopher Haraway, have put forward ideas about the partial or 'situated' nature of knowledge, suggesting that women have a different knowledge of the world from men (Haraway, 1988). Sociologists have gone further. Partly on the basis of different sets of values and different ways of knowing and partly on the basis of empirical studies they have suggested that women have different ways of doing things (Cockburn, 1991; Coyle and Skinner, 1988). All these differences together constitute a cultural difference between women and men and this is what we refer to when we write about the cultures of femininity and of masculinity.

We do not intend to suggest that all women hold precisely the same values and share precisely the same culture. We recognise that diverse experience gives rise to diverse identities, value systems and cultures. However, we do suggest that beneath the diversity there is a core set of gender-specific values which supports a core culture of femininity. Moreover, we are identifying tendencies, not invariable relationships: the complexity of life is such that individuals even with similar life experiences may differ markedly from one another. So we refer to core values and a core culture which are found 'among' women (Cockburn's emphasis, 1991:72), but which are not to be thought of as attributes of all women.

In our view the culture of femininity is a resource which can benefit the union movement. Aspects of this culture which are specially relevant to trade unionism are: the importance placed on affective rather than instrumental relationships; the emphasis on accommodation rather than confrontation; the priority accorded to social over purely economic factors; the connection made between home, employment and community; the acceptance of diversity and the belief that everyone's voice should be heard; a dislike of formality, hierarchy and top-down decision making and a belief in informality and the importance of grass-roots' opinion.

All the evidence shows that the trade union movement will not accept the culture of femininity without struggle. Changes will have to be made; claims to dominance and exclusiveness, embedded in the culture of masculinity, will have to be relinquished. This will take time. However, Segal in her book entitled *Slow Motion* presents evidence that men are changing. And some of her examples are taken from the trade union movement. Such changes will benefit not only women but the trade union movement as a whole.

A historical overview of women in the union movement completes the introduction. The remainder of the book is divided into three parts, followed by a conclusion. The first presents case material and deals with the development of consciousness and challenges to men's control at branch and workplace. The second assesses union policies designed to encourage women's greater involvement in the movement. The third examines the extent to which recent trade union negotiation expresses women's culture of femininity. The conclusion looks at the implications of this culture for the union movement.

Note on terminology and oppressed groups

Conventional terminology is defined by the powerful and in consequence words commonly used for oppressed groups often carry connotations of contempt. One reaction of such groups is to reject the conventional term and adopt their own. Another is to use it, but to do so with deliberate pride. As oppressed groups grow in self-awareness two other elements enter in: a strong wish to define themselves; and a recognition of common cause with other oppressed groups and the search for a term to name it. The situation is compounded by the fact that skin colour, ethnic differences, and cultural differences overlap in a complex fashion such that referring to any group by one of these criteria can imply something about the other two.

'Black' for example was originally used only to describe people with dark skins. Because black people were widely oppressed it carried derogatory overtones. However, they now affirm the term with pride. It has also acquired a wider political meaning: it can, in some contexts, be used as a catch-all to refer to all groups discriminated against on account of skin colour or ethnic origin. In this sense 'black' can include Asians, Arabs and even 'white'- skinned Irish and European Jews. However, not all oppressed groups are willing to accept the term black, preferring designations characterising their particularity.

The terminology used in this book is that which is current in the equal opportunity movement. Since this is a matter of practice rather than formal rule, it is not entirely consistent. 'Black' is used to refer to workers discriminated on account of skin colour or ethnic origin. It is so used in the trade union movement. But we also employ particular terms such as 'Asian' where it is used in self-definition, or where it gives cultural rather than political information; and 'minority' and 'minority ethnic' in context of discrimination primarily on account of ethnic identity. We also use 'race' and 'racial discrimination' as these are terms in which anti-discrimination legislation has been framed. Race is used too in its sociological sense to refer to broad ethnic divisions in society most commonly associated with skin colour.

'Lesbians and gay men' is used in preference to homosexuals; and 'disabled women' rather than women with disabilities. With regard to gender, equal opportunity practice is clearer: 's/he' or 'they' and 'chairperson' are preferred to 'he' and 'chairman'. However, in reporting situations where a strong culture of masculinity prevails, we tend to use masculinist language appropriate to that culture.

ii Historical overview

Women and men, united and divided

Women have taken part in the struggles of the trade union movement throughout its history. They have been involved in defending and promoting working class interests, as trade unionists in their own right and in support of fathers, husbands and sons. However, within the movement itself, they have had to struggle against male power, to defend their needs and interests against those of working-class men. An overview of this latter struggle from the early nineteenth century to the 1980s, provides a historical context for the main part of the book.

The character and extent of women's involvement in the movement has differed consistently from that of men's. Nevertheless, there have been significant changes in the form and direction of women's involvement and it is on these that we focus. We bring particular attention to the ways in which women have striven to get their interests accepted onto the trade union agenda and to the character of the issues over which they have fought.

We use the term 'women's issues' as a shorthand to refer to issues which are of particular interest to women, which women tend to see as significant but men do not. There are two major strands to their promotion. One is the pursuit of equality in respect of traditional union issues, previously defined in all-male terms. This strand includes issues such as equal pay, equal representation within the movement, and the way women's work is valued. The other is the attempt to broaden the union agenda to include issues such as sex discrimination, women's health, housing and other community matters, family concerns and issues surrounding women's caring role. Trade union women have not been alone in pursuing the interests of working women: they have always been part of a wider women's, or feminist, movement which has been a source of mutual assistance. Formal and informal links between different sections of the women's movement have been, and still are, important factors in the growth of their influence within the unions.

The early union movement

In the late eighteenth and early nineteenth centuries, the trade union movement consisted of small locally-based trade or friendly societies in traditional workshop-based occupations, such as the tailoring and boot and shoe trades. Run by men, they existed largely to provide benefits for their members in the case of sickness or death and as a source of information about jobs. Most women who were members of trade unions belonged to these societies. A few societies were composed solely of women: an early example, recorded in 1780, was the Sisterhood of Leicestershire Wool Spinners (Lewenhak, 1977:17); a later example was the Edinburgh Maidservants' Union Society of 1825.

From the nineteenth century until the First World War the cotton unions, federations of local weavers', spinners' and other cotton workers' trade unions, organized more women and more workers than any other section of the movement. In the early nineteen hundreds, in the face of falling wages, women handloom weavers rioted alongside men. Traditionally men had possession of this highly skilled work, but as wages fell, women also entered the trade. However, when power looms were introduced into the newly opened factories, women not men formed the new workforce. The men stuck to their handlooms and when lack of work eventually forced them into factories, the women were already established. With both sexes working at the same job, a system of equal pay developed. However, men were still hostile to the women. In 1840 in evidence to a Royal Commission male weavers, pronouncing that women's place was in the home, suggested that married women be excluded from weaving and that instead men should be paid a family wage (Lewenhak, 1977). Women were under-represented in official posts throughout the cotton unions (Turner, 1962). Nevertheless they established precedents which have inspired later women unionists. These included the presence of women in mixed-sex craft unions, the right of married women to work outside the home, and among weavers the right to skilled work and to equal pay.

Early in the century feminist values were promoted by the Owenite movement. Their aims, set out in a pamphlet entitled *An Appeal to One-*

Half of the Human Race by William Thompson and Anna Wheeler, included equal pay, women's right to paid employment and to work in jobs hitherto dominated by men, a new relationship between women and men where independence replaced subordination, and social rather than personal responsibility for childcare (Taylor, 1983:19-24). The political and industrial ideals of the Owenites led them to set up a single national trade union for all working people, thereby introducing the idea of general unionism. The Grand National Consolidated Trade Union was founded in 1833. Ideals of equality failed to overcome men's fears of women's cheap labour. Most of the organizations making up the GNCTU refused to admit women and in consequence separate organizations for women were created. The organizational and financial structure of the GNCTU was very weak. In 1833 it proved unable to finance the first major strike of its members; ironically this was part of a campaign by London tailors to exclude women from certain types of work (Taylor, 1983:Chapter 4).

The GNCTU lasted less than a year. Though its practice fell short of its ideals, Owenite ideas about equality for women within the trade union movement did not completely die. However, the 'new model unionism' which followed Owenism was unashamedly male-dominated. The new unions were craft-based and limited to men. They established a monopoly of their respective crafts by means of controlling the numbers entering apprenticeships. This put them in a position of power vis-a-vis employers, from which they were able to negotiate high wages. For the most part women had no place in these unions. However, where men were unable to maintain a male monopoly over craft skills, they allowed women to join. Their strategy then was to keep women out of the better paying jobs (Walby, 1986). These craft unions created a loose national association, formally established in 1868 as the Trade Union Congress (TUC). From its inception therefore, the TUC - the collective voice of the trade union movement - was heavily dominated by men.

Pre-eminent among the new unions was the Associated Society of Engineers. As the industrial base of the country expanded, the engineering industry grew and drew in more women. Because they were excluded from craft unions, women could only do unskilled or semi-skilled work and they became defined as unskilled, low-paid labour. A stereotype of women emerged, which depicted them as incapable of understanding and controlling machinery, and was later used to justify their exclusion from many jobs connected with engineering and technology (Cockburn, 1985).

The new unions made no attempt to organize the growing numbers of low-paid semi-skilled and unskilled women. These were therefore seen as in need of state protection. Protective legislation, limiting the hours and conditions of women's work, was initiated by male parliamentarians and philanthropists. It was supported by male trade unionists because of the ever present threat of cheap labour. Acts were passed in 1840, 1844, 1847, 1864 and 1867. Protective legislation was at first opposed by the feminists who campaigned against it during the 1840s. Later however they changed their minds and by 1850 praised it for checking employers' ability to exploit women. Protective legislation is still a contentious issue among feminists, although most union women today support it and also call for its extension to men.

Separate development and merger

The 1870s saw a new departure, separate trade union organizations for women. This development was closely connected with the feminist movement. In the first half of the century feminists had promoted women's rights in education, property and access to employment, mostly on behalf of middle class women. In the second, their main focus was the vote. But they also took up the causes of working class women. In 1874 Emma Paterson founded the Women's Protective and Provident League (after 1888 called the Women's Trade Union League) to promote separate unions for women. This was partly in reaction to women's exclusion from men's unions and partly in order to promote women's self reliance and enable them to produce their own leaders (Boston, 1980). From 1874 to 1886, the League helped establish between thirty and forty societies in England and Scotland. In 1875 it established the right to send delegates to the TUC conference. From this platform, despite fierce male opposition, it promoted issues such as women's right to work, protective legislation, the appointment of women factory inspectors, and equal pay. The latter became TUC policy in 1888. In 1889, after concerted campaigning by the League, feminists and philanthropists, the TUC agreed to assist the League in recruiting and organizing women. By 1900 some sixty unions had affiliated. In 1889, another organization, the Women's Trade Union Association (re-named the Women's Industrial Council in 1894) was founded to promote unionism in the East End of London. Though unsuccessful, it helped to publicize the problems of working women and lobbied the government on their behalf.

In 1892 the first official estimate of women's trade union membership was 142,000, only 3.1 per cent of all women workers recorded in the 1891 census. By 1913, the estimate had risen to over 433,000. Cotton unions still accounted for nearly half of this membership (Lewenhak, 1977:97).

The rapid increase in membership was, however, mainly due in part to the growth of general unionism among unskilled and semi-skilled workers. Unlike craft unions, general unions which emerged in the 1880s did not specifically exclude women, although their main membership was among men. General unions organized over a wide range of occupations. They provided a pattern for the National Federation of Women Workers, founded in 1906 by Mary Macarthur through amalgamating the small societies of the Women's Trade Union League. Macarthur regarded a separate women's organization not as a matter of feminist principle, but as a temporary necessity. Her aim was to join up with the men's movement. The NFWW was very active. It 'organized more women, fought more strikes and [did] more to establish women trade unionists than any other organization' (Boston, 1980:60).

It was formed during an upsurge of union and political activity which lasted from the late 1880s to the First World War and which began with a strike by women and girls at the Bryant and May match factory. The 'match-girls' strike', strongly supported by middle-class liberals and the labour movement, won most of its demands. The London Dock Strike followed in 1889. Industrial action peaked again in the 1890s, from 1910 to 1914, and during the First World War. From 1910 onwards it focused largely on demands for national recognition and national wage bargaining.

In the twentieth century women trade unionists obtained the support of MPs, mostly Labour, to assist their fight for equal pay, protective legislation and other matters. After working class men gained the vote in 1867, Liberal and Tory parliamentary candidates sought their support, but gave little in return. A demand arose among trade unionists and socialists for a new radical political party whose specific aim would be to represent the interests of the working class. The Independent Labour Party (ILP) was founded in 1893. However, the TUC's parliamentary committee refused to agree to formal union support of ILP parliamentary candidates. Within the TUC a struggle ensued between the socialist ideas of the general unions and the more traditional ideas of the miners' and cotton workers' unions. In 1900 an accommodation was reached when trade unionists and socialists from the ILP combined to form the Labour Representation Committee which in 1906 was reconstituted as the Labour Party. The close links between trade unions and Labour Party forged at this time remained more or less unquestioned until the 1990s (Lewenhak, 1977; Liddington and Norris, 1978; Saville, 1988; Simpson, 1973).

In the early twentieth century, the state assumed some of the welfare functions undertaken by the first unions. The 1911 Insurance Act established, for many workers, basic health and unemployment insurance including maternity benefits. Women unionists, led by Mary Macarthur, campaigned for minimum wages for women who worked in the 'sweated' trades. Middle class reformers and Fabians, men as well as women, supported this campaign. In 1904 they put on a 'British Sweated Industries Exhibition' and following that formed an Anti-Sweating League (Cadbury et al., c. 1907; Lewenhak, 1977:120-1; Mayer and Black, 1909:1-3). In 1910 the Trade Boards Act brought four trades under statutory wage control; more were added in 1913 and 1918. There were also campaigns on issues traditionally outside the trade union agenda such as maternal and child welfare.

Other organizations were active on behalf of working women. The Women's Co-operative Guild campaigned from the 1890s to the 1930s. By 1910 the National Union of Women's Suffrage Societies was organizing a vast number of meetings and mobilising huge processions. Women in northern textile trades and unions proved untiring suffrage campaigners. In 1890 a petition of 29,359 votes, signed exclusively by Lancashire cotton women was presented to MPs (Liddington and Norris, 1978:148). In 1910 a woman's suffrage motion was introduced at the TUC by Helen Silcock, President of the Wigan Weavers. When the more radical suffragists (women who saw violence against property as a way of furthering their cause) split from the suffragettes, a number of salaried organizers from the Women's Trade Union League joined their ranks.

During the First World War several campaigns, including that for the vote, were dropped. But women's new and crucial role in the civilian workforce brought them new influence with the government and women's right to vote was included in the Representation of the People Act passed in 1918. The right was limited to women over the age of thirty, householders and wives of householders.

Women's contribution to the war effort, their performance in 'men's' jobs and their willingness to join trade unions all facilitated their final merger with the mainstream of the movement. The leadership of the women's unions had worked to this end since the 1890s. Leaders of women's and men's unions were drawn together by common involvement in the socialist movement and common struggles for protective legislation. Common interests were fostered by the nationalist spirit of the First World War, and the shared goals of postwar society. The desire for unity became so strong that the importance to women of the difference and particularity of their interests was at least temporarily forgotten.

In 1921 NFWW merged with the Workers' Union, a general union catering for both women and men, to form the General Workers' Union. Women were given special representation in the new union. However men predominated; they had greater organizational skills and soon weakened or abolished most of the measures for special representation. The special Women's District (which cut across the union's other territorially-based districts) was abolished in 1922 and the Women's Department in 1928. Only the national post of Chief Woman Officer (filled by Margaret Bondfield) remained.

In 1920 when the Women's Trade Union League merged with the TUC, women had fared little better. Only two new seats were reserved for women on the General Council. A new committee of the General Council, the Women Workers Group, was formed to deal with the interests of women members. Heavily male-dominated, it soon came under criticism for failing to do so. The price of women's acceptance into the mainstream movement turned out to be costly. Both women's need for unions and the movement's need to organize women were now accepted, but women were not regarded as equal.

Welfare feminism and equal pay

During the war women had been encouraged to do men's jobs. Afterwards they were made to return to low-paid women's work. During the interwar years women's position was further eroded. National bargaining agreements were negotiated which upheld the principle of a family wage for men and confirmed unequal pay. Women's right to work was challenged. The high unemployment of the interwar years encouraged male trade unionists to collude with employers in preserving jobs for men. A marriage bar was widely enforced by local authorities against teachers, civil servants and other white-collar workers (Walby, 1986). Women were still feared as cheap labour, and their unionization was encouraged because it offered men possible control over this threat. Unionization of women also helped to stem the dramatic decline in union membership, consequent on economic stagnation, unemployment and industrial strife. These were the reasons behind union campaigns urging male trade unionists to encourage their wives and daughters to join unions and even to pay their subscriptions for them (Boston, 1980).

A strand of feminist ideas known as welfare feminism became dominant in the thirties. It focused on the experience of women as wives and mothers. The main thrust was towards financial independence for women, to be achieved within marriage. The welfare feminists - in the shape of the family endowment movement - argued that women needed financial support for their children from the state and that money should be paid directly into their hands, not given to their husbands. They offered the first consistent feminist argument against the family wage for men. The unions adamantly opposed the family endowment movement, arguing that allowances would be used to keep down wages. Women trade unionists also failed to give the movement any support. Their activities were primarily involved with regaining their lost influence in the movement and in equal pay. In this respect they had more in common with the less prominent, but still active, strand of equal rights feminism supported by such women's organizations as the Six Point Group and the Open Door International for the Economic Emancipation of the Woman Worker (Alberti, 1989:219-20; Riley, 1983:179).

Having lost control of their own movement, women tried in various ways to gain influence in the mainstream. At the 1923 TUC Conference a women's advisory delegate conference was proposed. The first was called in 1925. Women were angered by the tight control exercised over the conference by the male-dominated national Women's Group of the TUC. They felt the men ignored their wishes. No further conferences were called until 1931 when, in an attempt to stem the decline in women's membership, a second advisory delegate conference was held, renamed the Conference of Unions Catering for Women (CUCW). Advisory conferences have been held annually ever since.

Earlier, in 1925, the independent Scottish TUC had established an Annual Woman's Conference. From 1928 onwards the Conference met at changing locations. At each one it ran a local women-only day school, encouraging women who attended to form a women's committee of the local trades council. In 1931, the TUC (England and Wales) set up the National Women's Advisory Committee (NWAC) to organize the annual CUCWs. Some of its members were elected from CUCW, some were appointed directly by the TUC General Council. NWAC followed the Scottish example in promoting trades council women's committees in England and Wales: thirty-five were set up in 1931-2. The TUC General Council agreed to women from these committees attending the annual CUCWs as non-voting delegates (Lewenhak, 1977).

During the thirties the campaign for equal pay was an important issue for women trade unionists. It was led by the teaching and clerical unions which were active from the turn of the century until after the Second World War. Most of these unions were not affiliated to the TUC. The Civil Service Equal Pay Committee was formed to co-ordinate civil service unions, the London County Council Staff Association and a non-union group - the Status of Women Committee. At this time the TUC represented mainly private sector unions and was reluctant to support the campaign, arguing that responsibility for the matter rested with individual unions not the TUC.

Later the public sector unions led a campaign based on the findings of the Royal Commission on Equal Pay (1944). Again the TUC did not support it, this time arguing for delay because of the risk of inflation. However, the public sector unions continued to campaign and equal pay for white-collar civil servants and local authority employees was phased in between 1951 and 1961.

New wave feminism

The Second World War strengthened the position of women trade unionists. Membership increased during wartime and continued to grow afterwards. Shop stewards, introduced first into private industry began to appear in the public sector. A new group of militant women stewards, collectors and local committee members emerged. They influenced the views of the women's advisory structures, persuading NWAC in 1957 to withdraw its opposition to day nurseries and to mothers of young children going out to work. By the sixties, women had some influence in the policy-making councils of the TUC itself.

As trade union membership amongst women workers continued to grow they became more important to the movement, numerically and financially. Their increased membership resulted from a rapid growth in women's white-collar and service employment. These sectors were growing alongside a decline in traditional male employment. The union movement was buoyed up by a positive political relationship with the Labour Government. Government consultation with unions, developed in the War, continued until the late 1970s. An important consequence was the growth in state protection for workers.

While acknowledging women's new importance, the leadership did not consider their objectives to be as important as the traditional male-defined goals of the movement. For example in the mid-sixties the TUC temporarily withdrew its support for equal pay, citing again the threat of rising inflation and unemployment. However, women continued to campaign and in 1968 the strike of the Ford sewing machinists brought matters to a head. In 1970 the Equal Pay Act was passed. It applied to all workers. The Sex and Race Discrimination Acts were passed in 1975 and the Employment Protection Act, giving maternity provision in 1975.

The new wave of feminism in the late sixties, known as the Women's Liberation Movement, made equality a public issue. The movement became closely connected with the contemporary student and socialist movements. New wave feminists, operating mainly through consciousness-raising groups, were active trying to make the connection between 'the personal and the political'. They were also active in public life where they created the Women's Aid movement to protect women against domestic violence; established women's publishing houses and new journals and magazines; lobbied for equal opportunity in employment and education and campaigned for wages for housework. New wave feminist ideas resulted in a widening of the trade union policy agenda, in structural changes to encourage more women to participate, and in a new understanding by working women of their role at work and in society.

In 1974 feminists established the Working Women's Charter Group. It aimed at effecting social change through the trade union movement, but to do so by enabling women from the community and women trade unionists to campaign side by side. Campaigning was carried out through women's committees of local trades councils. The broad goals were to improve the pay and conditions of low-paid women and to make the Women's Liberation Movement relevant to their lives. In fact the movement proved more successful in advancing the interests of white-collar women unionists (Rowbotham, 1989a:223). Charter members, including non-unionists, tried to get themselves coopted onto local women's committees of trades councils. Many trades councils were reluctant to allow full membership to non-unionist Charter campaigners, and several women's committees were expelled or disbanded (Rowbotham et al., 1979). In others union and non-union Charter members worked together exploring how feminist ideas could be applied to branch meetings and other union activities.

Several Charters and Lists of Aims have been proposed, on behalf of working women, by different groups. In the union movement the idea was first raised in 1938, but trade unionists first produced a Charter in 1963 (Ellis, 1981:46). It failed to get TUC support. In 1974 another Charter, published by the London Trades Council and promoted by the newly-formed Working Women's Charter Campaign, was widely discussed in the unions. It won national support from NUPE, NUJ, NALGO, CPSA, ACTT and AUEW and numbers of local branches. It too failed to get TUC support (Phillips, 1987). However discussion at the TUC Women's Advisory Conferences led to NWAC producing its own List of Aims and this did gain TUC support.

The 1963 Charter had been concerned with issues of equality in pay and education and employment. The 1974 Charter was broader, including issues of sex discrimination in law, tax and mortgages; it also claimed the right to paid maternity leave and to adequate childcare provision. But it did not call for abortion on demand, and it did endorse women's responsibility for family care (TUC, 1975). In 1977 the TUC produced another List of Aims, this time incorporating demands for free abortion, more public provision for childcare and shared childcare with men (Stageman, 1980). A specific Charter concerning the provision of childcare and nursery facilities was also published by the TUC (1978a).

In 1979 the TUC drew up its own *Charter for Equality for Women within Trade Unions*. This departed from previous Charters by focusing on women's equality within the movement. It asked each union to commit itself publicly to involving women in union activities at all levels (TUC, 1979a). It acknowledged the need for positive action, recommending that special women's advisory committees be set up at national, regional, divisional and district levels and reserved seats established on decision-making bodies. It also drew attention to some of the obstacles facing women in attempting to combine union activity with family responsibilities, suggesting changes in meeting times and the provision of childcare during meetings (see Appendix 1).

New challenges

By the end of the seventies trade union membership reached a peak of over eleven million (TUC, 1979b). Women made up 29 per cent of this membership - between 1968 and 1978 women's membership had grown at more than three times the rate of men's (Stageman, 1980). Approximately 40 per cent of working women were now union members. However, the movement itself was soon threatened by profound social changes.

1979 was a critical year. Under pressure from the International Monetary Fund the Labour government of the day imposed a five per cent ceiling, well below the current rate of inflation, on the wages of low-paid public sector workers. This provoked a long national strike, commonly referred to thereafter as the Winter of Discontent. The strike brought about the government's downfall. It was replaced by a Conservative government led by Margaret Thatcher. Government policy and popular ideology shifted sharply to the right; the idea of the free market replaced that of the welfare state. The decline of manufacturing which had begun during the sixties gathered pace. Unemployment, particularly in men's traditional manufacturing jobs, began a seemingly inexorable increase. Although women's employment continued to grow, jobs were mostly low-paid and part-time.

The government adopted a policy of confrontation towards the trade union movement. New legislation limited both collective and individual rights as in the Employment Acts of 1980, 1982 and 1988, the Trade Union Act of 1984 and the Wages Act of 1986. Trade unions could now be sued for a range of previously legal activities. The closed shop was made illegal as was secondary picketing thus outlawing political and solidarity strikes; the definition of a lawful trade dispute was narrowed. Secret ballots were imposed in certain areas of decision making; the period of time needed to qualify for a number of employment rights was extended and small firms were given exemption from some of the legislation. Government and employers challenged union power in traditional strongholds already depleted by unemployment and restructuring, such as steel, mining, transport, print and the public services. In the public sector, the government also introduced policies of privatization and compulsory competitive tendering and encouraged the introduction of performance-related pay and decentralization of national pay bargaining.

The trade union movement defended itself stoically. A wide variety of workers was involved in industrial action and lengthy disputes. For example, in 1984-5 a miners' strike against pit closures lasted for twelve months. Recession and restructuring brought a sharp loss in membership which dropped between 1979 and 1989 by 21 per cent. In reaction the unions, competing against one another, increased efforts to recruit new members and retain old ones. A process of mergers and amalgamations commenced involving, by the end of the decade, seventeen out of the twenty largest unions. By 1990 the membership had dropped to around eight and a half million. A higher proportion were now women, 34 per cent as against 29 per cent in 1979 (TUC, 1991e). But they were still under-represented in union government (LRD, 1991; SERTUC, 1989) and unable to wield an influence proportional to their numbers. Women unionists, paid and lay, worked hard to prevent women's issues from slipping down the union agenda.

Lay activists worked to increase the influence of women's special structures. In 1986 a number of reforms were brought in and the term 'advisory' dropped from the women's conference. The TUC stepped up positive action for women. In 1988 seats reserved for women on the General Council were increased from two to six and in 1989, when the total Council was fifty-five, to twelve. In 1990 the TUC *Charter for Equality for Women within Trade Unions* was updated. The updated version, entitled *A Charter for Equality for Women in the Trade Union Movement* (TUC, 1990a), included a commitment to a policy of 'proportionality', and called for women to be represented on all committees in parity with the proportion of women in the membership. These reforms activated divisions between feminists and non-feminists. At the grass-roots, however, women-only trade union education helped to reconcile the two groups (Elliot, 1984).

In the same year the TUC passed a second and more inclusive *Charter for Women at Work* (TUC, 1990b). Sexual harassment and discrimination against lesbians and disabled women were among the new items. This Charter was meant to act both as a policy statement and a negotiators' guide, part of a new policy of practical support to unions pursuing women's interests. This policy was shown most clearly in the setting up, in 1988, of a TUC Equal Rights Department.

The 1979 and 1990 TUC Charters are a clear indication of the movement's unfolding commitment to women. The earlier Charter recognises the crucial importance of achieving equality within the movement, acknowledging it to be a precondition of equality at work. The later Charter shows a growth in understanding of the nature of women's subordination. It now accepts that equality for women, both in employment and in the movement itself, must address - in addition to issues directly related to employment - those of domestic life and of systematic discrimination along lines of race, sexuality and disability. Getting the movement to accept these ideas has involved challenging deeply established beliefs and attitudes, some of them present long before the beginning of the nineteenth century. It has been no mean achievement. Nevertheless fair representation for women is still a long way from realization. In 1990, although women made up nearly a third of TUC membership, they comprised only 20 per cent of national executives, 23 per cent of delegates to union conferences, 21 per cent of TUC delegations, 20 per cent of delegates to union conferences and less than seven per cent of general secretaries (LRD, 1991; see also Appendix 4).

Part One
BRANCH AND WORKPLACE

1 Male control at the branch: Case 1

Women's supposed lack of interest

Trade unions appear to be less relevant to working women than to working men. Proportionally fewer women than men join unions. Fewer regard their unions as relevant to workplace problems. Fewer attend local branch meetings regularly and, once they are there, fewer participate actively or are elected to office.

The lack of interest among women at the workplace has been well documented. Pollert and Wajcman in 1972, Cavendish in 1977-8, Westwood in 1980-81 and Purcell in 1980 each studied factory women at work (Cavendish, 1982; Pollert, 1981; Purcell, 1982, 1986, 1989; Wajcman, 1983; Westwood, 1984). With the exception of Cavendish, each found that the women perceived their own union as largely irrelevant to the general run of problems they faced. Survey reports about women and unions confirm this (Charles, 1983; Munro, 1990; Purcell, 1979:89). Westwood puts this most strongly:

> The world of the trade union presented itself as a frustrating irrelevance which seemed, from the women's point of view, to promote ignorance and powerlessness rather than knowledge and control. (Westwood, 1984:236)

Pollert writes of young women 'whose experience of the factory unionism was just a blank' and describes the attitude of the women after the failure of a strike as being 'bored with the whole business' and cynical about the union (Pollert, 1981:215). Wajcman says that the women at Fakenham were indifferent and passive towards the union because of its failure to provide them with support, encouragement or even information while they were struggling to create a cooperative and so retain their jobs (Wajcman, 1983:161-2).

That is not to say that women were against unions in principle. Most of the studies, in common with our own, report that women are generally supportive towards their unions and of the idea of trade unionism in general. Pollert reports that the women in the tobacco factory she studied 'regarded trade unionism as a necessary, basic defence of their rights', though at the same time they 'expressed many of the inconsistencies of sectionalism, peppered by the prejudices of an anti-union right-wing press' (Pollert, 1981:163). The telephonists interviewed by Charles had no time at all for trade unionism, but in this they were an exception.

Of the workplaces studied, the car factory researched by Cavendish is the only one where the women felt that the union belonged to them:

> Most of the women were highly in favour of the union and often said that they, the women, were the union. If they did not stand up for themselves, no one else would. (Cavendish, 1982:137)

But it is not clear how far this trade union consciousness was forged through the experience of a strike which took place during the study and how far it may have been a consequence of trade union organization in the motor industry.

Most commonly women, although they might support the union in principle, felt excluded. In this chapter, using a case study of a hospital-based branch of COHSE, we examine mechanisms by which male control was perpetuated and the consequences of this for women workers. A summary of the research on which this and following cases are based is found in Appendix 2.

The band of brothers

The research we refer to was a study in 1977-78 of branch of the Confederation of Health Service Employees (COHSE), the main union organizing ancillary staff, nurses and other workers in one of three large hospitals in a northern city. The period of the research was one of industrial stability. At such times, trade union activity tends to be very much a minority concern; most people are willing to sit back and let others speak for them. The analysis in this chapter applies to such a period. The branch had between six and seven hundred members the majority of whom were low-paid women cleaners and kitchen workers.

The branch is the basic unit of trade union organization, to which all members belong and upon which the hierarchy of union government and administration rests. The vast majority of branches are territorially based, but they vary greatly in extent and size. Some - like the COHSE hospital branch - are attached to a single workplace; others cover more than one. The territorial extent and and the number of workplaces covered by a single branch depend among other factors on the structure, traditions and history of the particular union, and the branch's rural or urban location.

Trade union membership was expected and indeed recommended by the NHS management on the grounds that it both provided insurance cover in case of accidental mistakes at work and facilitated wage negotiations. Wage rates were negotiated nationally with the unions. Bonus schemes however, then under active consideration, were negotiated locally.

In the words of the women canteen workers the union was 'the men's thing'; it was a subject they rarely mentioned. Men, in contrast, would sometimes discuss union business at break times in the canteen. The main branch business at this time was the introduction of a bonus scheme among uniformed porters which, like most union business concerned only men. Though women did not talk about the union, some - mainly nurses - would occasionally approach a union steward when they had failed to resolve a work problem through talking to management. No women from the canteen or kitchen went regularly to branch meetings although a woman cook who acted as branch auditor occasionally put in an appearance. In their eyes their obligations to the union were fulfilled once they had paid their dues. They became interested and involved only once during the year of the research, when they attended a large meeting held to protest about inadequate meal facilities for nurses on night duty.

The branch as a homosocial club

The COHSE hospital branch, more than any other of the branches we discuss later, had developed into a small exclusive male club, a 'Band of Brothers' (Purcell, 1979:129; Walton, 1991:162). The central core consisted of five men, a barber, a joiner, a uniformed porter who dealt with patients and two porters who did labouring jobs. All were shop stewards and all came regularly to monthly branch meetings. The three main officers, Secretary, Chairman and Treasurer were men. Two women cleaners, shop stewards, also attended regularly, but they never contributed to discussion and were never asked their opinion. Attendance at ordinary branch meetings was usually limited to these seven people, sometimes with one or two porters and very occasionally a nurse. The AGM and meetings about pay claims attracted more members.

The meeting place was unattractive and uncongenial. This and the fact that almost everyone was male, that only men spoke and that they spoke about men's concerns made women appear and feel out of place. The atmosphere was 'unfriendly' to women.

The hospital had provided the branch with a small dilapidated office, a room in a derelict terrace of small houses which it owned. This office was the organizational base of the COHSE Band of Brothers. A few male officers and their friends met there regularly to brew up, to spend the lunchtime in chat and to conduct union business. Women members never went there. In fact the 'club' was regarded by men as a refuge where they could be free from members' demands. One of its implicit functions was to exclude women from union business conducted there. It also excluded and marginalized a lot of men.

Occupational segregation and male control

The customary system of shop steward representation builds male domination into most trade union branches. It seeks to supply each occupational group with a steward who works within that group. In that way stewards in negotiation with management can be properly informed about both the relevant terms and conditions and the particularities of the job. There is no representation by gender, race, sexuality or disability. The distinctive interests and problems of these different groups are not acknowledged in the shop steward system. Neither is there usually much attempt to provide representation proportional to the numbers in each occupation.

By this simple custom of having each different job represented by a different shop steward, male domination in the COHSE hospital branch was ensured. The gendered structure of occupational segregation in UK society, in common with most industrial societies, results in men occupying a far larger range of jobs than women, who tend to be crowded, or ghettoised, into a rather narrow range. Around eight hundred women were employed at the hospital. Most were nurses and ancillary workers. The ancillaries were mainly cleaners and canteen workers. Around one hundred men occupied a far wider range of jobs. In addition to male nurses there were five different kinds of craftsmen, five different kinds of porters and also drivers and cooks.

Although the COHSE branch was numerically dominated by women, of seven shop stewards, only two were women. The male stewards consisted of two craftsmen (barber and joiner) three porters (kitchen, uniformed and laboratory). The two women were both cleaners. The kitchen porter represented all the women from the canteen and kitchen. In spite of efforts at recruitment no nurse of either sex could be found to act as a steward. Nurses were usually represented by the barber, the shop steward most frequently on the wards. Formally the two cleaners had a constituency of several hundred between them, but in practice their willingness to represent more than their closest workmates was unclear. The idea of achieving a better proportional representation for women was never raised.

Each of the male stewards in the COHSE branch represented only a small number of workers. The men were thus in a far better position than the women to argue for and push the interests of their members. The women felt over-burdened by numbers. The prospect of large constituencies of members to be serviced may have been a potent factor in discouraging women from becoming shop stewards.

When a woman shop steward cannot be found or when women's constituencies are very large, it is usual for men stewards to represent the women. In contrast women seldom represent men. Women members tend to be dissatisfied with representation by someone outside their occupation; they prefer a steward who knows the job through doing it. Men stewards, however, gain in experience by representing workers outside their own occupation and this can be useful if they are ambitious for branch or regional office.

There is evidence that authority patterns at the workplace tend to be replicated, through the election process, at the branch. Officers as in the COHSE branch tend to be men; women are pushed to the margin (Ledwith et al., 1985; Munro, 1990:441, 450; Rees, 1990). The wider experience of men stewards was only one element in this. There is a tendency in a patriarchal society such as ours to equate authority with men and thus for women as well as men to vote men into office. In part this is based on the observation that men run most of the institutions in governmental and industrial life. In part it is based on men's position in the family, on the persistent idea of the father as head of the family and primary earner.

Of particular significance is the fact that men's jobs are more highly graded than women's. At this hospital, except for the nurses, nearly all men held higher grades than the women, most of whom were on an exclusively female grade one (cf. Munro, 1990). Both men who held the office of branch secretary, a kitchen porter and barber, were on higher grades than the two women shop stewards who were cleaners.

Proportionally few women were present at elections which were carried out formally at branch meetings. And when the COHSE hospital branch changed their officers during the study, the change was planned in advance at the union office. It was a mere formality, a 'palace revolution'.

Family ideology and trade union culture

The introduction to the book drew attention to the different ways in which women's and men's lives are structured by the systems of production and reproduction and how women have a double identity, lodged partly in the family and domestic life and partly in paid employment. The family and paid employment are to a large extent discrete, though linked, social spheres, separate in time and place. The union is firmly situated in the sphere of work. Each sphere may be seen as making demands on women's time and energy. When these conflict, choices have to be made. Women on these occasions, it is often suggested, tend to place demands of family above those of paid work and of the union.

Many married women members are linked to the movement both through their own employment and that of their husbands or partners. The link through men is supported by ideologies of class and family and on the practical importance to women (especially women with children) of men's earnings (Hunt, 1980). It may account for the generally supportive attitudes of women to trade unions noted at the beginning of the chapter. Such general support can co-exist quite easily with feelings that the movement is not particularly relevant to women's own working lives.

The research studies of Cavendish, Pollert, Wajcman and Westwood all suggest that women's sense of the irrelevance of trade unions is located primarily in the structure and ideology of the family. They come to this conclusion despite producing evidence of exclusion and even, in Pollert's words, the betrayal of women by their unions. Westwood lays a great deal of emphasis on the way in which ideologies of marriage and family life shaped women's daily experiences and she documents their salience in structuring social life within the factory. Pollert comments on the women's attachment to the unreal myth that 'retirement' and escape from factory life are just around the corner, even though most women know they are likely to be in paid employment until formal retirement age.

These researchers argue that women's conventionally defined responsibility for family care makes material demands upon their time and energy which limit their ability to participate in other areas of social life. Women's failure to attend union meetings is not seen as a result of low interest or job commitment, but to unavoidable commitments in their domestic lives (cf. Stageman, 1980). Pollert describes the combination of motherhood, work and activity in the union as 'simply incompatible' (Pollert, 1981:171)

There are reasons for thinking this card may be overplayed and that women questioned about their failure to attend union meetings find domestic duties a conventionally acceptable explanation (Cunnison, 1983a). Instances exist of women who do combine work, family and union, though they need a high level of organizational skill to do so. There is an alternative, that of restructuring trade union organization to fit in with women's family lives. Research studies have produced a few examples of attempts in this direction, mainly changing times of meetings. Meetings during working time tend to generate the best attendance but are difficult to arrange where there is shift working. A few unions, as we note in Part 2, are suggesting adventurous initiatives, either providing a creche or paying for childminding.

Munro's study of four hospital trade union branches strikes a different note. She reports a situation where the trade unions were of very limited relevance to the women workers. In one branch, a questionnaire to women identified thirty-seven work-related problems; of these only three were taken to the union, most went to supervisors or managers; in another branch the figures were nineteen and one. Munro sees the reason for this not in 'familial ideology' or the structure of women's lives and their domestic and caring responsibilities, but in the exclusion of women's issues from a male-defined trade union agenda and in the gender structuring of the labour market which places women at the bottom of the job hierarchy, a hierarchy of power which, as noted earlier, is reproduced within the organizational structure of the union movement itself.

We argue differently. We see familial ideology and the structure of women's lives on the one hand, and men's marginalizing tactics on the other, as interdependent rather than alternative factors in explaining women's lack of interest in trade unionism. The union brothers of the COHSE branch made use of familial ideology to define women. But the familial ideology on which they drew was defined by the culture of masculinity. Women's character, interests and responsibilities were interpreted in a way which marginalized them within the branch and subordinated their interests to those of men. Defined thus, familial ideology provided grass-roots men with a 'respectable' rationale for their oppressive behaviour.

Stereotypes of women based on patriarchal ideology were propagated and elaborated by COHSE men. These stereotypes stressed the second earner status and were used to invalidate the importance with which women

41

viewed their earnings. The male branch officers were convinced that most women worked for 'pin-money', for 'holidays abroad' and 'bingo' while men were assumed to be breadwinning for their families. A woman who let her wages accumulate for several weeks was cited as evidence that women as a category did not need their money. It was said of the two women who regularly attended branch meetings that money did not matter to them because their husbands were in work. The secretary claimed they only came to meetings because their husbands were active unionists, thereby denying both the branch's relevance to them in their role as domestic workers and their relevance to the branch. A corollary was that the men did not regard women's earnings as deserving the same support as those of men.

A double standard operated. Male stewards sat in the social club after a union meeting; with a pint on the table and a fag in the hand, they criticized 'women who go out to work for booze and cigarettes'. They did so with no sense of irony. Beside them sat the two cleaners, saying nothing. The stewards regarded their own attitudes towards work as the norm; they saw women's attitudes as different and 'strange', something that 'you can't really understand' (cf. Cunnison, 1989). Their confusion no doubt encouraged their reliance on stereotypes.

In so far as men define women as primarily domestic creatures, they define the union as being of limited relevance to them. In so far as women collaborate with this definition, they confirm this limited relevance. There are many pressures on any subordinate group to collaborate with the views of their oppressors; many members of a subordinated group who may not fully accept the views of the dominant group may yet, for a variety of reasons, be unwilling to voice a protest.

Appropriating the agenda

Most trade union branches operate according to formal procedures laid down in a union rule book. A list of issues or items for discussion is generally drawn up beforehand by one of the officers. This comprises the formal agenda. Issues which are not listed but which members wish to discuss can usually be raised at the end of the meeting as 'any other business'. Whoever has control of the making of the agenda has a large degree of control over what is discussed. There is also an 'informal agenda' which arises from tacit agreements between members, particularly officers, about what sort of items should or should not appear on the formal agenda and where priorities should lie.

The branch agenda is important in three ways: it indicates the range of union concerns and hence the extent of its relevance to members' lives; it is the basis for local negotiation with management; and it is the first step in forming national policy which is constructed from motions put forward by branch committees for consideration at national conference.

In the COHSE hospital branch the formal and informal agendas were completely controlled by men. Four different mechanisms operated to keep women's issues off the branch agenda. The first was an unspoken agreement to restrict discussion to traditional men's issues, i.e. to the informal agenda. The omission of women's issues, is a more important indicator of male control than the marginalization and subordination of issues which are at least articulated (Munro, 1990). Issues may be excluded because of their origin rather than their content. White working class men appropriate the agenda to their own ends, excluding not only women but black workers, disabled workers, lesbians and gays. This mechanism operates on a barely conscious level - the consequence of men confining their attention to 'proper', traditional, male union issues, enabling them to feel they are 'right' in what they are doing. Childcare problems are an example of the kind of issue which, although of crucial importance to the canteen staff who had to work a complicated system of shifts and rosters, was never raised at the COHSE branch. Problems about caring for elderly and disabled people concerned several of the hospital women, but they too found no place on the union agenda.

The second mechanism was domination: by numbers, by familiarity with procedure and by the confidence which comes from long practice of running and speaking at meetings. In the COHSE hospital branch this resulted in an agenda devoted almost exclusively to men's issues. During the year's observation, most branch business centred on the introduction of a bonus scheme for uniformed porters; up to eight porters - instead of the usual one - attended meetings where crucial decisions were made about this. Bonus schemes were part of an NHS drive (a result of public spending cuts) to get costs down. Labour costs bulk large in NHS spending and the bonus schemes aimed to increase productivity thereby allowing a reduction in the numbers employed; this was to be effected by wastage rather than redundancy. The increases in productivity were to be achieved through time study and job analysis carried out by management consultants; those presently employed would benefit by increased wages. The schemes were introduced on a voluntary basis.

Union and management both thought bonus schemes more appropriate for men's jobs (like portering) than women's (like cleaning). They are easier to introduce in jobs where productivity is easy to measure, but it is difficult to argue that portering and cleaning differ much in this respect. In the COHSE branch, the bonus scheme would bring immediate financial benefit to the porters currently employed. So this might be seen as an example of men using their power to further their own interests. But there is a tendency in some service jobs for women to work with greater effort than men. Where workers are putting out maximum effort, productivity cannot be increased and bonus schemes have nothing to offer. The women's pace of work may have indicated that the schemes would have no effect. That is open to question, though it was certainly found to be the situation among women in the school meals service (see Chapter 4). Also, the women were wary of bonus schemes, they had less understanding than the men of the technicalities and procedures attached to them and thus relied more on advice from officers. Paid officers were also wary of the schemes because of the wastage of jobs.

The third mechanism was to treat women's issues as personal problems and handle them through individual casework rather than branch discussion. Nurses, for example, took their issues to the barber whom they regularly met on the wards; he passed them on to one of the officers who then dealt with them as personal problems. The opportunity to identify difficulties as members' issues rather than personal problems - in C. Wright Mills' terms, to transform private troubles into public issues - was lost (Mills, 1970:14-15).

The steward was reticent about the nature of the casework undertaken on behalf of women; often he just said it was something 'not worth discussing', 'petty' or 'something they should have seen to themselves'. However, the main issues which he disclosed concerned intimidation by management (including failure to follow agreed disciplinary procedure), and excessive sickness (in management's definition). The branch never discussed, let alone raised, a *general* formal complaint about the intimidatory attitudes and style of supervisory staff. Neither was the connection between sickness and stress discussed. Stress has been identified as a hazard of hospital work which causes abnormal rates of sickness and absence (cf. Norfolk and Stirton, 1985). At the hospital it was common knowledge that wards were understaffed and nurses overworked, especially at night. Such matters were never explored at the branch; sickness due to stress continued to be defined as a personal rather than as a job-related problem appropriate to casework.

Fourthly, there was a failure to take advantage of the rare occasions when women's enthusiasms were aroused and their interests were articulated. At one point the night nurses lost patience with management about their failure to ensure that the vending machines provided proper meals for the night shift. They approached the union. The management was asked to attend a branch meeting. About sixty trade unionists attended, mainly nurses, nearly all women. The manager was roughly questioned and tempers ran quite high on both sides. Following this meeting meals improved, at least for a short time. The meeting provided the occasion for the nurses to raise other grievances, but the officers failed to pursue them and the nurses did not attend any more meetings. No attempt was made by the branch to transform the grievances into branch issues. The only move made was by the branch secretary who tried to persuade the most articulate of the nurses to become a shop steward. But fearing victimization by management, she refused.

The self-fulfilling prophecy of irrelevance

Trade union ideology and rhetoric revolve around establishing and defending the rights of the powerless against the powerful. The values aspired to are those of fairness, justice and solidarity, the latter often expressed as 'brotherhood'. Yet we have argued here, using the case of the COHSE branch, that the union brothers consistently behave in a way which effectively precludes their union sisters from equal participation.

The contradiction here between values and practice is one that might be expected to create tensions. For several reasons, these tensions are contained. First, the men's behaviour, for example in defining the informal agenda and in following particular methods of representation, is sanctioned by trade union custom and practice established when men were dominant in trade union membership. The traditional practice remains in COHSE even though women are now numerically dominant. Second, the definitions of women drawn from the culture of masculinity are supported both by the traditional values of the trade unions and by the mores of a patriarchal society. These enable men to translate their oppressive behaviour into victim blaming, with women as their victims, and to explain women's lack of interest as a result of their 'natural' and primary role in family matters. Finally the subordination and neglect of women's interests bring to pass the situation about which men complain: women are alienated from their union, trapped by the self-fulfilling prophecy in a circle of irrelevance.

The major links of this circle are five. The first is male-formulated definitions of women located in the trade union culture of masculinity. The second is obstacles for women stemming from their practical role in systems of reproduction, reinforced by men's cultural definitions and by women's own complicit acceptance of their low rates of pay. The third is male-dominated structures of representation supported by gendered patterns of occupational segregation. The fourth is male-dominated structures of authority which rest both on common cultural equations of men with authority and on occupational segregation. The fifth is a male-dominated agenda which excludes many work-related issues of potential interest to women and marginalizes those which are included.

Though we have talked of mechanisms maintaining male power within the branch, we are not even hinting at conspiracy theory. The mechanisms operate largely subconsciously through the values of a patriarchal society. However, later when we come to look at ways in which women are trying to break the circle of irrelevance and at men's reactions to this, we enter a realm where subconscious attachment to the culture of masculinity is combined with conscious attempts to hold on to power. Here there may indeed be a whisper of conspiracy theory.

The circle of irrelevance may appear self-perpetuating. Two factors make it open to challenge. First there are the traditional union values of fairness, justice and equality to which women can appeal; they are likely to find support from among union men. Second, women's acceptance of patriarchal values and the culture of masculinity is incomplete. There is available to women, as we said in our introduction, a culture of femininity which can provide them with resources to challenge patriarchal values. A culture with a muted voice, it is nevertheless a potential source of women's empowerment.

COHSE branch has shown men in very tight control with women in compliance. We have raised the notion of the culture of femininity and its qualities of empowerment to show the possibility of breaking such a male stranglehold. In the next chapter we look at another union branch which is also under tight male control. This time our main focus is on what men have to gain by their power and the ways in which they exercise it when they are under challenge. We also look briefly how one woman challenged that control.

2 Collective bargaining at the grass-roots: Case 2

The financial pay-off

Male control within the union brings rewards. These are not just the comfort of a homosocial club or the pleasure of exercising power. Control over the collective bargaining agenda and the negotiating process leads to tangible advantages for men: better money, more control over the job and a quieter life (cf. Cavendish, 1982; Westwood, 1984:72). Collective bargaining operates at different levels - workplace, regional and national. Many workers are covered by agreements at more than one level. As public sector workers, the wage rates of COHSE hospital workers (**Case 1**) were negotiated at national level, but bonus payments were negotiated locally. The wage rates of the workers presented in **Case 2** were negotiated at the workplace by the TGWU branch based on the company which employed them. Consequently the men who controlled the union branch had a significant influence on the relative levels of women's and men's pay.

The creation and maintenance of higher levels of pay for men must rank as one of the most important consequences of, and reasons for, their continued dominance within the union movement. Privileging men's earnings goes against the grain of union principles of fairness, justice and equality, but also of the formal policies of many individual unions and of the TUC itself. It also runs counter to the intentions of the law of the land. However, it conforms with union custom and practice, with traditional patterns of earnings distribution in society at large, and with prevailing myths about the male family breadwinner.

A TGWU manufacturing branch

The setting for **Case 2** was a branch based in a large manufacturing company, employing around eight hundred women and two hundred men. It was a long-established company of importance in the local economy, with a history of paternalism. The TGWU organized the bulk of the workforce. A paid officer of some standing at the regional office, which was sited in the same town as the company, oversaw the affairs of the branch and had established a harmonious working relationship with management. Men dominated the union branch: more men than women attended branch meetings; men occupied all the official posts; more men were shop stewards and the works convenor, a man, had been in this post some years, but had never been elected.

On the face of things, both management and workers appeared content. But there were underlying problems, namely unequal pay and unfair union representation. At the factory women and men tended to do different jobs. A grading system had been agreed with the union; as is common, the women were bunched on the three lowest grades and consequently earned far less than the men.

A woman's story: challenging men at the annual wage round

There were several women stewards at the factory, but with the exception of our informant, a part-time cleaner, they were not active because 'women believe that it is men's place to run the union'. The union encouraged all shop stewards to follow basic trade union education courses as soon as they took office. But women did so only reluctantly: they were always outnumbered by men who took advantage of their unfamiliarity with union procedure to make them uncomfortable.

> Women lose contact at home having babies. They become convinced they're not clever enough. I was like it. I wouldn't go on basic training for ages. You're always in a minority. Some women go and they're overwhelmed and cold-shouldered by the men and they can't continue. Then the men say it proves a lack of commitment.

After she had finished her basic training, the woman steward went on a woman-only course and found it a liberating experience. She began to feel a new confidence in her own views. She got to know one or two other women from the course. Then the factory went on strike and she spent a lot of time picketing and helping run a soup kitchen. She had not been at the factory for very long and as a cleaner she worked on split shifts. Nevertheless, she had developed relationships of mutual trust with the women who worked day shifts on the assembly line, as well as with the cleaners.

For the 1980 wage review the workers were, as normal, represented by a union review body, responsible for making recommendations to the branch. Out of eight workers on this review body, only two were, in the words of our informant, 'allowed' to be women. One of the decisions to be made each year was whether the wage increase should be taken by flat-rate or by percentage - the former favouring the lower grades and women, the latter the higher grades and men. The woman steward discovered that the review body was likely to favour a percentage increase; it was to be combined with a bonus system and paid over a period of several years. At the end of the period those on the top grades (the men) would have an increase of around £10 a week in take-home pay, while those on the bottom would only get around £1.

She was anxious that women in the factory should understand what was happening, and be able to express their views. The procedure laid down was for the review body to discuss the different proposals, then to get the shop stewards to report on the views of the members and, on this basis, to come to a decision about members' preferences. Finally the review body would report this decision to management. What usually happened was that only selected stewards were told of the wage proposals. Few ever consulted their members and of those who did, not all explained the full implications. As a result the review body, dominated by men, was usually able to choose the deal that suited them best.

Filled with confidence from her new course, the woman steward decided to intervene at branch level and propose a change of procedure: that the pay deal be decided by a ballot of the members rather on recommenation of the review body. She had spoken up at the branch in the past and this had attracted some hostility. 'We're not having this clever part-time worker telling us what to do' said one man voicing the views of the majority. In time-honoured fashion she mobilised her followers; calling to her aid women whom she had helped in the past, she persuaded them to attend the branch meeting and got one to agree to propose a ballot, and another to second it. But plans went wrong: the person who was seconding failed to appear. She herself seconded, but the branch chairman said this was out of order because her name was not on the motion paper. He tore it up: the motion fell. Afterwards when she consulted the rule book she found that his ruling was incorrect.

Time was getting short; if a ballot could not be arranged soon the percentage system would be adopted, so she proposed an emergency motion. This time, in spite of there being only three days notice even more women attended and the motion was passed. But notice of the emergency motion should have been posted before the meeting, allowing time for discussion. The vote was disallowed. The matter would have to go to the next branch meeting. There followed a period of harassment by the men who were becoming frightened of being outnumbered and losing control. The branch chairman tried to silence her by declaring that as a part-time worker she had no right to vote. She insisted she did, and asked him to put his views in writing. He would not do so. The men were angered by the effrontery of a part-time steward trying to change their ways of doing things. She was threatened: a male steward driving a fork lift truck suspended a bale of straw over her car. She received a message that if she did not give up the idea of a ballot she would be out of a job.

There was ill-feeling and the woman steward became angry. Eventually, she went for help to the local union office. She hoped the office would see the case as one of women's rights and would support her. But the office stood with the men and she was warned to take the matter no further.

Despite this warning she contemplated complaining directly to the National Women's Officer. She drafted a letter but did not sent it: she was scared of going over the heads of the local union bureaucracy and officials of her branch. The message from the local office was clear; it was 'keep off - otherwise your life will become really difficult!' and she accepted it. If women's rights in this particular factory were going to be advanced, some other way would have to be found, perhaps involving co-operation with the local union bureaucracy rather than confrontation. What she had achieved, however, was to make the men, the stewards and the union bureaucracy, aware that things were changing, that women were becoming more conscious of their rights, and that it was only a matter of time before men were going to have to make some concessions.

Issues raised by Case 2

Collective bargaining and unequal pay

This case has shown men at the grass-roots of the union movement using power for their own material gain. It has shown the leadership of the branch controlling the negotiating process to achieve higher wage increases for men than for women. Informal practices and procedures, developed over the years, kept power in male hands: numerical dominance of men in the negotiating body was ensured; information was largely restricted to the negotiators and kept from the membership (cf. Pollert, 1981:178; Purcell, 1982:58; Stageman, 1980); male financial privilege was validated by appeal to the union tradition of maintaining differentials.

Pay differentials are usually thought of as corresponding to differences in skill and training. Skill, however, is largely a subjective notion: conventional ideas about what factors determine skill have been socially constructed over many years. Trade unions have been largely instrumental in this process. Countless agreements made at grass-roots level and others made at national level have contributed to currently accepted definitions and hierarchies of skill. Nearly all such agreements have been dominated by men. And this is one of the main reasons why men's jobs have become regarded as skilled while women's are seen as unskilled, why men's wage rates are so much higher than women's (cf. Westwood, 1984:233). This is why women argue that free collective bargaining, so beloved by the trade union movement, has over the years served them very ill. They do not argue that trade unionism itself is not to their benefit, but that they might have fared far better if women as well as men had been in control.

The woman steward challenged the widening of pay differentials, but she did not question the grading structure on which they were based. Skill gradings and pay differentials serve men well. However, as the union movement tried to reform and restructure itself for the future, grading systems have been challenged both through equal value legislation and through national negotiation. We discuss these developments in Part 3.

Men as 'the problem'

Male trade unionists and academics seeking to explain women's low participation in trade unions usually begin by defining women as a problem for the unions. In fact, it is more realistic to see things the other way round. **Case 2**, like **Case 1**, indicates that it is men not women who are 'the problem'. On this occasion it was men's attempts to keep control over collective bargaining, rather than women's lack of interest, which excluded women from the bargaining process.

The TGWU men fought to hold on to their power and the social and economic advantage it brought. They fought hard, they fought dirtily and they bent the rules. They fought from within a trade union culture constructed around men's experience and their ideas about the kind of work with which trade unions should be engaged. Proper work in this context is full-time work for which specialized training is needed and jobs which entail hard physical effort, in other words traditional men's jobs. Part-time work and the caring, cleaning and catering service jobs whose skilled are learned in the home are devalued, and thought of as second-class work. These tacit assumptions are part of the trade union movement's 'hidden agenda'.

Men's struggle to retain control emerged from this hidden agenda. Hence the attack was made upon the woman steward, not in terms of what she proposed, but because of who she was and what she did - a *part-time, woman, cleaner*. Each word carried a message of second-class status; in the heat of the quarrel the words were used as terms of abuse. The men tacitly agreed they could not allow a person in this position to share control of branch business. Looked at in this way it is easy to understand the men's lack of compunction in bending branch rules, in tearing up the branch motion, in trying to deny part-timers their right to vote: trade union ideals of fairness and justice could not prevail against the local masculine culture. The strength of feeling unleashed in this case suggests that it will be a hard struggle to get the men to share their power.

Failure to support women

The role of the paid officer   When the woman steward went for assistance to the local union office the men activated their well-established links with the paid officer who normally dealt with this branch and she got no satisfaction. The role of paid officers can be critical to the success or failure of women's struggle to get themselves heard. In introducing this case we mentioned the close relationship which existed between management and union officers, paid and unpaid. In the eyes of the woman steward the relationship was far too cosy: seeking help from the local office, she found the paid officer already aligned with the branch officers, against her. The officer in question did not want to enter an already fraught situation. He was nearing retirement and in poor health; it was rumoured that all he wanted now was a quiet life. The job of a paid officer is demanding. The daily representation of the powerless is a struggle; the inevitable accommodations which have to be made can be demoralising. Furthermore, paid officers deal daily with business people of no greater ability than themselves, but who pull in considerably higher salaries. For many the ideal of a better, more just society which in their youth seemed attainable, in mature years appears to be further away than ever. Old men who retain the fire and mental energy of their youth are unusual; they are more likely to settle for a quiet life, unlikely to be willing to rock the boat for the principle of women's equality.

At the regional union office the officers were all men, and most of them were unsympathetic to national policies supporting equality for women. Attempts to activate such policies would upset their established routines. The unpopularity of women's rights within the union office was fanned by competition between the union and local educational institutions. The latter provided TUC-sponsored courses for shop stewards and health and safety officers, and had recently pioneered a successful series of courses where both tutors and students were women. The TGWU itself ran a variety of courses. The TGWU education officers resented the success of the young women tutors from the educational institutions in generating enthusiasm and activity among shopfloor women, particularly since the tutors had limited trade union experience. Thus generational and institutional factors set, as they were, in the context of traditional trade union culture, were inimical to the interests of women.

Women's Advisory Structures Set up in response to the 1979 TUC *Charter for Equality for Women within Trade Unions*, the TGWU Women's Advisory Structures were intended to act as a forum for debate between women, as a channel of advice from women members to those (mainly men) in the unions' mainstream structures, and as a support to women members. In the TGWU the Women's Advisory Committees should have provided communication between the grass-roots and the top of the union. However, the regional TGWU Women's Advisory Committees which included men as well as women, appointees as well as elected members, often came under male control (cf. Westwood, 1984:72). In this case they seemed to be irrelevant. There was also, supposedly, a direct line to the National Women's Officer. But the National Women's Officer seemed very remote and, as we said, the woman steward did not try to get in touch. But most important of all, the steward had to consider her continued relationships at workplace and branch. It was time to call a halt in this particular battle; the struggle would go on, in another place or at another time.

Conclusions

Male culture and male control

The mechanisms by which men kept control of branch affairs operated within the context of a culture of masculinity, one of the most prominent features of which was male bonding. Men bonded together against women:

they did so within the branch; across the boundary between members and the union bureaucracy; and across the boundary between union and employers. Within the branch bonding proved effective because most of the regulars at branch meetings were men. Across the member/bureaucracy boundary its effectiveness was guaranteed by the absence of women paid officers. Male bonding was probably also a factor in maintaining good relationships across the union/employer boundary. As the case illustrates, men and management both had an interest in keeping down the wages of the large numbers of low-paid women.

At branch meetings, within the supportive culture of a male-bonded group, men used their own stereotypes of women, defining them as primarily domestic creatures, out of place in union affairs. This justified them in regarding women's interests as outside proper union business, 'private' troubles appropriate to casework rather than 'public issues' of importance to the branch (Mills, 1970). It enabled them to regard women's grievances as trivial and to devalue women's work.

Because men attended more meetings and conducted more union business, they were more familiar with union procedure. In the COHSE branch men were accustomed to ignore women. In the TGWU branch, supported by the group's culture of masculinity, men were prepared to use and misuse union procedure to prevent women's views from being put to the membership and so risk men losing their pay advantage. United by the male bond, the union bureaucracy was prepared to turn a blind eye to deviations from procedure. The brothers in the branch were able to block all the normal procedural moves women could make from within. The Women's Advisory Structures should have acted as an escape route, but male domination of the appointed members made them appear inappropriate. Finally fear of retribution made a direct approach to the National Women's Officer unappealing.

Interest, activism and consciousness

Both chapters have reported much lower participation in union affairs by women than by men. Yet each has also reported an issue which generated a great deal of activity among women, indicating that in certain situations women show great interest in union affairs. In **Case 1** the women confronted management; their activity was short-lived; they received full support from the men of the branch; their immediate grievance was redressed and they took no further part in branch life. In **Case 2** the women challenged men's control of the union branch; male mechanisms of control were brought in to repulse that challenge and the women lost their battle.

Women's challenge to male control at the grass-roots of the movement is a theme which we develop in the remainder of Part 1.

We end this chapter with some brief comments on the TGWU women's 'rebellion'. Initially it was based on the women's conviction that they were being cheated by men of their just financial rewards. Later, the women's grievances centred on the refusal of men to acknowledge their democratic rights and men's disrespect for them as women. Furthermore an awareness was dawning among these women that their low pay was not a fact of nature but was the result of deliberate decisions taken by the union in favour of men. The women became aware they might remedy this by exercising their rights to participate in the negotiating process. This seemed a straightforward choice. However, the men rendered the women's efforts ineffective; the women's interest and enthusiasm waned; their activity dwindled and the woman shop steward was left on her own.

The rebellion was clearly sparked and led by this one woman steward, who, unusually, took an active part in union affairs, particularly in the workplace. She had come to understand how collective bargaining operated, at this workplace, to the grave disadvantage of women, and her story relates her unsuccessful attempts to seek redress.

She was at that time the only woman in the branch with a clear consciousness of class and of gender relations. She came from a background of trade union commitment by the men in her family. She had the moral support of her husband, a factor said by other women activists to be important. Her years of juggling domestic responsibilities with low-status service jobs meant she knew from experience that women were exploited. She had been helped to articulate and theorize this knowledge, she said, by exposure to women-only trade union education. In the next chapters we examine further, and in very different situations, some of the factors affecting women's trade union and gender consciousness and the relation of both to their participation in the unions.

3 Changing consciousness and political ideology: Case 3

Ideology, experience and consciousness

The previous two chapters have examined how women at the grass-roots are controlled and subordinated by men. The next three deal with aspects of the theme of changing consciousness, with its connection to male power and control and with women's resistance to that control. But they do so in very different ways.

The focus in this chapter is on the influence on consciousness of ideology, which we define as a body of ideas through which the social structure of society is explained. We distinguish between conventional ideologies which refer to society as it is, and alternative ideologies which seek, additionally, to develop ideas about how society should or will develop in the future. **Case 3** is that of a local association (branch) of the National Union of Teachers, a union representative of white-collar, basically middle-class, professional unions, and an association typical of many found in large urban areas.

We do not set out, in this chapter, to test hypotheses about the role of ideology in changing consciousness. We seek rather to examine the influence of one alternative ideology of the political left, held by a small group of activists, on the trade union consciousness of the members of their local association. We ask further whether trade union consciousness raised in this situation tended to advance or marginalize the development of gender consciousness. (It must be stressed that we are in no way concerned with the effect of such ideology on the practice of teaching.) We argue that left-wing ideology, which is a valuable analytic tool for explaining the class structure of society, has been largely appropriated by men, has become male-centred and now tends to block the development of gender consciousness among both women and men. We refer more briefly to the role of experience in raising gender consciousness. We touch - but only lightly, as the data warrant - on the role of feminist ideology in raising gender consciousness.

We see changing consciousness as a crucial aspect of social change. People resist in situations when they are aware of something amiss in the way they are treated. There are different types of resistance, some which attempt to change an oppressive system, others which may challenge it symbolically but do not try to change it. Women workers resist not only control by management, but also control by men, as illustrated by Purcell (1979, 1986) in her analysis of cross-gender joking in the factory. Pollert (1981) too reports women factory workers who resist management control by using their femininity and sexuality; she describes it as 'symbolic' rather than organized resistance. Westwood (1984:101, 238) recounts a far greater degree of organized resistance, expressed by means of a shopfloor culture based on 'friendship', 'solidarity', and the 'collectivity of sisterhood'. It competes with management for the women's time, for example in the celebration of rituals, and for resources. The sisterhood of the shopfloor was powerful, but it gave contradictory messages: it was based on women, but on their position in a patriarchal, sexist society. Relationships with other women provided the factory women with the 'essential support for their lives', support for one another 'through pregnancy, death, illness, marriage breakdown and sadness'. In a sense these relationships were the trade unionism of the women, or a substitute for it (Oakley, 1981:272). But they did not offer the kind of challenges we are interested in. We seek to identify, at the grass-roots, the seeds of challenges to the mechanisms and structures of male power within the unions.

The issues discussed below are those of changing consciousness - class, trade union, and gender. Women's route to gender consciousness is not always direct; there is evidence that many working class women achieve consciousness of gender after having first become conscious of their role within the working class and within their trade union. We define consciousness as a twofold awareness: firstly about the structure of constraints attaching to particular sets of social relations; secondly about the need to change those relations.

It has been argued by Hunt (1980) and Wajcman (1983) among others that, although experience makes people aware of their subordination and may give them some understanding of the structures and processes by which it is maintained, the development of a sustainable consciousness needs a deeper and more coherent understanding of structures of oppression. They argue further, that this requires the support of an alternative ideology. They see appropriate ideologies to be those of the political left, based on social class as defined by the relations of production. Wajcman's views arise from her study of a sit-in during the seventies where women resisted redundancy by forming and running their own co-operative. Their project folded. They became disillusioned. Wajcman, who joined them towards the end of the experiment, noted that they failed to develop a consciousness of their identity as trade unionists, as members of the working class or as women. The only change was a strengthening of their consciousness as workers in their own small local factory. Wajcman attributes this failure to their isolation and lack of access to any alternative ideology: they were industrial workers in a rural culture and they were rejected by their own trade union. For Wajcman the case shows that experience alone is insufficient for the development of new areas of consciousness; exposure to an alternative ideology is an additional requirement.

Women's willingness and ability to challenge their oppression depend in large measure on their becoming conscious of an alternative way of ordering social life. Alternative ideologies assert that change is possible. They offer both an analysis of the present and a vision of the future. They provide individuals with new ways for interpreting old experiences, give support to those who are seeking new understandings or who are working for change. They are a fertile ground for changing consciousness, but only within their own terms. Feminism and trade unionism provide such ideologies.

Historically trade unionism as a working class movement has been closely allied with the political left. The movement together with the Fabian society were the roots from which the present day Labour Party developed, and links remain close. The dominant ideology of capitalism endorses the existing class structure of society. The alternatives to which workers have readiest access at branch and workplace are the ideologies of the left, those which to varying degrees challenge the existing class structure. At the local association the left ranged from the Revolutionary Communist Party through to the Labour Party.

Ideologies of the left tend to emphasise class at the expense of other social divisions. Their analysis of gender tends to be rudimentary; until recent years they were almost gender-blind. A masculine bias pervades their theories. These rest on an analysis of the relations of production, in which wage earners are referred to almost exclusively as men, heads of households and family breadwinners. Women workers are conceived of mainly in their role as a reserve army of labour. The theorists and leaders of the far left tend to be men. Traditionally they have had heroes rather than heroines: Marx, Engels and Trotsky are revered far more rather than Alexandra Kollontai and Rosa Luxemburg; nearer to home Keir Hardie, Ramsay Macdonald and Aneurin Bevan more than Ellen Wilkinson, Jennie Lee and Barbara Castle. For all these reasons, the influence of the political left on the development of gender consciousness tends to block rather than catalyse its development. From the seventies on, the male bias within Marxism has been subject to theoretical challenge, in the labour process debate (Beechey, 1978a, 1978b; Bruegel, 1979) and in the domestic labour debate (Creighton, 1985; Dalla Costa and Jones, 1973; Gardiner, 1975; Seccombe, 1974). The attempt to weld gender relations onto Marxism has proved problematical and has been likened to an 'unhappy marriage' (Hartmann, 1981). However as noted in the Introduction there have been recent advances in that area (see *Sociology* 1989; Walby, 1990).

Feminism has also developed a fairly coherent ideology based on gender as a major source of oppression. There are of course differences of emphasis within feminism as there are within the ideologies of the left; the ways in which gender relates to other social structures are the subject of much debate. The ideology of feminism, however, is far less likely to be accessible at workplace and branch than those of the political left. Feminism, as a named social movement, has flourished more in the context of community than the workplace, more among the middle than the working class. Yet a minority of working class feminists have made important contributions to women's advance within the union movement, for instance the Lancashire cotton women in the late nineteenth century and the civil service clerks in the interwar years.

In considering the role of ideology in changing the gender consciousness of trade union women, we keep the following questions in mind. What kind of ideology? How do the class-structured ideologies of the political left and gender-structured ideologies of feminism relate to one another among the grass-roots members? If both individual experience and ideological understanding of oppression are necessary before consciousness changes, what is the balance between the two? Will it differ in different situations and with different groups of trade unionists?

Gender consciousness and political ideology: a local association of the NUT

Gender in the profession and the union

Gender, in the form of discussions and struggles about women's rights, has been an issue in the teaching unions and in the teaching profession itself for the whole of the twentieth century. Contradictory forces have been at work, some highlighting the issue of women's rights, others tending towards their suppression, resulting in a somewhat ambivalent attitude towards gender.

The NUT is a middle-class union, different from those already discussed. As professionals, teachers are subject to pressures to conform with the dominant ideology of society. Such pressures emanate from their employers, head teachers, the parents of the children they teach and the government. But there is another element. During their training, both in study and as part of the student experience, teachers are usually exposed to alternative ideologies, including often those of the far left. Some find that these provide a more satisfactory explanation of social relations than the dominant ideology, and a better hope for the future. A small minority continue to hold and propagate ideologies of the far left after taking up posts as teachers. Such teachers find a natural home in the trade union movement with its historic left-wing connections where, as hard-working activists of their local associations, they often become influential.

If ideologies of the political left are associated with teachers through the student experience, so is feminism. And feminism too finds a place within the trade union movement, though not such a secure one as the political left. Middle-class feminist teachers and women's rights workers have exerted considerable influence on the NUT and teaching unions. Founded in the 1870s, the NUT was first numerically dominated by men. But since the end of the nineteenth century women have been in the majority; they comprise roughly 60 percent of the membership today. However men have always dominated union organization, on the NEC and other committees and as officers. The outstanding women's issue championed by the NUT has been equal pay, which was first raised within the union before the first world war. During the war many women became active trade unionists and in 1919 persuaded the union to make equal pay a national policy. However, male interests, inside and outside the union, ensured for the next twenty years that no serious attempts were made to implement it. Rather the reverse; for example in the thirties the NUT collaborated with various local authorities in barring the employment of married women; it also agreed to greater percentage reductions in women's salaries than in men's.

Contradictory attitudes to gender were embodied in the creation of two further teaching unions. The NUWT (National Union of Women Teachers) was founded in 1907 by women members of NUT angered at the union's refusal to support the equal pay motion proposed in that year. NAS (National Association of Schoolmasters), a male union, broke away from NUT in 1919 immediately after equal pay was accepted. Its explicit purpose was to fight against equal pay.

NUWT, together with the women's clerical unions, was largely responsible for keeping equal pay a live issue during the 1930s, disbanding in 1961 when equal pay was formally achieved. In 1975, after the Equal Pay Act, NAS merged with UWT (Union of Women Teachers) - founded in the 1960s to cater for the 'career' woman teacher. NAS/UWT does not show the gross chauvinism of the old NAS, but its support for women has been stronger in rhetoric than practice (Cunnison, forthcoming). The NUT, in contrast has, from the late seventies, worked to improve the position of women within the profession and the union.

The role of the NUT in reflecting teachers' aspirations to professional status introduces another dimension. Teachers' professional (or semi-professional as some people would insist) status rests on the special training and qualifications required to practise within the state system. Teaching, however, is not a self-regulating profession; there is no control over standards and training. But teachers do have a strong professional identity. This carries a notion of professional equality which overrides women's actual experience of discrimination and inhibits the development of gender consciousness.

The structure of the teaching profession is, and has for years been, marked by gross gender inequality which has been accompanied by a strand of gross sexism (Littlewood, 1989), expressed within the structure of the unions. Although women constitute some 60-70 per cent of all teachers, men occupy a higher proportion of top posts leaving women crowded at the bottom of the salary scales. Even with equal pay, women still earn less than men largely because they are less likely to be promoted. Women and men work with children of different ages: proportionally more women in nursery and primary teaching, more men in secondary teaching which carries higher prestige. Women and men work in different subject areas: more women in the arts and domestic subjects, more men in science and technology. Men tend to be more ambitious and more confident in their ambition than do women. In this structured inequality tensions between women and men are defused by a belief in the myth of 'professional equality'.

Of the activists in the local association, most had become politically conscious during their student days. Political activism was characteristic of the student generation of the sixties when student uprisings occurred throughout Europe and America. At the same time the second wave of the feminist movement was emerging. It too was international in scope, linking women in America, UK, the continent and beyond; it transformed the gender consciousness and the lives of many of the women it touched. Of the two movements, left-wing politics has had a greater effect on teacher trade unionists: the ideology of the political left is already deeply embedded in trade union philosophy, while the ideology of feminism challenges some of the union movement's most hallowed traditions and practices. Again the early feminist movement has tended to direct itself only to women, rejecting and excluding men. It did not fit so easily with a mixed-sex movement.

The salient features of the teachers' background were thus: a professional identity carrying contradictory messages about the significance of gender; a trade union which talked about equality but was both dominated by men and strongly associated with professionalism; exposure to alternative political ideologies with a resultant small minority strongly attached to the politics of the far left and an even smaller minority attached to the politics of feminism; and a strong pressure to conform to the existing conventions of society.

Gender consciousness, feminism and far left ideology

Case 3 concerns the relation between gender consciousness, feminism and left-wing ideology within a local association of the NUT, the largest of the teaching unions. In 1978 the local association had approximately 1,700 members; three-quarters were women. The average attendance at association meetings, with around 40 men and 20 women, showed the dominance of men. The proportion of members attending was higher than in **Case 1** or **2**. Men spoke more at meetings. A count of speakers sampled over a six-month period revealed more than three times as many men as women; men and women, on average, each spoke three times, but the men spoke at greater length. A number of married couples came regularly. Usually the husband played an articulate role, the wife the part of silent consort. Most of the officers of the association were men although the secretary at this time was, unusually, a woman; the minuting secretary as usual was a woman.

The most frequently debated issues were those of professional interest such as salaries, class size, temporary contracts etc. Those and routine union business took up most association time. Industrial action undertaken over teachers' pay was prominent for a period. Issues of wider interest were discussed occasionally including the effect of public spending cuts, civil and political rights abroad, specially in connection with South Africa and Chile and occasionally issues of concern to women. But issues where gender was central were few and far between. We discuss them in detail later in the chapter.

The association at this time was concerned with a power struggle between the moderates and the left wing - between the current office holders and the Socialist Teachers. The salient sets of beliefs which structured teachers' thinking, political ideology, professional identity, feminism and conformity were all drawn into the struggle for power and aligned with one faction or the other. The ideology of the left wing was demonized by the moderates, who sought to monopolize the theme of professionalism, and with whom conformity found a natural home. Feminism and feminist ideology became more or less attached to the left.

Socialist Teachers was an informally organized group of trade union activists drawn from parties and factions of the far left, including the left wing of the Labour Party. The moderates were a much more loosely defined alliance, including Labour, Liberal and Conservative Party supporters. The far left had two beliefs which were unacceptable to the moderates: that real improvements could be achieved only by changing national policy; and that teachers, as trade unionists, had a duty to show solidarity with workers in struggle throughout the world. The moderates were pragmatists who believed in limiting business to issues directly affecting teachers and addressing these on a local or professional basis, and who felt strongly that wider political issues should be kept separate. They outnumbered the far left at association meetings; their support among the inactive membership was far greater and could be called on when necessary, for example on the occasion of a 'vote of confidence' in the leadership. This central struggle focused members' attention; it relegated gender to a side issue.

Gender-related trade union issues

Gender issues arose from three distinct sources each with a different ideological perspective. Most arose from the Socialist Teachers group, some from socialist-feminists and a very few from a handful of women who, while asserting their professional identity, claimed that politics should not be discussed in a trade union setting.

Socialist Teachers were mainly men; their ideology was based on class relations where class was defined in terms of productive (male) occupations. They reflected the male-dominated culture associated with parties of the political left. Although relations of gender were not part of their ideology, gender was accorded some importance - due partly to one or two socialist-feminist women, and partly to a general sympathy with alternative ideologies. The group was small but well-organized, often holding caucus meetings in advance of ordinary meetings. It was loosely connected to the national London-based Socialist Teachers' Alliance. Each year, in liaison with STA, a programme of conference motions was produced. It included a number of gender issues which appeared to be taken straight from the Working Women's Charter (see Introduction). Subjects of motions sent by the association to Conference in 1979 included: parental rights (with paternity leave), abortion, contraception, and parity in the payment of pensions to widowers - all proposed by men; and a flat rate salary increase (of benefit to women), improved access to a career for women, the adoption of the Working Women's Charter - proposed by women.

These conference motions were passed by the membership, some rather reluctantly: the idea of fathers having birth leave was described as 'ludicrous'. The reluctance sprang mainly from the source of the issues rather than from their content. When Socialist Teachers put forward a proposal, the gut reaction of many members was to object. They suspected the left wing of using gender to widen its support; they perceived the motions as coming from the central STA rather than from personal experience and they resented this as they did the patriarchal overtones of wives of the group appearing just to second proposals put forward by their men. The raising of gender issues by Socialist Teachers did little to change members' gender consciousness; for some it was counter-productive.

A further example of Socialist Teachers' failure to respond to gendered (not feminist) differences of interest among teachers, occurred during prolonged industrial action in support of a pay claim. In the action teachers refused the usual cover provided for absent colleagues. A consequence was that children were sometimes sent home from school or advised not to come because there was no one to teach them. From the outset women were less keen on action than men. Working more often with the early years, women teachers anticipated the problems and dangers that might arise for young children and their mothers, many of whom were employed during school hours. Older children would be in less physical danger. But both young and old would lose hours of schooling which few could afford. As the action dragged on without response from the employers, enthusiasm dried up. The hard core of support - and it was very firm - came from the male-dominated senior high schools where most of the Socialist Teachers were. Their determination prolonged the action and drew high levels of attendance at association meetings from teachers, mainly women, who wanted to end it. The insistence on maintaining action which did not appear to be producing results alienated a number of teachers from the union, particularly women. After it was withdrawn, attendance fell. It did not recover its previous level.

Three self-acknowledged socialist-feminists were the second source of gender issues. No more than one was active at any one time. All were already committed socialists when, through feminism, they became aware of the singular importance of gender in shaping women's lives. With like-minded women they were part of a loosely-knit nation-wide socialist-feminist 'movement'. This had little impression on the basic thinking of the political left. However, the naming of socialist-feminism provided, for feminists concerned with class inequality, a distinctive identity and a standpoint from which they could cooperate pragmatically with the male-dominated far left. The three socialist-feminists in the local association were allied with Socialist Teachers. They acted independently in association meeting but were confident of the group's backing. The issues which they raised included the preservation of the 1967 Abortion Bill, creche facilities for local meetings, funding for a local Women's Centre and Women's Aid and a 'Reclaim the Night' march against male violence. Members, women especially, respected the socialist-feminists' courage and commitment to their beliefs and they gave more support to these issues than those raised by Socialist Teachers. But where they could see no direct relevance to teaching, they remained sceptical.

The third source of gender issues were women who, though holding political views and even party attachments, thought politics and unions should be kept separate. The issues from this source were directly connected with teachers' problems and were raised infrequently. They were received with respect and judged with open-mindedness. The women spoke from the standpoint of experience and professionalism and the female membership, recognising their own experience and problems, was able to identify with them. One proposal suggested a single intake in the first year of school, arguing it would enable all children to secure an equal grounding and to reach a similar standard before moving to the next class. This directly concerned women who usually taught the early years. In this example, gender and professional issues were fused. The proposal received wholehearted support.

In an association dominated by men and secondary teachers, few women (except for the socialist-feminists) felt sufficiently confident to stand up and speak. In two years' observation, only one woman, a primary teacher, consistently presented gender-relevant issues arising from her own experience. She came from a family background of intense political activity. She knew women members who held strong opinions on these issues. She reflected on their silence. All this led to a change in her own consciousness, to a new awareness of the powerful influence of gender on women's and men's contribution to public debate. Her consciousness was reinforced by joining a local women's educational pressure group, by reflecting on both her daughters' education and her own problems in gaining promotion.

Summary: gender consciousness, ideology and experience

What emerges from this analysis? First, the political ideology of Socialist Teachers, though it resulted in a strong trade union consciousness within the group, failed to raise their gender consciousness much beyond the level of rhetoric. Second, their ideological message failed to have any impact on either the trade union or gender consciousness of the majority of members, who tended to resent their proselytizing. Third, the interventions of the socialist-feminists, although they provoked less resentment than those of Socialist Teachers, also failed to make any impact on the gender consciousness of ordinary members. Fourth, the gender-related ideas and issues which gained most acceptance were those grounded in experience and put forward without reference to ideology or politics.

What relevance have these findings from **Case 3** for an exploration of the role of ideology and experience in changing gender consciousness? The reluctance of the membership to engage with the gender issues presented by the Socialist Teachers group may be explained in two ways. The first is that rhetoric on its own is not persuasive. The second is that socialist ideology, as formulated within a male-dominated culture, does not provide women with any new understandings of the gendered nature of their social position. It is thus most unlikely to lead to any change in their consciousness of gender. Teachers were far more willing to support women's issues which were directly relevant to teaching experience than those associated with socialist rhetoric or socialist-feminist ideology. This suggests the primacy of experience over ideology. However, ideology still may have an important role to play in both raising and sustaining gender consciousness. In the next chapter we comment on where we think its role is appropriate.

The primacy of experience over ideology for this group of professional middle-class women teachers is also suggested by the rapid rise in gender consciousness which took place a few years later. This centred around sex-discrimination in promotion and linked immediately to the experiences of women teachers who were, along with other women professionals of the period, becoming more career conscious and more frustrated by sexism. Within the NUT it was underpinned by a survey *Promotion and the Woman Teacher* published in 1980, by an increase in feminist activity within the NUT bureaucracy, by national activity of feminists on behalf of the education of girls and by pressure from feminist members living in some of the larger urban areas. NUT organized, on request, a series of workshops throughout the country on sexism within teaching. The women of this association took advantage of the offer. Some thirty attended a local workshop. In an informal atmosphere and in the context of small group discussion, all felt able to give their views. Promotion was the most popular topic. Networks of mutual support were established, but the women did not continue to meet as a group.

In the intervening years the numbers attending the association had contracted; the moderates had ceased to attend, leaving the left wing in control. With the exception of socialist-feminist women, the newly gender conscious NUT members did not seek out their trade union association to assist them in their struggles against discrimination within the profession. They saw their local association as being more interested in issues of social class and education than in strictly professional issues. Their experiential route to gender consciousness had not raised their class consciousness and they preferred to reserve their energies for their professional careers.

4 Male power, industrial action and changing consciousness: Cases 4 and 5

The 'Winter of Discontent'

In this chapter we continue our exploration of changing consciousness and its relation to experience and ideology, but place the discussion within the context of organized male power within the unions. The chapter takes two case studies: a workplace employing only women and a mixed-sex trade union branch. In both the workers were organized by the National Union of Public Employees. This chapter deals with a broad range of data, gathered during workplace participation, meetings organized by trade unions (including monthly branch meetings) and on other formal and informal occasions. There are three closely related themes: the development of trade union consciousness through the experience of industrial action; the capacity of male power in the union for encouraging this development; and the extent to which growth of trade union consciousness encourages or inhibits the development of gender consciousness.

The industrial action to which we refer took place in the public sector in 1979. In contrast to that of the teachers, it was of major national importance. Unrest began in December and culminated in a strike in February and March; the period has gone down in history as the Winter of Discontent. The late seventies was a turning point in the political and economic life of the country and in trade union affairs. Recurrent crises in the balance of payments during the late sixties and early seventies had resulted in uncontrolled inflation. The government obtained help from the IMF in controlling the balance of payments, but only on condition that public spending was severely cut. In consequence, it decided to impose a five per cent limit on public sector wages, well below current inflation. An announcement to this effect was made at the beginning of the annual round of public sector wage claims. The unions' claim proposed a minimum wage of two-thirds of the national average (amounting to £70). The result was impasse in negotiations and industrial action by the public sector unions (COHSE, GMWU, NUPE and TGWU). A strike-ridden period followed during which selected groups of local authority and NHS workers took action: grave-diggers, refuse collectors, hospital cleaners, drivers etc. In the locality where the case studies were carried out, the action was confined to hospital workers. Nationally it was not successful, ending with a commission of enquiry and a payment on account of £1 per week to all full-time workers. Soon afterwards, in the autumn of 1979, the Labour government fell. The subsequent election returned a Conservative government under Mrs Thatcher.

The action of the Winter of Discontent was significant for the workers who took part. They shared experiences across different occupations, unions and regions and across gender. They organized in strike committees across these differences; they picketed, went to meetings, took part in massive demonstrations, listened to skilled union orators and talked among themselves. It was a heady, eye-opening experience and for some it began to transform the way they thought about the world, about the place of the working class, about the role of the unions and - for a few - about the place of women in the world of work. In drawing attention to these processes we are not blind to the fact that it was also a very bitter experience for the unions and their members, a major defeat and - as it turned out - the herald of a darker period in which the unions have undergone a severe battering both from the recession and from government attacks. In terms of employment conditions, women were particularly hard hit. However, in terms of the progress of women within the unions, there were some very positive effects.

A school kitchen - Case 4

The thirteen women in this case worked in a school kitchen; most worked part time. The kitchen was a hive of industry. The job was hard graft: when work study experts examined school kitchens with a view to introducing a bonus system (cf. the COHSE uniformed porters, **Case 1**), they found the women were putting in a degree of effort comparable to top bonus. The idea was abandoned. The kitchen was also like a hive in that it seemed to run by instinct. Apart from the daily menu, most information - like the preparation and cooking times for the various dishes - was held in people's heads. Yet it ran smoothly and meals were never late. A great deal of unrecognised skill went in. The cook was like a queen bee; the kitchen revolved around her. She had authority to engage temporary help and to apportion overtime. But she was unlike a queen bee in that she was always willing, especially when things were rushed, to work alongside the women. School cooks tended to be powerful people and it was from among them that strong union representation eventually emerged.

The women were organized into a general branch of NUPE along with school cleaners, a few school caretakers, refuse collectors, lollypop ladies, traffic wardens, sheltered housing wardens and others. Refuse collectors and caretakers dominated the union branch. Although women comprised the majority of the membership, they hardly ever attended branch meetings. All the shop stewards were male. School caretakers (men) represented the kitchen workers, cleaners and others employed by the education service.

The kitchen was a women's world. No men were employed there. The union had limited relevance to this world of women. School meals, like many women's public service jobs, had no tradition of union organization; systematic union recruitment went back only ten or twenty years. Moreover, although public spending cuts and privatization were looming, the women did not yet feel threatened and in need of support; that was to come. Trade union consciousness was low, gender consciousness rudimentary. The feminine, home-based identity played a lively part in conversation and personal relationships.

Encouraging women: the role of the paid officer

In **Cases 4** and **5**, consciousness developed in context of contradictory influences of male union power: paid officers encouraged trade union and (to a lesser extent) gender consciousness among women; lay officers pointed in the opposite direction. Participation of the school meals women in union affairs was mainly limited to occasional social events. But NUPE's policy was clear; it intended to increase the women's participation. Moves to this end included the reservation in 1975 of five seats for women on the NEC - a clear and public commitment. Other measures included production of union literature targeted at women; research into the position of women in the union; the creation of women-only education courses, and education for part-timers. Most important perhaps was advice to paid officers that part of their job was to encourage women: as members, as participators, as shop stewards, as branch officers, as consumers of union education, and as delegates to conferences and committees.

In many unions, NUPE among them, paid officers have resources and a degree of authority to intervene in local union affairs. Their informal authority may be considerable. They can challenge the traditional culture of masculinity when they see it discriminating against women. They can have a critical role in raising women's trade union and gender consciousness. However, not all paid officers use their power in this direction. They can choose whether to implement, ignore or even block their unions' pro-women policies.

The branches in **Cases 4** and **5** both came under the same paid officer. He was active in promoting the union's pro-women policies. He was intellectually convinced that the future viability of NUPE depended on involving women in union affairs, at all levels from the branch to the top. His encouragement and support of women significantly increased the proportion of women shop stewards in local branches. However, by the Winter of Discontent he still had not persuaded any of the city's school meals workers to become stewards. He had tried: mini-branch meetings had been held on estates where many of the members lived, but there had been little response. During the industrial action, however, he was able to persuade two school meals women, one from this kitchen, to sit on the public service workers' strike support committee. Afterwards she agreed to become a shop steward. He was also instrumental in starting regional union conferences for school meals women. At one of these, under his encouragement, a school cook made her first public speech. She later went on to become secretary of a new women-led NUPE education branch (see **Case 7**). This officer exemplified the benign use of male power.

Lay officers' lack of support

The attitude of lay officers was quite different and frankly discouraging. Work-related problems reported to the officers by the women, for example the danger of slippery floors or the lack of hot washing-up water, were ignored. Other problems, like those related to combining work and caring, although of critical importance to several, were never raised. Such problems, the women understood, were not recognised as part of a male-constructed union agenda. The women regarded the union as basically the 'men's thing'. They approached their problems on a personal basis, first with the cook then with the manager. The union was a last resort.

But when they did turn to it in this way, they encountered a stone wall of male exclusion. They reported what happened when they decided, for the first time, to take a particularly intractable problem to the branch meeting. They were apprehensive. They were the only women present at the meeting. The officers, all men, sat at a long table, opposite the ordinary members.

The women had prepared their case, but unaware of union procedure, had failed to put it on the agenda beforehand. According to procedure it could only be considered at the end of the meeting, under 'any other business'. What followed recalls **Case 2**. The men, who by custom had 'always' run the union branch, used rules and procedures to freeze the women out (cf. Walton, 1991:162-3). As soon as the meeting started the women tried to present their problem. The officers seated at the table acted 'like judges'. 'Not now' the women were told, 'later'. But there was no further explanation. A little later the women tried again and then a third time. But still it was 'not the right time'. They gave up and left. They did not go back.

When next they had a problem - one of understaffing - they went instead to their steward, thus entering another field of male dominance. All school meals stewards were caretakers and thus on higher grading and pay. Each one represented a number of different schools near his own. Caretakers were able to undertake steward responsibilities fairly easily because they worked a split shift and had few domestic responsibilities to occupy the time in between. The caretakers, however, had no experience or understanding of working in a school kitchen. These women were unlucky: their steward was also lazy. He came infrequently; when he did arrive his relationship to the women was well defined by their greeting: 'Hullo stranger!' He took over eight months to solve their problem although it could have been done without delay. While it remained unresolved the women were overworked and someone new was deprived of a job. Nevertheless they expressed only gratitude when it was settled.

Experiencing the Winter of Discontent

The experience of union action during the Winter of Discontent brought change to this kitchen. The critical event was a union-organized trip to a public service workers' demonstration in London. The women were strongly affected by this experience. The mass of people in common cause was a physical representation of union solidarity; it made them feel the potential strength of the union movement. The ritual of the march and the rally, the banners and the oratory, generated a great deal of emotion. The women may be said to have entered a state of liminality (Turner, 1969) from which they emerged with stronger ideals about fairness and justice, and with firmer convictions that a better way of organizing social life must be found.

They met workers from other public service jobs and other unions. With feelings of sisterhood and brotherhood, communication was easy and they learned from one another. They returned to the kitchen slightly different people, with a greater knowledge of the extent to which their problems were shared and with a greater belief in the movement's potential for remedying them.

Apart from this emotional impact there was an ideological one, a new way of understanding the world. It came from two major sources. First from the political parties and factions who while supporting the action also publicized their own views. The Labour Party had an input; the Communists, Socialist Workers, Militants and others from the far left were tireless in their propaganda. They introduced new ideas; they talked about the power and wealth of drug companies, financing the NHS and class-based inequalities in health care. Underlying their contribution was the male-centred class-structured ideology of the political left.

The second major ideological input, from the trade union movement itself, was also male-dominated. Although women predominate among the public sector workforce and among low-paid workers, strike meetings stressed the low pay of men, their problems as family breadwinners and as mortgage holders. All implied an acceptance of the family wage. The unions also spelled out the inequalities between the classes and their own role in redressing them. Women's low pay was highlighted only once, at a public meeting addressed by a school cleaner. For women the emphasis was more upon their role as wives and daughters than as workers in their own right. Nevertheless women did identify themselves with these roles and through them with the union cause; their consciousness was raised.

Locally strike action was taken only by health service workers. However, the women in the kitchen supported the strike enthusiastically: they even claimed they wished they had been called out instead of the health service workers. Some began attending local branch meetings and as mentioned earlier, one joined the strike support committee and later became a shop steward. The kitchen workers' conversion from lukewarm card carrying members to enthusiastic supporters of industrial action is similar to that reported by Walton (1991:170).

Trade union and gender consciousness

The trade union consciousness of the school kitchen workers was raised through a combination of industrial action and the benign use of male power. Industrial action expanded the women's horizons, revealing the relevance of the union to their working lives and opening their minds to the movement's ideology. It brought them into closer contact with paid officers one of whom took the opportunity to encourage them into more active involvement.

But did this growth in trade union consciousness help the development of gender consciousness? Contradictory influences were at work. Encouraging women to become stewards and use the union to deal with their own problems had a positive effect on both trade union and gender consciousness. But the industrial action and supporting publicity were both heavily infused with the culture of masculinity. Though encouraging trade union consciousness they were counterproductive of gender consciousness.

The basic education which all new stewards were expected to take aimed to raise trade union consciousness; for women it probably also stirred gender consciousness. In thinking about trade union ideology (as any alternative ideology) people must take the important step of questioning their customary opinions and this always opens up the possibility of further questioning. Trade union ideals about equality and justice, are likely to prompt questions about sex equality and sex discrimination - the kinds of questions which are addressed on women-only courses (Beale, 1982; Elliot, 1982) to which the new women stewards were directed.

A NUPE hospital branch - Case 5

Case 5 examines the impact of the Winter of Discontent on another trade union branch, a hospital-based branch of NUPE. Here the workers, who already possessed a degree of trade union consciousness, were directly involved in the action of the Winter of Discontent. We use this case to explore further the effects of industrial action and the power of union officers on women's trade union and gender consciousness.

This NUPE hospital branch was slightly better attended and much more active than the COHSE hospital branch (**Case 1**). There were, however, similarities. Each had a large (500-700) membership, captive in the sense that the NHS advised all employees to join a union, and overwhelmingly female. The women's jobs were in a narrow range carrying low status and pay, the men's in a broader range with higher status and pay. The NUPE branch operated some similar control mechanisms to those in the COHSE branch. Shop steward representation was through occupation so there were fewer women than men; the male shop stewards had a lower workload and tended to 'help' the women, thus gaining greater negotiating expertise. Men filled most union offices. Branch meetings were small; there was virtually no competition to join the self-selected group of activists who ran them and they became, in effect, shop steward meetings. One difference was that in the NUPE branch a woman chaired the meetings during the first months of the research.

Intervention by the paid officer

Although the branch was dominated by men, women's issues were not ignored. It was looked after by the same paid officer involved with Case 4. The internal running of branches was the responsibility of lay officers; paid officers attended meetings only periodically and for a particular reason. The periodic presence of this officer was enough to ensure that women's issues were not overlooked: for example the problem of supervisors who ignored agreements to advertise internally and gave plum jobs to friends and relations. Careful monitoring of vacancies kept this problem under control.

The officer had worked with this branch for several years and had been impressed with the ancillary women's support during a recent strike. He was anxious to increase their involvement. His particular interest was in education. In 1978 when adult education put on a women-only evening course in trade union issues, the NUPE office publicized it and three women from the hospital branch attended. In 1977 the hospital laundry steward refused basic shop steward training (now compulsory for all NUPE stewards). She was intending to get married, start a family and leave work. She thought her training and the union's money would be wasted. The paid officer convinced her otherwise and she became one of the most articulate and capable of the local stewards.

Commitment, energy and personality help explain the effectiveness of the paid officer. That he was locally based was also important, enabling him to give regular support to women who showed interest, which they would be unlikely to get from lay officers and branch members.

Industrial action and trade union consciousness

The effect of the Winter of Discontent on hospital branch activists was much the same as among the school meals women: a drawing together of workers of different occupations; a heightening of emotional ties and feelings of solidarity; exposure to class-based trade union ideology; and, for some, a new or renewed commitment to working for the union. A small core of workers who already had a well developed trade union consciousness, was very heavily involved in planning and directing the action, picketing, attending and speaking at meetings; but other members were also involved. Many found trade unionism had a new relevance for them, but others - feeling patients were being put at risk - found the reverse. A steward and a lay officer both resigned from the branch.

Gender discrimination and the settlement

Despite the unions' appeal to solidarity the action privileged the concerns of men and men's trade union consciousness was changed more than that of women. Out of an elected strike committee of twenty-four, only two were women. Both were from strategically important departments, central sterile supplies and the laundry; both had been active at their particular workplaces; both were elected to the inner committee of twelve which met daily to assess and plan. Control of these departments together with the stores and the drivers, enabled the strike committee to virtually close the hospital except to emergencies. Other women activists could have been elected, notably an ancillary ward housekeeper from the NUPE branch who had been active for over sixteen years (she appears later). No representative of the ancillary women domestics was nominated even though they were the largest manual occupation in the NHS.

Although they welcomed the two women elected to the strike committee some found it difficult to acknowledge their ability. The laundry steward, intelligent and articulate, had a lot to contribute to committee discussion. They did not all respect her for this. Instead she was criticized and labelled as a loud-mouth, and 'jokingly' nicknamed 'Miss Piggy', a brainless chatterbox from the Muppets television show. One man addressed her thus in a public street, an example of resentment of women who step 'out of place' into areas traditionally occupied by men.

Breakthrough to gender consciousness

The ward housekeeper from the NUPE branch did not resent the women ancillaries' lack of representation on the strike committee, but worked energetically in its support. The women ancillaries carried the public face of the strike. They picketed throughout, ignoring the spittle of irate nurses going in to work and the taunts of an angry public whipped up by local newspaper reports making claims (later denied by the strike committee) that patients were suffering, for example, from shortage of bed linen and use of paper sheets. They stood in the early morning in the cold, they explained their point of view to anyone who would listen, they went to meetings, they collected money from union branches round the city.

When the strike ended, the terms were announced at a large multi-union meeting. Predictably the union had got nowhere towards its aim of a minimum wage of £70 a week. A commission of inquiry was to be set up. Meanwhile full-time workers were to get £1 a week on account. Part-timers, the majority of whom were women, were to get nothing.

There, in the middle of the public meeting, the injustice suddenly struck the ancillary ward housekeeper. Shaking and overcome with anger she stood up and spoke her mind. 'Women are being discriminated against. Women have carried this strike and yet they are to get nothing.' She made her points briefly. Her speech was greeted with applause, mostly from women. But she got no further support. Later that night the situation went round and round in her head. She could not sleep. The next day she wrote down her views in a letter to the General Secretary of her union. He replied, but made no comment on her claim. She raised the matter with her branch, they made sympathetic noises but that was all. Yet they had taken note: later, as has already been recorded, a motion calling for equal rights for part-time workers was submitted to the annual conference.

The ward housekeeper's initial contact with trade unionism had come sixteen years earlier, shortly after she had been sacked from a local factory for standing up to management and a supervisor who had been cheating the factory women over the purchase of tins of Christmas biscuits. She was dismissed on the spot, without payment in lieu of notice and with only a small proportion of the holiday pay due to her. She found another job. She asked her old firm for the money, but they refused. In casual conversation at a bus stop, someone suggested that the local TGWU might help her recover the money. She joined, the TGWU took up her case and to her amazement recovered all that was due. From then on she was an active trade unionist, spreading the good news that the workers had someone who would fight for them, recruiting members, taking her part in action. She went to trade union education classes. Learning basic negotiating and public speaking skills she became confident enough to represent workers to management and took office as a shop steward. She learned about the structure and organization of the TGWU and about the history of trade unionism and the labour movement. She joined the Labour Party. She did not let family commitments stand in her way, neither a sick husband nor three children: when her husband was in hospital she took her seven-year-old to branch meetings (some of the men objected but were overruled by the regional office).

When family circumstances forced her to leave engineering, she found a job at the hospital. She was surprised by the apathy there. She became a steward and tried to get the members to take their problems to the union. She was an active caseworker. She encouraged two other women domestics to become shop stewards. She attended branch meetings regularly and spoke up on behalf of the domestics. She attended the first women-only trade union education course in the locality where she was introduced to feminist ideas about the labour market and trade unions. She was very active during the strike. She became aware of a contradiction between the unions' claims to represent the interests of women and their practice. With the settlement, she became convinced of the existence of sex discrimination within the movement.

With this steward we see a committed trade unionist, whose consciousness of the specific disadvantages which women face was just beginning to emerge. Her new insight meant she had something to say to her branch and union colleagues. The irony was that she was already fifty-eight and nearing retirement. Time deprived her of the opportunity to develop her insight: and the branch never had a proper opportunity to learn from her. Her story suggests an urgency to the unions' efforts to utilize the abilities and enthusiasms of such women.

The aftermath: male power at the branch

The industrial action of the Winter of Discontent on the hospital workers' branch was to increase trade union consciousness among men more than women. It produced a stronger branch but one where men's dominance was increased. Almost the same number attended as before, but a few more men and a few less women. The political input into the action was reflected in increased (male) political activity at the branch. A small coterie involved in left-wing politics arrived at meetings together and giving the others the impression of having worked out a common approach to branch business.

The new male secretary had a big influence. A theatre porter and COHSE member during the strike, he had been one of the two main local lay spokesmen. He had a penetrating, analytic mind and considerable organizational ability; he was also a powerful speaker. These talents became evident during the course of the action. But their use was blocked in his own branch which was under the grip of a long-established and traditionally-minded secretary. The suggestion that he should join the NUPE branch was welcomed by both members and paid officers whose respect he had gained during the dispute. He joined the branch and was almost immediately elected as secretary. (The previous secretary had resigned through illness.)

His election was clearly set up in advance. He did not fulfil a NUPE requirement of having a pre-existing period of membership. The failure to adhere to democratically framed union rules caused some resentment in the branch, particularly among the women. They, notably, were not involved in discussions which took place behind the scenes. The election was openly discussed at branch; but it was clear that no one but the theatre porter was prepared to take on the secretary's job, so the election stood. The ward housekeeper was very upset about the failure in democracy; she absented herself from branch meetings for several months but then became reconciled because of the new secretary's evident dedication. He proved innovative, energetic and reliable; he continued to work for the branch for the next ten years. Under his leadership new local organizing structures were set up between steward groups and the local management; there was more discussion about the implications of government policy such as privatisation, contracting out, and closure of long-stay mental hospitals.

Ironically more attention was now paid to women's issues. The motion put up by the branch to the annual delegate conference concerned part-time women. The new secretary was personally responsible for framing it. There had been a clear change of attitude among a new generation of lay officers. The paid officer was no longer alone in promoting pro-women policies, the secretary worked with him. The branch's acceptance of gender as a union issue was perhaps more of matter of accepting national policies on gender than of understanding the structures and experience of women's subordination. It thus indicated trade union rather than gender consciousness, but maybe a step on the road to gender consciousness.

Action, ideology, male power and consciousness

What do these cases say about the role of industrial action and of ideology in changing trade union and gender consciousness? There are two main points. Firstly, in major industrial action, experience and alternative ideologies are not separate but interwoven. Mass meetings and demonstrations are occasions for the proclamation of trade union ideology, often in situations of high emotion. But during the conduct of any dispute there will also be a constant flow of ideological messages, from the unions and the political left, through leafleting and through trade union and public meetings. At the same time major industrial action creates and enlarges experience, brings workers into new relationships, breaks down isolation, and extends knowledge and ideological perspectives. It is the interweaving of these new experiences and new ideological perspectives which makes the 'experience' of industrial action a fertile breeding ground for changes in consciousness. That the change is likely to be towards trade union rather than gender consciousness and is likely to be more marked among men than women is a direct outcome of the ideology of the movement and the fact that is controlled by men.

However, as the story of the ward housekeeper shows, the outcome is not always predictable. Her breakthrough towards gender consciousness is best understood in terms of her past experience of injustice and oppression, her attachment to the trade union movement with its professed aims of fighting injustice and her strongly developed trade union consciousness. The new experience for her was not taking part in demonstrations and meetings, but the dawning, and painful, awareness of the union movement's almost cavalier neglect of women's interests in the current dispute. She had no feminist ideology or feminist network with which to easily sustain or develop that insight.

The second point is the importance of the context of male power. More often than not this power acts to prevent women developing trade union consciousness. But just because men are powerful they are able, if they wish, to exercise that power to encourage women's development of trade union consciousness. The NUPE paid officer provides a prime example of positive influence. He was able to get women into shop steward positions where they had at least an opportunity to develop their union interests, monitor union branches to see that women's issues were not put to one side, and set in motion processes such as women-only education leading possibly to raised gender consciousness. There are limits to the beneficial influence of male power, since men tend to speak and act on behalf of women rather than let them speak for themselves. Thus after the industrial action was over, when NUPE branch began to pay more attention to women's issues, men not women took the initiative. In the next chapter we look at the experience of some women who challenged male power and set out to create a union branch where they could speak for themselves.

5 Taking over from the men: Cases 6 and 7

The will to change

The last two chapters have discussed some of the ways changes in consciousness are brought about at the grass-roots. We have shown women coming to recognise the trade union movement as a collective means of defending their rights and confronting the injustices which inhere in capitalist relations of production. We have shown, also, women becoming aware that the movement's overt role in defence of justice and fairness is paralleled by an unacknowledged, and largely unrecognised, role as an oppressor: that it is an instrument by which women (and various minority groups) are subordinated and disadvantaged. A new understanding of this mode of oppression may make women determined to achieve an equal voice with men. We call this determination the 'will to change'; its success depends on women being able to maintain their new levels of consciousness.

Women's path to trade union and gender consciousness as expressed by this will is not easy. It involves learning to operate in a culture of masculinity, and doing so without suppressing the identity, interests and aims of women. The struggle to maintain a new level of consciousness is hard. Several research studies report failure to hold on to new enthusiasms and levels of consciousness (for example Pollert, 1981; Purcell, 1979, 1982; Cavendish, 1982).

This chapter looks at two trade union branches where the will to change was evident. In each case women at a predominantly female branch felt overwhelmed by the male minority and tried to establish a branch under their own control. In each case the experiences surrounding the Winter of Discontent had raised trade union consciousness. The events of 1979 had also stirred their consciousness of gender. They began a process of self-questioning; they talked together; a few attended women-only courses. By the time of the miners' strike they felt gender to be such an important issue that, on a visit to West Yorkshire, they went into the miners' clubs and talked with the men about the desirability of freeing their wives from domestic chores and starting to brew their own cups of tea.

By 1981 a few women had begun to openly question the whole male culture of their union, especially men's influence over women's jobs and pay. They saw their own branch as the place to tackle this issue. In their trade union activity they drew support from left-wing political views and party affiliations. In their activity on behalf of women they were more on their own although they had limited contacts with feminism through friends, networks and women-only education.

Like the ward housekeeper referred to in the last chapter, all were grandmothers in their third working lives. They were articulate and powerful women who wanted to share their new understandings with other women. We look at the different responses of their two unions, the one supportive the other antagonistic, and see how they affected the outcome of their struggles.

These took place between 1980 and 1984, after consciousness had been raised by the Winter of Discontent. The women were manual public service workers - school cleaners and school meals workers. One group, **Case 6**, belonged to GMWU where they were organized with caretakers and drivers in a predominantly female education branch; the other, **Case 7**, belonged to NUPE where they were organized in a general branch covering all local authority manual workers. The NUPE branch had proportionately fewer women. It included the school meals workers discussed in the previous chapter. The officers of both branches were men and, at the outset, attendance at meetings was almost totally male.

Manual jobs within the local authority were segregated into women's and men's jobs; women's jobs were crowded on the lowest scales, men's placed on short career ladders. In the education service at this time caretakers had direct authority over cleaners, with powers of engagement and (in practice if not in law) influence over dismissal.

Cleaners challenge GMWU men - Case 6

The move to form a new branch in the GMWU was instigated by a woman cleaner. She had two main supporters, a cook and a Labour councillor who was not in paid work, and the support of her husband, an active trade unionist. But she bore the brunt herself. She was around forty with four children. She and her husband became interested in trade unionism and politics five years previously. A year later, when her youngest child was three she took a job as a school cleaner and joined GMWU. Attending branch meetings she was disturbed to find that women seemed to have no place. The GMWU branch at this time numbered nearly three thousand, including about 250 men. Most of the men were caretakers, most of the women, cleaners. Fourteen years previously, before the unions had begun to recruit women in the public services, the branch had consisted of 200 women and 200 men, with men in control.

Having established her presence at meetings the cleaner persuaded the branch to delegate her to the local trades council. This too she found dominated by men, though less markedly so. Though she belonged to no feminist group and felt uneasy in the company of middle class feminists, she was aware of current ideas. These confirmed her view that male control over a largely female branch was wrong.

She tried to present the cleaners' grievances to her union branch. But her efforts were bedevilled by the fact that the caretakers who ran the branch were the cleaners' bosses at work. Caretakers were responsible for hiring cleaners and saw themselves as bosses. The branch secretary referred to himself as a 'good employer' because several of 'his ladies' had been with him for fifteen to twenty years. He had no power to sack anyone, but could refuse to rehire: 'If a lady leaves of her own accord' he said 'I never take her back on again'. The caretakers filled in time sheets on behalf of cleaners. This presented them with opportunities for fiddling. A caretaker might record that he had done a woman's work when she was absent and claim payment for it. In fact other cleaners might have helped him, but nevertheless he might keep the lion's share of payment for himself. The final irony was that the caretakers acted as shop stewards for the cleaners, though with the proviso that they should not represent cleaners at their own schools.

Nearly all the school caretakers in the city were in GMWU. They were well organized. Pay and grading structures were negotiated nationally, but locally the caretakers had their own agreements covering overtime (a large component of their pay) and promotion. The union had negotiated the right to observe job interviews and could see that management followed agreed promotion procedures. As in **Case 2** these agreements brought greater rewards to men.

The 'band of brothers' who controlled the branch consisted of about twenty caretakers, very regular attenders, who acted as shop stewards, each representing eight or nine schools. Around eight men formed an inner core. A further sixty came to meetings fairly regularly. The branch secretary had been in post for ten years; his wife was the only woman who had held office, as social secretary. Most women did not attend the branch: many had young families and were content to leave union work to others. When the cleaner insisted on her right not only to attend but to participate in debates, she was made to understand she was unwelcome. This part of trade unionism was for men only.

GMWU's local union culture

We now examine the attitudes and values of GMWU paid officers from the regional office (sited locally) and of the lay officers from the local branch.

GMWU paid officers It is important to understand the strength of masculinity in the union culture which the cleaner had to confront. GMWU national policies towards women were progressive. However, interviews with local paid officers gave no sign of attempts to implement them. At this level, women were stereotyped according to family roles, their contribution as paid workers was devalued, their voices deemed irrelevant.

In 1977 the man in charge of the local office explained women's low participation in the union by their family commitments:

> The biggest thing stopping cleaners from getting involved is their families. They work from 6. 30 to 8. 30 a.m. and then again from 4. 30 till 6. 30 p.m. Then they want to be with their families.

There was no suggestion that the union ought to make itself accessible to women nor that men should share family work. Union meetings were held on Sunday mornings to suit the men's working week of daily split shifts and evening overtime; but it did not suit the women. The idea of changing meeting times had not arisen. And a burst of laughter greeted the suggestion that men might cook the dinner on the days that women had union meetings.

The same officer claimed he rarely saw 'his' women members. He boasted of making an agreement on behalf of 400 workers, 300 of whom were women, without 'ever having seen a woman member'. He had not felt the need to consult their opinion. In 1981, a disastrous agreement resulted from another failure to consult. Under pressure from the local authority, officers agreed to a cut in cleaners' hours which brought a number of them below 16 a week thus automatically lengthening from two to five years the employment qualification period entitling them to redundancy money.

Paid officers from GMWU (in contrast to the NUPE officer in the last chapter) did not promote women's participation. And they failed to encourage those who were eager to become more involved. The cleaner was not seen as a resource who could mobilise inactive members, but as an interfering problem. No attempt was made to assist her in her work as steward, for example getting round her scattered school constituency. For a long time she was denied access to trade union education.

The lay officers Lay officers and shop stewards when interviewed appeared even more sexist than the paid officials, seeing women as family 'servants', judging them by male ideas of femininity and belittling the problems they raised. Issues relating to men's work formed the only true union agenda. A branch officer and shop steward together explained how

> women have no idea. They don't understand the way things are done or what is important. They raise trivial issues.

A request to wear trousers on cold winter mornings was regarded as trivial. The steward was reluctant to forward the issue because

> trousers are unfeminine; they shouldn't be worn in the kitchen; I like to see women properly dressed.......The children in the school see them too; we don't want them to see women dressed in trousers.

Never mind about the women's comfort. What mattered was how men thought women ought to look. However, the women persisted; negotiations took place; management agreement was obtained. Then when women asked to be allowed to go without tights in summer when the kitchens became almost unbearable, the request provided an opportunity for sexual innuendo, with one of the men suggesting a further state of undress.

> The best kind of uniform the women could wear would be that of a bunny girl. Those dark stockings with long black seams up the back. Then everyone would say what a marvellous dinner, never mind what crap it was!

Other issues which would probably have been followed up had they been raised by men were simply ignored: health and safety issues such as the well-documented accident risks attached to large food mixers, sterilizer-sinks, slippery floors, hot chip fat and so on.

Again women were considered unsuitable for the post of shop steward simply on account of their sex: they were stereotyped as being 'not tough enough'. Yet the woman manager of the school meals service, a tough negotiator, was described by the men as 'truculent'. Later when women did become stewards they dealt with their tough manager just as efficiently as the men.

Behind these views of women lurked the notions of the male breadwinner and the family wage. Women were seen as financial dependents. In one interview they were described as belonging to three types: 'she who supplements the family wage from necessity, she who goes out to work for luxuries and she who is earning for herself'. The numerous women with dependants for whom they were wholly financially responsible were ignored.

In negotiation, men still unashamedly used the family wage to privilege their earnings, arguing the need of extra money to support their wives. They had even devised an argument to show that women, in contrast to men, could not be classified as low paid, whatever their earnings. It ran as follows:

> A man looks at things in this way: he sees himself as low paid if he earns less than an average wage or a fair wage. A man discounts his wife's wage in this, whereas when a woman looks at her wage, she will also count her man's.

The men firmly believed that women did not want equal pay and to some extent the women agreed. As the GMWU lay officer expressed it:

> Basically women are not for equal pay. They look at a wage differently from a man. They depend on men. After the Equal Pay Act came in when the union was phasing women's wages up, they [the women] actually voted in the branch against equal pay.

The women took this line because they too thought that men with young families, whose wives often were unable to work, should get extra money. At the same time they fully acknowledged the justice of equal pay for equal work. Not so the lay and paid officers connected with this branch. For them equal pay was a dead letter. Most of the women whom they represented were undervalued and underpaid, yet they never thought of using the Equal Pay Act. Of course it is not possible to generalize on the basis of this branch to GMWU as a whole: after a few years GMWU made union history by lodging the first equal pay case under the 1983 Act. The case of

Julie Hayward gave the union a reputation as a supporter of women's rights.

Excluding the women

The caretakers who ran this branch had considerable control over their day-to-day jobs, their career paths, and also over the jobs of women cleaners. They feared that if women attended the branch they might lose this control. As one put it: 'We don't want women in the branch in a position where they dictate to us'. The threat was specially poignant because it was seen to issue from their inferiors, inferiors in the hierarchy of employment and in the family; moreover it came from women whom they themselves had 'employed'. They sought to exclude women from participating in branch affairs.

They achieved this by splitting the branch meeting into three: caretakers, cleaners and kitchen workers. The caretakers alone, as branch officers and shop stewards, had access to all three. In practice only the caretakers' meetings regularly took place. They were not formally constituted as branch meetings, but because there was no one to challenge them the caretakers' meeting became nominally the branch meeting. However, when issues of particular interest to women arose, special mass meetings of cleaners, kitchen workers or both together, were convened.

The caretakers' meetings began ten years earlier after the women had actually outvoted the men on the issue of overtime on Saturday mornings. The men were chagrined and decided they would never again be 'ruled by part-time women'; they would take their own decisions when the women were not present.

Although women were ineligible to attend caretakers' meetings, a few were allowed in on sufferance. Among them were the cleaner and her two supporters. The cleaner alone attended with any degree of regularity. However, the men expected her to moderate her opinions. She refused and when she protested about the use of non-union buses to take members to a union demonstration, she was asked to leave. She was excluded on several occasions; this, as much as anything, convinced her of the need for a women's branch.

The men were reluctant to accept women as shop stewards. Most women were equally reluctant to serve. The cleaner, however, volunteered. She was voted in, but the branch refused to accredit her. They said that as a part-timer she could not do the job properly. She was voted in five times before she was accepted. The cook, persuaded to volunteer by the women in her kitchen, faced similar difficulties. She was refused on the grounds that she would not be able to leave the kitchen. Then she met some cook-stewards from another part of the country and realised she had been conned. In fact most school meals stewards were cooks: being less involved in physical work it was easier to arrange for absence.

Campaigning for a women's branch

The women's experiences of industrial action in the Winter of Discontent destroyed a number of myths about what women could and could not do. The cleaner had been elected to the local government support committee for the hospital workers' strike. For the first time in her life she had spoken from the platform at a public meeting. Such experiences, combined with the general disaffection with the way women were being treated in the existing branch, led her to campaign for the new branch where they could run their own affairs.

The way that part-timers were treated in the final settlement strengthened her resolve. At one of the caretakers' meetings, supported by a group of other women, she proposed a new women's branch. The move met with initial support from the men, who saw that the women would no longer be able to outvote them, but the paid officer was against it.

Still determined get their branch, the women met informally and looked for officers. The cook was willing to stand as chairperson, two other women as shop stewards. However, because they had not followed union procedure, these arrangements were ruled invalid. After a few weeks, a special meeting of cleaners and kitchen workers was called to nominate officers according to procedure. But by then, confidence had been lost and women refused to stand. Only the cleaner and her original two supporters were still eager: 'We were pushing it' she said 'but the women just didn't want to'.

The next special women's meeting saw a further fall in confidence; they had become fearful about their lack of negotiating experience. 'We can't just jump into things' said one 'we need to learn'. Finally the cleaner alone remained as shop steward. The cook withdrew in order to stand for the local council. It was decided that, for the next few months, the new branch would operate under the current male officers. The branch structure which resulted was very similar to the old tripartite system. Now it was bipartite with the caretakers in one branch as before, but the women all together in the new branch. Men still ran both meetings.

A number of women's meetings were held but were not well attended. When the time came for election of officers it was clear that the branch was not viable. No one wanted to stand; support for a women's branch had dissipated. The women were asked to vote about returning to the old branch. The return was to be on the men's terms: they had to agree to support the caretakers' action against cuts in education expenditure although they had wanted to conduct their own. Nevertheless, the women voted almost unanimously for a return to the old branch. Before we see what can be learned from this episode, we look briefly at the struggle over who should control the industrial action.

Cleaners attempt industrial action

Towards the end of the seventies, cuts in education expenditure were posing new threats to manual jobs. As soon as she was accredited the cleaner began bringing these cuts to the notice of women cleaners and preparing them to resist.

In 1981, while arrangements for a new branch were under way, she got wind of a new round of cuts. Drivers were being dismissed, assistant caretakers not reappointed and cleaners expected to cover greater areas of floor space. There were rumours of worse to come. In her opinion, a strike was the best tactic. First she raised the matter at the regular branch/caretakers' meeting but got little support. Then she called an informal meeting of the cleaners who voted for strike action, expecting to be given support by the caretakers. However, the paid officer pointed out that if the whole membership was to be involved, proper procedure meant that the matter be put to the whole branch. A special meeting of the branch was fixed for the next week.

Meanwhile at the shop stewards' meeting the caretakers were up in arms about the women's strike proposal:

> No woman's going to tell me what to do! No woman's going to tell me whether I open my school or not!

There was angry talk about who was going to make decisions and who was to control whom. When a refuse cleaner from another branch supported the cleaners' wish to strike, he was asked to leave the meeting or be silent. 'Marvellous isn't it' said the cleaner later 'when you have to get your support from another branch!' When the special meeting of the branch duly took place several hundred people attended, mainly women. But the cleaner was not present: her father had been taken ill and she was at the hospital.

Four men, three branch officers and the regional secretary presided. They sat at a long table on a raised dais at one end of a large hall. It was an intimidating place to those unused to public speaking. Even with a microphone the acoustics were bad. The women's resolve and decision to strike was talked away by the officers one after the other. The meeting began with congratulations to members for the 'passionate concern' shown at a recent lobby of the local authority. After that the heavy hand of control came down. The union policy was underlined: never strike before exhausting procedure; the next step should be a further meeting with the council. In the meanwhile, the caretakers, not the cleaners, would take some kind of action. A strike on the part of women would be stupid: the authority would be sitting pretty, saving the expense of the women's wages - which was what they wanted to do in the first place. They added that the shop stewards' committee had voted against action. The men thus pre-empted the women's action, taking control themselves. They refused to say what their own action would entail. 'Probably the action will be not filling in forms; we can't say exactly; you don't let the other side know what you are doing' the officers explained - to their own side!

After this dose of cold water the meeting was opened to discussion. Eight women and four men spoke from the floor. Officers replied to each one. One of the men spoke in support, not of the strike, but of the women's 'right to know' what action the caretakers proposed. He got no clear answer. No women spoke in support of the strike. Reference to procedure confused them: they could not make sense of the arguments. 'We don't know what you're on about' was how they put it. They knew they were overworked and the cuts would mean more problems: 'We're already doing extra work for people who are off sick, what will happen if there are more cuts?' A strike would express their determination to refuse a still greater load of work. They did not see the relevance of the men's proposed action, only that it would give the men an easy time.

> Why don't *we* do something. If we do it your way, you're sitting back not doing your work, but we're still slogging our guts out.

But they got no satisfaction. They were told to take their complaints back to their branch meeting.

The women were without their leader. They had been bamboozled and pre-empted. Any fight had gone out of them. Only one woman voted against the men's plan. As they went out of the door they talked to one another fatalistically: 'They've done it again. The caretakers have stopped us again. They always do'. An observer at the meeting reported that the women near her were all in favour of striking, but were too shy to say so.

Lessons from the GMWU branch

The GMWU story has implications for those involved in furthering the interests of women trade unionists. To begin with it was evident that most women were reluctant, after the first flush of enthusiasm, to support the activists. This is a point of some practical importance. The factors underlying this reluctance are complex. One factor is a visible association in our society between men and authority, a pointed noted by trade union researchers (Ledwith et al., 1985; Rees, 1990; SERTUC, 1989). In the Introduction we suggested that women have a double identity one part of which relates to their caring roles in domestic life. Women may see the caring identity as inappropriate to leadership, especially in a movement imbued with macho culture and this may be a source of ambivalence towards women in authority.

Because of this ambivalence, women aspiring to leadership find more difficulty in gaining acceptance than men, even in predominantly female unions. As compared with men they usually lack both confidence and experience. Men are likely to stress both handicaps thus undermining aspiring leaders' self-confidence and the confidence of their supporters. Moreover by accepting men's images of women as their own, women often aid and abet men. Morris writing about disabled women refers to this process as the 'internalization of *their* values about *our* lives' (Morris, 1991:22); others have spoken of men's 'colonization' of women's minds.

In summary, this case illustrates first the power of the trade union bureaucracy over the grass-roots, both women and men; second, men's power over women. At a critical point in the struggle a small band of men, paid and lay officers, combined together to defeat a very much larger number of women. The women looked for aid neither to the union's women's officer nor its advisory structures, but relied on their own resources. The cleaner, however, was so incensed that she felt she must let someone outside know: she contacted the local women's committee of trades council to let them know

> how we were held back by the caretakers and the full-time officers, how they twisted things and lost us our chance.

NUPE establish a new branch - Case 7

In **Case 7** three factors come together: a rise in women's consciousness; support of women trade unionists by local paid officers; and individual women looking for interest outside the home.

The NUPE branch was formed with the support of paid officers. It was a gradual process in which women were helped to undertake greater responsibility in the union: encouraged to become stewards, to take training, to take part in negotiations and to speak in public. When the occasion to form a branch arose, the women were prepared. The two women who led the move towards a new branch and the industrial action which followed were, like the GMWU women, already well into their third working lives. One, after her children left home, had made a conscious decision to become involved with politics and trade union affairs. She had got her house how she wanted and was looking 'for something else - the television was not enough'. The other, in difficulty with her marriage, was also seeking interest outside the home. Both husbands were union men, supportive of their wives' union activities.

NUPE's local union culture

A NUPE paid officer   Nationally NUPE had clear pro-women policies which were taken seriously by the local union office. The branch and the paid officer referred to in this case (**Case 7**), are the same as those featured in **Case 4**. This officer was a key figure in implementing the unions' policies for empowering women. Here we report his views in more detail. He was well aware that women's position in society was changing and that unions would have to move with the times:

> Women will impose their demands on management with regard to working hours, to creches and so on. Women will want to work just the same as men work......Then there are further questions, questions of redundancy, of looming unemployment and of the overworking of those who remain. Women are much more likely to accept overwork than men. Some old questions are coming back: whether women should work when men are unemployed.

He saw these changes as posing particular problems for NUPE which, with over 60 per cent female membership, still thought 'in terms of the paid man'.

The Winter of Discontent had taught the union about the need to communicate with women members before acting:

> We were beaten in the strike......Before we go into action again, we must get the support of our workers who are women. It's no use going into action against the support of the majority of our members.

He saw a need 'to create conditions where women could identify with the union' including their appointment as paid officers. In his own area he had seen a woman paid officer give up. She had taken 'a great deal of stick', especially from older men secretaries. She did not succeed, but the next woman did.

He had confidence in women but thought that they needed 'a bit of positive discrimination'. This was doubly necessary because of the great degree of exploitation in many women's jobs:

> Poor bloody women and I say that with no disrespect.

He was constantly seeking women stewards:

> I'm always on the lookout for anyone who shows any sign of real interest. When I'm in a meeting I'm always watching. Now and again a woman will get up to speak and she'll begin sparking off and getting everyone's attention. I'll sit there at the back nodding, then afterwards I'll go along and have a word and ask her up to the union office.

Later he might persuade that woman to become a steward. Many women stewards, in his opinion, had considerable ability and were underused by the union.

He saw lack of confidence as a problem for women. When they faced management or men at branch meetings, it could result in feelings of 'confusion' and these, in turn, could incline them to accept male leadership. But he thought the problem could be overcome by education. In practice however, he did not feel entirely comfortable with women whose confidence led them to transgress male stereotypes about proper female behaviour: he did not like 'aggressive' women.

His own members regarded him as still 'a bit of a chauvinist', but as one said: 'we're teaching him'. He admitted that his attitudes had changed. Before the Winter of Discontent he had reported dismay at an encounter with a woman paid officer:

> This dolly bird came in. It quite put us out. She was right out of place in a meeting like that.

And he was equally scathing about women executive members:

> You can't let your hair down with them like you can with a man. The executive are our employers. With men, you can joke, swear, bugger around and it doesn't affect your professional relationship. But with a woman, you wouldn't dare do that. They'd get their knife into the professional relationship.

He thought women were unsuitable because they could not, like men, be just given a car and expected to travel. By 1979 he had rid himself of prejudices about women paid officers and presumably about lay officers as well.

However he still saw that family work disadvantaged women: 'They can't just do the washing up and go'. When a married woman did a lot of trade union work, he praised her relationship with her husband, accepting that she needed his consent. He thought most women put their domestic lives first and this led them to regard their paid employment as 'part-time' even when it was not.

Men were different: 'For a bloke, work is his natural habitat'. He did not suggest that men needed any education about the division of labour in the home. And he volunteered that he did not have full confidence in women. 'Can you imagine' he said 'fighting a dispute with a committee of women?' Nevertheless his actions were a clear challenge to certain aspects of the dominance of masculinity within union practice and culture.

NUPE lay officers One of the tasks of paid officers was to encourage men to take a more positive attitude to women members. This could be an uphill struggle, especially with older men accustomed to power within their small coterie. The secretary of NUPE general branch, then nearing retirement, had joined NUPE when it was a predominantly male union. He did not take easily to its changed character. He had a low opinion of women as trade unionists:

> I believe that women are lax......They are obsessed with money...... They don't take the interest they should. When there is talk of closing a school for a day their first question is "Are we being paid?"

He spoke pejoratively of women who worked only for money to spend on bingo. However, in a small way he was beginning to follow the union policy, and boasted of having taken two women cleaners with him on a union demonstration. His support, however, was laced with patronage.

Some of the shop stewards were more prejudiced. The steward representing the school meals women in the last chapter had transferred from GMWU. He disagreed with NUPE's national policy of sex equality. He did not want women attending the branch because he knew they could outvote the men. He held conventional male stereotypes about women, that they worked for their own pleasure, for 'pin money', 'bingo' and 'beer', while a man worked 'to support his family, for a loaf of bread and a bottle of milk'. In his opinion women did not merit the same protection at work as men. His views were not entirely consistent: he acknowledged that some women worked to support their families and he thought all working women were 'entitled to a bit of pleasure, to a holiday abroad, why not?'

Other stewards were more responsive to the union's policy. One, spoken of highly by school meals staff, had been enrolling many women from a new estate. With the paid officer he had called a series of special local meetings for school meals workers. He had also negotiated improvements in working conditions for the members whom he represented.

The new NUPE branch

After the Winter of Discontent, some of the school meals women wanted their own voice in local union affairs. They found it galling to be 'controlled by refuse collectors who know nothing about school kitchens'.

They had gained confidence. One of them described how she had changed:

> I used to be a little grey mouse, sitting back and saying nothing. Now I will say what I have to. I'm not afraid. If I know I'm right I'll speak up.

Trade union education had helped her, though slowly:

> The first course was ten weeks and I didn't think I'd learned anything. But then later, back at work, things started falling into place. The second one was better.

She became a delegate to trades council, joined its women's committee and become interested in women's issues. She began to resent her husband speaking on her behalf:

> I get fed up with John always telling me what I ought to say and then telling me what I am saying. It's always, 'What Joan really means is......' and then he says what he thinks I ought to have said.

She even told him off in public. 'O frig off John! I know what I mean!' She was ready too to challenge the men in the branch.

The occasion for creating the new branch was the retirement of the old branch secretary. The women were not happy with the heir apparent. This was a man, the husband of a sheltered housing warden, who had been a physical education teacher but was now unemployed and registered as disabled. He might know about sheltered housing, but they considered his knowledge of school kitchens was minimal.

As an unofficial steward for wardens of sheltered housing he had achieved several improvements in conditions of work. He had also helped to persuade a woman warden to become their first official steward. The paid officers had confidence in him. But at the same time, they were quite agreeable to splitting the branch, seeing as a way of getting more members, especially women, involved in local organization. The branch was big and covered many different jobs. It would simplify matters administratively if the education workers were in a separate branch. So the NUPE local office gave its blessing to the new branch.

It was not a women's branch; men belonged as well as women. But it provided a voice for women. At its inception, the secretary was a woman, a cook who had been a member of the strike support committee in 1979 and active afterwards regional school meals meetings (see **Case 4**). Two women agreed to act as stewards, one for school meals workers and one for cleaners. No woman was at this time prepared to chair meetings and this job was taken by a retired caretaker, the steward responsible for recruiting so many women. On his death six years later a woman agreed to become chairperson.

The branch grew in numbers and strength. It began with 124 women and 20 men; seven years later there were nearly 800 women and 250 men. It ceased to be purely an education branch: attracted by numbers and by a reputation for reliability, the refuse collectors and the rest of the general branch had elected to merge with it. When the woman secretary left the area, the woman chair took her place and a male caretaker moved into the chair. Then when this woman retired, both key officers became men. The new branch was a place where women felt at home, where their voices were heard and their interests were attended to. It remains to be seen whether, under all-male leadership, these gains can be held.

Perceiving their disadvantage compared to caretakers in terms of both pay and job control, the women in the new branch early laid claim to become caretakers themselves. Several applied in writing to the local authority. But by 1989, despite a local authority training scheme, only a handful of women had succeeded in getting the job. They also joked about their daughters putting their names down for that most macho of jobs, dockwork, where sons had a traditional right to follow after their fathers.

School meals women take action

The first problem addressed by the new branch concerned school cash cafeterias. These had been introduced into senior schools after 1980 when the government abandoned nutritional requirements for school meals. A large range of snacks and desserts was added to the standard dinner. The new system meant more work. More dishes had to be produced; choices were less easy to predict and that led to last minute cooking. The pace of work and stress increased. The union asked for a reassessment of staffing scales in the kitchens working under this new system.

In this already fraught situation, a national agreement awarded a two-and-a-half percent wage increase at the same time reducing the 40-hour week to 39 hours. The implementation of this agreement was left open to local councils. The council in question decided to implement it unilaterally. It took no account of the fact that workers would have put in more effort to carry out their jobs in the shorter working week. No extra staff were allocated to the kitchens. The women felt they had been put under unreasonable pressure. Though they took home a little more money, they felt this was offset by the extra effort required and they were angry at the lack of consultation. They wanted to take action.

The union produced some Guidelines for Industrial Action: these stated that work should be left unfinished as evidence that workers were being asked to do more than they could manage. A mass meeting of school meals women was called jointly by the GMWU and NUPE. Strong support was expressed for union action, especially by staff from cash cafeteria kitchens. The women were angry: the 39-hour week was supposed to improve not worsen their conditions. They insisted that more hours should be assigned to the kitchens. At this meeting the new education branch came out in strong support of the proposed action and an official dispute was declared.

For the women in kitchens which still operated the traditional two-course dinner, the situation was different. Their workload was not so heavy and they soon managed to fit it into fewer hours. The workforce was thus divided, and the dispute soon became one between the cash cafeterias and the authority. After a few weeks most of the cash cafeterias began to weaken; eventually three out of eleven remained in dispute; they were all headed by activists in the new branch. They remained in dispute from November 1982 until February 1983. Negotiations about the correct hours to be assigned dragged on into July.

In normal times all dishes were washed at the end of the day, floors and work surfaces were left spotless. During the action the women left a few dishes unwashed each day and a small area of the floor uncleaned. Gradually the piles of dirty dishes increased and the floors got dirtier. Each day they had to begin with the previous day's washing up. In addition, cooks refused to hand in their administrative work to head office.

Dinners began to get later but not too late. If they became so late that children stopped taking them the women would no longer be able to claim they had too much work. The kitchens, however, were allowed to get much dirtier than usual. And eventually health and safety workers were called in. More than once the cooks were given a large number of overtime hours in order to clear the backlog. But there was no admission that more hours were needed for normal working. The employers insisted that the problem could be solved if the women agreed to operate new work rotas. This they refused to do.

The dispute attracted publicity in the local press with articles and letters in support and in criticism of their case. Children from the school wrote letters in praise of their dinners and their dinner ladies. But relations between the women and their employers became very acrimonious. All the women in the kitchens taking action eventually received letters threatening them with loss of their jobs.

The dispute resolved itself into a battle of wills. But the employers had more power and time was on their side. As the dispute lengthened so the numbers taking dinners began to drop. The women were expecting a further drop in numbers as Spring and Summer approached and children customarily chose to go out at dinnertime. The argument that the women could not get through their work would then look suspiciously thin. The women in the kitchens began to tire of the action which condemned them to work in a dirty and disorganized environment.

In February, at a branch meeting, the paid officer persuaded the women that it was time to settle. They were reluctant, but could see no alternative. The settlement involved an agreement that a peripatetic cook, a part of the local management team, should work for a few days alongside the women to assess whether they were understaffed and advise on new rotas.

As a result of this investigation, management agreed to reconsider the staffing of all the cash cafeterias. Despite the drop in the numbers taking meals, most cafeteria kitchens were reassigned the hours they had lost. This resulted in the creation of new jobs. A number were assigned further hours. However, new rotas were imposed which diminished the cooks' control over the organization of the work of the kitchen. Though it was not wholly successful, the women's action did gain some redress for the increased workload and it did provide a few new jobs. Other workers in the education service, caretakers and cleaners who took no action, got no redress.

Conclusion

This chapter has analysed the story of two groups of women whose consciousness of gender oppression had been raised to the extent that they set out to contest the dominance of men in their local branches. We see in these aims a challenge to male power and control and to masculine cultural practice and values. The women wanted to be free to define their own interests, often ignored or belittled by their shop stewards and union branches. They wanted to get away from the stifling effect of traditional union procedure and men's manipulation of it, to run meetings in a language they understood and one which would give everyone an opportunity to express themselves. They wanted relief from being stereotyped by men and told what sort of person they were or ought to be; they wanted to be free to define themselves.

The GMWU women failed, the NUPE women suceeded. Why? First, the GMWU women had a harder task. In aiming at a branch exclusively for women, they were trying to push further. Second, the structures of their employment and of the union branch overlapped; in confronting the caretakers they were taking on their 'bosses'. Third, the caretakers had considerable power: they were were well organized, active within the local union hierarchy and in close relation with the local union office, and they had contacts in local government. Initially they were happy to be free from women's interference, but when the women began to take independent action, they saw their own power to be under threat and changed their minds. They decided to keep the women in their control and the women not strong enough to break free.

Finally, GMWU women failed because they did not get the support of their local office. This can be partly explained by the traditional culture of masculinity. Partly, however, it may be attributed to the structure and membership of local organization. The potential conflict between the caretakers and cleaners (as 'employers' and 'employees') was a force which the union wished to keep in customary balance; this might be achieved more effectively by organizing within a single branch.

NUPE women's success was partly because the goal they set themselves, a branch catering for men as well as women, was more in keeping with the union value of solidarity. Further, the goal was also more acceptable in organizational terms and likely to make the paid officers' jobs easier rather than harder. The new branch was not faced with the institutionalized power of caretakers: as cooks, the new leaders, were not in the same 'boss' relationship with kitchen workers as caretakers and cleaners. A final element was the support received from their paid officer.

The lesson to be learned is not that NUPE is good and GMWU is bad - it is quite inadmissible to draw this type of conclusion from a case study. And it would be wrong. The national policies of both unions were strongly in support of women's interests. The real lesson to be learned from these cases is that, given the will on the part of paid officers, national policies can be effective in bringing about change, they can be used to challenge the culture of masculinity and to empower women at the grass-roots. But, in the context of existing male power, the commitment of paid officers becomes almost a necessary element in this endeavour. The primary necessity, however, is some expression of the 'will to change', a spark from women at the grass-roots to fire the process.

6 Grass-roots women speak to the movement

Women-initiated action

So far our examination of women's consciousness and challenge to men's control at the grass-roots has focused on the single branch or workplace. We have looked at the effects which major industrial action has had on raising women's consciousness and their will to challenge men's power. And we have seen how union encouragement of women can support these challenges. In this chapter the focus widens to see how action initiated by women at the grass-roots has influenced the trade union agenda. We examine how it has pushed the movement to implement equality policies and to broaden the agenda to include women's and community issues; how it has made visible and audible both the interests which women share and the particular concerns of oppressed women long ignored by the movement. Taking examples of action in the seventies and eighties (see Appendix 2), we consider what the women involved were saying about the relevance of trade unions to their lives.

The industrial action discussed in this chapter constitutes an implicit challenge to male domination within the movement. However, most of the women we report did not deliberately set out to challenge the authority of their unions. Some purposely sought out unions as defenders of the working people's interests. They assumed their interests would be given the same importance as men's. Challenges emerged only because the women felt marginalized; they could not persuade the unions to listen, or if they listened, to accept their views. There was an underlying failure in democracy; women's views were simply not represented in the structures of union government. And this led them to take control of the industrial action themselves.

A common theme was that the women wanted to fight for aims beyond the boundaries of the traditional agenda. Defence of jobs, pay and conditions was high in the women's priority, but they were also concerned with other community- rather than work-based values: the preservation of public services and community institutions. Their challenge was not new; it harked back to old and almost forgotten union values. But it was radical in that it called for profound changes in attitude and practice. It called on the union movement to widen its horizons, to find a way of representing not only the women and men at the grass-roots, but also the interests of the community. Though the challenge may have been radical, the consequences were not. Some actions failed; some had limited success; others made small but significant advances. Yet for a brief space of time, with the miners' wives, it looked as though women might have begun to break the mould of UK trade unionism.

The qualified character of trade union support for women's issues has meant that women-initiated trade union action has relied quite heavily on support from outside the movement. The most important have been feminist, ethnic and community groups and networks. Although women have become involved with these partly because of failure in support from their unions, they have wanted to make contact because they see large areas of common interest. Collaboration between unions and community-based groups presents difficulties, but these can be overcome in times of crisis when short-term goals are agreed. When the crises have passed, collaboration is more difficult: to achieve it unions will have to develop new and more flexible structures of organization and representation. This is one of the challenges posed by the women's action.

Distinctive voices

Women's action in the seventies and eighties represented the interests of a variety of different groups: factory and service workers; full-timers and part-timers; Asian, black and white women; and women whose main link to the union movement was not through their own jobs but through men or shared community life.

Low-paid and part-time women - night cleaners

Among the groups ignored by the trade union movement were low-paid and part-time workers, mostly women. In the early seventies the second wave of the feminist movement, partly on principle, partly in order to spread the feminist message to working class women, tried to assist low-paid women to help themselves. An example was the support given in 1970 by the Dalston Women's Liberation Group to the London Night Cleaners' Campaign, organized and run by May Hobbs. The Campaign sought not only to raise the women's abysmally low wages - only half what was paid to men in similar jobs - but also to achieve greater recognition and social value for their skills (Alexander, 1974; Hobbs, 1976; *Shrew*, December 1971, quoted in Rowbotham, 1989a:326). Their aim was to have their own branch within their trade union, TGWU. In spite of the fact that the TGWU was unhelpful throughout (Carter, 1988), they succeeded in this, went on to take industrial action and won some improvements in their wages and conditions. Feminist support was crucial to their success.

Women's action for equal pay

Equal pay is a long-standing goal of the feminist movement. By this is meant not only that women and men doing the same job should be paid the same money, but that they should be rewarded equally for work of equal value. Equal pay is an area where blue collar women have used industrial action to implement a national TUC policy which has never had the mainstream movement's wholehearted support. Although unions have given more support to struggles for equal pay than to those against low pay, their attitude has been ambiguous: policies are in favour, but practices often run contrary. There are exceptions: for example in the 1970s TASS, where feminists held influential positions, negotiated substantially greater improvements in women's pay than the rest of the movement (Coote and Campbell, 1982:144-5).

Women's earnings have never equalled those of men. This is partly because women work fewer hours. Partly it is because of unequal rates of pay: in whatever sphere of employment, the work that women do is almost always held to be of lower value than that which men do. Until 1975 when the practice became illegal, employers paid women less than men for doing exactly the same work. However, women usually do different work from men. Yet, when different types of work are compared by job evaluation 'experts', women are found to earn less than men for work of the same value.

As we reported in the Introduction, women trade unionists began their struggle for equal pay in the nineteenth century. But it was not until the late twentieth century that legislation was passed to bring it about. Equal pay for equal work was granted to civil servants and white-collar local authority employees in 1961. But manual workers had to wait. With the

second wave of the feminist movement, equal pay emerged into public consciousness and began to catch the imagination of working class women.
The fight for to extend equal pay widened to include a variety of pressure groups including feminist organizations. But manual workers began to take action on their own account. In 1968 a strike by women sewing machinists in the Ford motor company brought matters to a head. The women, who sewed car upholstery, were dissatisfied by the results of a recent regrading exercise. They claimed that their skills had not been recognised and their jobs had been unfairly graded in comparison with men's. Ford replied that the grading scheme was objective, the women had no case. The women then went on strike. Their union, AEF (Association of Engineering and Foundry Workers), reformulated their complaint to include a claim for equal pay (Friedman and Meredeen, 1980). The women struck for several weeks; the men came out for a short period in support. The strike threatened to spread to other plants. An agreement was negotiated whereby the women got up to 90 per cent of their claim, but their jobs were not regraded and they did not achieve equal pay. However, during the course of negotiations, Barbara Castle, a minister in the Labour government, finally committed it to a date (1970) for the introduction of an Equal Pay Act that would apply to all workers. It was a step forward of great symbolic importance. The Ford machinists finally achieved equal pay in 1985 but only after taking further industrial action.

The Ford machinists had widespread national publicity. Other women were inspired by their success, among them the Leeds clothing workers who came from an industry which was over 90 per cent female but where men did the so-called skilled jobs earned the higher wages. In 1970, in defiance of their union, women from the Leeds clothing industry called a strike. Over twenty thousand women took to the streets in protest against an agreement proposed by their union, the National Union of Tailors and Garment Workers, awarding 4d an hour increase to women and 5d an hour to men. This agreement had been suggested after a resolution for an equal increase of one shilling (12d) for both sexes, put forward from the floor at the union's Annual Conference, had narrowly been lost (Roche, 1970). Many men came out in support of the women. Women and men stood together as leaders of the unofficial strikers, but a man emerged as the main spokesperson. Initially the union refused to recognise the strike, but when success was ensured it undertook to negotiate the return to work. The final settlement did not satisfy the strikers, but it was nevertheless a breakthrough in principle. Women were awarded a higher increase than men, 14d as against 13d. Their militancy had forced the union to move towards equal pay.

The Equal Pay Act proved to have serious limitations. Employers were not made responsible for paying women and men equally; workers were responsible for challenging employers when treatment was unequal; challenges could only be made on an individual basis, not as in the USA by a class action where one person could claim on behalf of a whole category. An individual had to go through a complex system of industrial tribunals and courts of appeal. A successful claim might take years. Furthermore the act, in practice, applied only to situations where men and women did exactly the same work. The extent of sex-related job segregation meant that the act was irrelevant to most manual workers. The Equal Value Act of 1983 remedied some of these faults (for a fuller discussion see Chapter 11).

Because of the weakness of the 1970 act, some women resorted to industrial action. Most of these equal pay strikes were given official support by their trade unions who were themselves disappointed with the Act. Attitudes of men at the grass-roots the varied from strong support to outright hostility. In *The Past is Before Us* Rowbotham (1989a) reports on equal pay strikes in 1975-6. In three the women had full support from their male colleagues. In a fourth the women were ridiculed. In a fifth, Trico, a London car components firm, where women had struck after an equal pay claim was turned down by an Industrial Tribunal, they were given limited support only. That particular strike, however, supported and celebrated by the feminist movement, was successful.

Taken as a whole the equal pay strikes of the seventies can be seen as an attempt by grass-roots women to force implementation of national policy on a movement unwilling to address the basic causes of the problem and reluctant to commit resources to legislative redress.

Asian and black women demand respect and equal pay

Britain is a racist society; women from Asian, black and other ethnic groups face discrimination at the workplace; they are accorded neither equal respect nor equal pay with white workers. In their resistance to this discrimination they have turned to the trade unions. But although the ideals and national policies of the unions set them firmly against racism, their practices and organization are pervaded by it. They have found it difficult to accept that Asian and other ethnic workers constitute a distinctive oppressed group, and as such need to be allowed a distinctive voice within the movement (Wrench, 1987:163), and that within this group women and men occupy different positions and need an opportunity to express their own views.

In the seventies, several attempts were made by Asian women to fight discrimination. Two strikes initiated by Asian women took place in Leicester in 1974. A third which took place in 1976 at Grunwick, a photograph processing factory, became a *cause célèbre* of the union movement, but not in connection with the women's original grievances.

All three strikes initially addressed problems of equal pay: equality with white workers and with men. Two were also concerned about the lack of respect, amounting to racial harassment, with which Asian women were treated by white supervisors. In Leicester the TGWU which represented the women strikers gave little support. The first Leicester strike lasted for three months, but was never officially recognised. A second strike was, but strike pay was denied. White women, also, failed to give support. Unqualified support came only from the strikers' own communities which enabled them to survive the unpaid weeks on the picket lines. The strike settlements did improve the women's earnings, but it did not address the issues of racial harassment and lack of respect. Neither did it bring them equal pay with men or white workers (Moore, 1975). On the face of things, Grunwick was a very different proposition: the union movement appeared to give full support to the women strikers. In fact the movement ignored the issues about which the women had taken action and used the strike to fight its own battles. Like the Leicester strikes, the dispute at Grunwick hinged on race. Asian women sought redress for contemptuous treatment by supervisors, for poor working conditions, for wages so low that practically no white women would work there (Wilson, 1978). Pushed beyond endurance, the women walked out. On advice they joined a union, APEX. But Grunwick refused to recognise the union. The women began a six-month-long fight for recognition. And it was this and not the issues of racial and sexual equality which galvanized the unions. They called up their big battalions; mass picketing was organized; socialist and feminist groups joined in; violence broke out. The government intervened and passed a law restricting secondary picketing. The employer refused to bend; the union was not recognised; the women did not gain redress.

Union recognition and secondary picketing became the main issue of the dispute, replacing the women's original demands while mass picketing swamped their physical presence. Women from the picket lines reported that men who came to support assumed they would take control. 'Alright dears! You can go home now!' was how they greeted the women pickets. 'We are right behind the ladies, here, they have our full support.' they explained to nearby journalists (Parmar, 1982:267). Thus a women-initiated action was hijacked by the white male trade union movement, and the racial and sexual wrongs were almost forgotten. A black writer puts it more strongly:

> From the outset of the Grunwick walk-out, its strikers [had] been led to believe that mobilising white workers had to be their primary purpose, that only this could deliver them from the jaws of bondage.

It was a tactic that failed and left the women 'in bondage' (*Race Today* quoted in Parmar, 1982:267).

In 1980 a strike by 96 Asian women at Chix bubblegum factory in Slough was similarly transformed. The Asian women were paid only 95p an hour compared to the £1.10 earned by white women. But the occasion for the strike was the behaviour of management. Conditions were bad: heavy and dirty work, four toilets for 120 workers, no sick room, workers sent home for the day if they were late. A pregnant woman asked to be moved to a lighter job; she was refused; she lost the baby. Most of the workers then joined the GMWU. The firm refused recognition and the workers struck. White male paid officers took over the strike and, despite support from local black women's groups, it became defined purely as a fight for recognition. No Asian women were on the strike committee; none spoke at meetings. A white male officer was heard to state categorically that the strike was not 'about Asian women or women's rights', though that is precisely where it began (Southall Black Sisters, quoted in Parmar, 1982).

Minor strikes by Asian women in Coventry's clothing industry in the seventies followed Grunwick (Hoel, 1982:91-5). Small workshops predominated; many workers were relations or friends of their employers who were often implacably opposed to union membership. Women found joining a union brought difficulties. Some joined secretly. A survey of twenty-two factories revealed only one that had become openly unionized, by TGWU. This happened during a two-week strike when nine women of a workforce of twenty-two were made redundant. Hoel found that women's resistance through trade union action often led employers to close factories but continue production through homeworking or reopening elsewhere. Where unions did become established, paid officers found that the new women stewards needed a lot of support. They labelled the industry 'excessively time consuming' saying that 'nobody within the union [wanted] to take it on' (Hoel, 1982:93).

Summary Asian women in the sixties and seventies resorted to industrial action largely because of the union movement's failure to address the discrimination experienced by their members. But their resistance to racism and sexism in these years was not recognised. Grunwick has become famous in trade union history not for that resistance but for the fight for recognition. The Asian women's militancy, staying power, leadership and organizational abilities have also not been properly acknowledged. The failure of the trade union movement to assign a place and voice to the Asian women was experienced by them as rejection. They turned then for support towards their own community and particularly to the Asian and black women's groups therein (Bryan et al., 1985).

The movement's failure to harness Asian women's militancy was a lost opportunity. Nevertheless the alliances forged between workers and local communities opened up new opportunites for understanding both the aspirations and priorities of black members and the ways in which employment and community life are interlinked. They can assist the unions to become more truly representative.

Taking account of the community

Next we turn to the hospital workers' strikes and the action of the miners' wives in the nineteen-eighties. We show how women used industrial action to assert a new agenda for the unions, to claim that they should look beyond individual jobs to the interests of the whole community.

Hospital workers take action

Compulsory competitive tendering, deregulation and continued checks on government spending all threatened jobs in the NHS. Health authorities were forced to put all service provision out to tender from private contractors thus exposing workers to a competitive wage market. Competition between contractors tended to force standards down to the lowest acceptable level and this resulted in significant job loss. The abolition of the Fair Wages Resolution (in operation since 1891 and designed to prevent undercutting among firms tendering for government contracts) removed an informally accepted wage standard which had helped to prevent the low wages of hospital workers falling further.

The job loss was largely a women's problem. Manual jobs in the NHS, poorly paid, are largely done by women. The threat to their jobs, wages and conditions of work was enormous. For instance, in 1982 of 220,000 NHS ancillary workers the biggest group was 102,000 cleaners, all women. By 1986 this group had been reduced to 73,000 (*Guardian*, 13.11.86).

The provision of public services was decreasing, a deliberate consequence of government policy. Women bore the brunt of providing care previously given by public service workers: for people returning early from hospital, for old people without places in residential homes, for people returned to the community on the closure of long-stay mental hospitals. They absorbed most of the family strains arising from longer hospital waiting lists.

Most women in the NHS responded to the threat to their jobs and to the deterioration of public services by private protest and public acquiescence. Some responded by taking direct action in the form of occupations to prevent closure and protests against privatization. Among the former, the four-year-long occupation of the Elizabeth Garrett Anderson Hospital in London - a hospital run by and for women - takes pride of place. Its closure was scheduled for 1974 and provoked one of the earliest occupations, bringing together trade unionists, feminists and community groups. The five years from 1976 to 1981 saw eleven hospital occupations (Tuckman, 1985). None lasted as long as Garrett Anderson, some only a matter of days. Few hospitals were occupied in the eighties; only one, in Bradford, lasted longer than a year (1983-4) (*PSA*: 1983, 1984, 1985). Women, as representatives of the labour force, played a crucial role in organizing the occupations and in picketing. Men, representing the community protest about the loss of services, also played a role. The joint nature of the protest made women trade unionists become aware of the important interests they shared with community groups and of the need to develop joint ways of addressing them.

The link between union and community interests became even more apparent in the anti-privatization strikes which began in 1984. They were mainly organized and led by grass-roots women, but most were supported by the trade unions. Between 1984 and 1989 union-backed action took place at ten hospitals in England, more in Scotland and Northern Ireland (*PSA*, 1984-89). Many short protests will have gone unrecorded. The strike at Barking in London lasted the longest, over eighteen months.

Barking was one of a number of hospitals already cleaned under private contract. A new contract, due in April 1984, proposed to cut cleaning hours by 40 per cent. Average earnings were to fall from £87 to £47; sick pay was abolished; holidays were cut from four weeks to three. New complex shift patterns were introduced, making childcare arrangements impossible for many women. The women went on strike. They ran the strike themselves holding weekly meetings, organizing public speakers and publicity campaigns. Their shop stewards took charge of funds (*Community Action*, 1986). Working with individuals from the community, with a GLC-financed resource centre and an independent health group, the Barking women were able to produce three environmental health reports into hospital conditions and - as an aid to other workers planning in-house tenders - a 'Workers' Plan' containing details of methods, standards and practices of cleaning at their hospital.

Links were maintained by Barking with other groups taking action in the UK. Additionally, because the main contract cleaning companies were large multi-national organizations, the women established international links: with women in Netherlands and New Zealand, employees of the same firm (in New Zealand a 24-hour sympathetic strike was held); with Sweden (Swedish cleaners and caretakers took sympathetic action); with Germany, Australia, South Africa, Canada and the USA. Sue Smith, a Barking shop steward and strike leader, was invited to address the Swedish union's national conference. In spite of this international recognition no national trade union officer involved ever visited the women on the picket lines.

The attitudes of the public service unions towards the hospital strikes were complex and inconsistent. The unions came out strongly against privatization. They ran national campaigns; they lobbied managements, health authorities and community health councils; they publicized issues among the general public. Their research departments studied the structure and organization of contract cleaning companies and investigated standards of hospital cleanliness. Reports by environmental health officers confirmed the deterioration of standards claimed by the unions, as did press and television coverage. Despite this the public service unions failed to enlist the support of the bulk of the trade union movement. The women never attracted '*significant*' support from the wider (male) labour movement' (Coyle, 1985:21).

Yet individual unions did support individual disputes. NUPE, the main public service union at Barking, gave formal but specific and limited support to the strikers (whatever their union) throughout the dispute. It helped with printing and publicity; it funded a support worker; it put a minibus at the women's service for use at evening meetings. GMBATU, in contrast, only supported strikers towards the end, and then only its own members. NUPE's support was crucial in enabling the women to keep up their action.

Women-initiated action raised serious questions for the unions: who was in control, the women or their union? And how could union structures and organization cope with the action jointly run by union and community groups? The women wanted to retain control at the grass-roots. Further, they saw privatization as a community as well as a jobs issue because 'the quality of cleaning and care affects everyone' (*PSA*, 1985:3). They saw close collaboration with community groups as integral to the action. However, traditional union structures of authority, resting on democratic centralism, made it impossible to cooperate on an equal footing with a variety of loosely structured community groups. At this stage unions were unwilling to experiment with new forms of organization.

The Barking women wanted to raise health service issues at their national conference. The failure of their branch secretary, a man, to call a branch meeting during the first five months of the dispute prevented them from doing so. The branch was unable to put forward a motion for the Annual Conference. No name could be suggested for the conference delegation. Nevertheless, at the 1984 Conference an emergency resolution in support of the strikers was passed unanimously; it resulted in a National Day of Action. The Barking women attended the 1985 Conference as visitors; they requested but were refused permission to speak. The women had intended to ask the union to set up a national co-ordinating committee for action against privatization. In the event they set up their own National Action Committee joining with other hospitals to do so. Without the resources, organization and authority of the mainstream union movement, it was a weak alternative.

Within a year of the start of action at Barking, women from four more hospitals came out on strike. Demonstrations and stoppages took place at three others. The women fought long and hard but in the end they lost. Not one group achieved its primary aim: no private contracts were withdrawn. Minor improvements in staffing and committees of enquiry were the only immediate achievements. (At some other hospitals union negotiation had managed to secure in-house tenders, thus preserving the jobs of women already at work, but usually at the 'price' of a wage cut (Coyle, 1985:20)). The women felt they would have stood a better chance if the unions had supported their community-based action more wholeheartedly.

There were positive outcomes. The women kept protest alive. They made their communities and the public far more aware about the drawbacks of competitive tendering in the NHS, a service which the public holds in the highest regard. This awareness may yet bear fruit. As one Barking woman said 'If in ten years' time somebody gets rid of the contractors, then we've won, and it wasn't all in vain'. Two years after Barking the balance appeared to be moving against the contractors and in favour of in-house tenders: in 1988, 80 per cent of contracts were in-house (*PSA*, 1988). In the 1990s however, the pressure to employ private contractors continues.

Summary The hospital workers, like the Asian women, began industrial action when the union movement failed to respond adequately to what they saw as a critical situation. As women they were concerned about standards of public service, a concern which was deepened during the action by their close contact with community groups. Defending jobs became only part of a wider aim of preserving public services. As a Barking striker put it: 'It's not just a matter of a handful of women fighting for their jobs, we're fighting for justice. People like us and the miners are fighting for the future of the working class' (*Community Action*, 1986:2). They collaborated with community groups, developing modes of joint working and responsibility. These alienated the unions already ambivalent in their support. Nevertheless the women continued their action seeing importance in their new goals and methods of collaborative working. Though their action had limited success in terms of the NHS, it did exercise pressure on the unions to put community issues on the movement's agenda.

The miners' wives

The biggest challenge to the trade union movement in the eighties came from the 'miners' wives' of the 1984-5 miners' strike. Their courage, tenacity and inventiveness captured the imagination of people all over the world:

> In the coalfields there is a new breed of women who are only as old as the strike, who have won the admiration of people the world over. They have fought not behind their men but shoulder to shoulder with them. When histories of the strike are written, all will agree that the women were glorious. (North Yorkshire WAPC, 1985)

This quotation captures some important features about the thousands of miners' wives or, to give them their proper name, Women Against Pit Closures. They were crucial to the strike: without them the year-long epic struggle of the miners would have been impossible; they organized much of the feeding and the fund-raising, although the miners' primary line of defence was undoubtedly informal family-based kinship networks (Allen and Measham, 1991). For the first time also, numbers of women joined the miners on the daily picket lines. What is perhaps more significant was that the women transformed a strike about saving jobs into a strike about saving communities. As Jean McCrindle put it, the strike 'clearly wasn't any longer about wages or even just jobs. It was about who's got the right to decide really how you live' (Rowbotham, 1989a:284). Furthermore, the women's own consciousness was transformed; their class consciousness was deepened, but at the same time a consciousness of gender was born: a new awareness, and rejection, of the structured subordination to men which had been integral to the mining way of life.

The WAPC movement began about a month after the strike started when the women, aware that strikes bring hardship, began to organize. By 1985 there were 34 groups in North Yorkshire alone, and many more in the different coalfields in Wales, Scotland and England (North Yorkshire WAPC, 1985).

The *raison d'être* and main structural base of the WAPC movement lay in men's jobs and the men's union, the National Union of Mineworkers (NUM). But the movement was also based in the community. Though miners' wives formed its core membership, many women were not directly connected with miners, but members of political or other community groups or unaffiliated individuals. The occasions for founding WAPC groups differed: Barnsley women got together after a newspaper article portraying women as against the strike, Kent women after publicity about Nottingham wives supporting their strike-breaking husbands of the breakaway UDM. A Sheffield group was based on the local Communist party. In other places, groups grew out of existing women's groups in clubs and pubs. When the national WAPC was formed in August 1984, Jean McCrindle who became treasurer was not a miner's wife but a lecturer from Northern College, a locally-funded institution with strong trade union links. At national level the WAPC remained basically an organization for miners' families, but at local level groups aimed to draw around 25 per cent of members from other members of the community (Stead, 1987:21-2).

Early in the strike NUM funds were sequestrated by the government and the union could no longer fund strike pay. But the government deemed the union to be paying at first £15, then £16, a week in strike benefit. Because of this hypothetical payment striking miners were denied social security benefit. This was paid only to wives and children, but had to provide for the whole family. Single men had no access to money. Food was the most crucial need. Women organized communal feeding and food parcels. They collected and exchanged clothing, toys and other goods. They advised people in financial difficulties over mortgages, fuel bills and hire purchase. They raised funds inside and outside their local communities. They also ran entertainments and activities to create an atmosphere where politics was a matter of enjoyment, not just of duty. This was a new 'feminine' idea for the UK labour movement, where politics had always tended to mean hard chairs, bare light bulbs and smoked-filled rooms, or public houses (Rowbotham, 1989a: Chapters 12 and 13).

Speaking from public platforms the women publicized the miners' case far and wide, attending small meetings and rallies with tens of thousands of people. They carried the message not only into the rest of the UK, but into the Soviet Union, Germany, Holland, Belgium, Switzerland, France, the USA, Chile, Canada. They tried to offset the image of miners' violence on the picket lines by presenting the other side of the story, police violence against pickets. And the women knew what they were talking about; they had joined the picket lines and some had been imprisoned along with the men.

But most of all they stressed the threat to their communities. As the miners' strike progressed it became seen as a struggle, not just to keep pits open but to preserve the mining communities for future generations. The women led this struggle. They had a slogan: 'Close a Pit, Close a Community'. In many villages the pit provided the only job opportunity for men; other jobs were often dependent on the continued existence of the pit. The strike did not succeed: the miners returned to work without any agreement limiting pit closures. At the time it was a bitter defeat, just how bitter, however, was not then apparent. In 1985 there were 170 pits, in 1990 only 76. Between March 1985 and February 1987 the number of miners fell from 172,363 to 114,974 (Stead, 1987). In 1992 further swingeing pit closures and job losses were announced.

The miners' wives movement brought profound changes to many of the women who were part of it. Their experiences gave them a new confidence and a new political awareness. Many whose lives had been focused before the strike on family and house found a great deal of satisfaction in contributing more directly to the community. Relationships with their menfolk changed as women spent hours away on support work, on picket, in meetings or speaking and raising funds. They could not help becoming aware of what, according to Vic Allen, they 'had always known in their bones', that 'they were exploited' by their husbands (Stead, 1987:28). But they have always known too, that their husbands were members of an exploited occupational group. They have become more aware of the value to them of their traditional mining communities, and starkly aware of the way in which those communities rested on pit jobs. Though their experience of the pit was secondhand, theirs was not a secondhand consciousness derived from that of their men (Porter, 1982), it was a different, community consciousness, based on deep firsthand understanding of the relation of pit employment to the life of their communities They could be said to have developed two new areas of consciousness, one of gender and one of community, both based on class-bound experience (see Leonard, 1991). On the other hand, Allen and Measham suggest that too much has been made of the WAPC experience; they agree that women's consciousness was raised, but see it more as a result of long-term change than of short-term industrial action (Allen and Measham, 1991).

When the strike ended the women were caught in a contradiction. Proud of being miners' wives, proud of their community with its sense of belonging and solidarity, they did not want to lose these things. Yet they did not relish returning to the old oppressions of family life and housework, of dependence on and domination by men (Leonard, 1991:145-7; Rowbotham, 1989a:117). They were eager for greater freedom of action, more independence and for the ability to contribute directly to the community. Yet they did not seek individual independence as avidly as their middle-class sisters did; they placed a greater value on communality. They kept a certain distance from the idea of feminism with its middle-class associations. They had a vision of a new life with family and sisterhood, with solidarity and a strong community spirit, which they would build with their men.

'There will be no going back once the strike is over' - so the North Yorkshire WAPC wrote in 1985 in the foreword to their book. In a sense this is true. The pits are closed, the jobs are gone. Without these structural supports will the women's groups continue to meet? With the tiredness that comes after long battle and defeat, and without constant crisis, will women find the energy to keep going to meetings? Some will. Some groups have taken up new causes, forming links with Greenham Common, Greenpeace, Friends of the Earth, anti-nuclear protesters, tenants' associations and others. For example, Castleford WAPC (North Yorkshire) opened a drop-in education centre aimed at people who would be unlikely to attend colleges. Academic and vocational courses were offered; there was a free creche for children over six months. The centre expanded to include an advice section which dealt with depression, agoraphobia, violence against women, child abuse and more. A group in Wales founded a credit union in order to give women greater financial control over their own lives.

The women's new consciousness of gender has led some to become active in their own unions and there to challenge men's power. In a television programme they criticized men's unwillingess to accommodate children at union meetings, their attempts to 'intimidate' and 'discredit' women speakers, their attachment to bureaucratic procedure and their tendency to raise a 'hue and cry' if a woman said anything out of order. They spoke with distaste of the tendency for men to keep in exclusive groups even in the union and of the male voice of 'rugby and freemasonry' which emerges from these groups. They wanted to demolish the movement's culture of masculinity (Channel 4, 1989).

The formal status of WAPC in relation to the NUM was a vexed question throughout the strike. In June 1984 three months after it began they applied to the union for associate status, but an NUM conference decision was required and no conferences were held during the strike. At the first WAPC annual conference after the return to work they pledged themselves to continue the fight against pit closures, 'to be there when the NUM calls us'. The women felt they belonged in the NUM by virtue of their work in the strike and by virtue of the need to defend pit communities as well as pit jobs.

Maybe the men did not understand or did not accept this need. Perhaps it was too painful to abandon their traditional masculine culture and control. At the first NUM conference after the strike they refused to grant the women associate membership.

The women at the 1985 WAPC conference in 1985 felt betrayed. Ann Lilburn Chairwoman of WAPC, saying she was 'putting it mildly', described them as 'disappointed, shocked or bloody angry'. She went on:

> It makes a mockery of every speech made by respected union leaders of every area that voted against the proposal. We know who they are and we lost count of the number of times they paid tribute to us during the strike......What were they afraid of? (quoted in Wintour, 1985)

However, the unique structural importance of WAPC was recognised by some NUM leaders: at the conference Peter Heathfield described it as a new form of organization, neither trade union nor political party. Mick McGahey, then NUM vice-president, said the women 'had created conditions whereby the NUM would no longer just represent miners, but whole communities'. He said the Scottish area would grant associate membership; Arthur Scargill called on all areas to do so (Wintour, 1985). But it was never done.

Summary WAPC benefited the union movement in a number of ways: it enabled the miners' strike to survive; it made available a vast source of energy, ingenuity and commitment; it established strong links with trade unionists in other countries. Perhaps most important it brought into the public consciousness a new and positive image of what trade unionism might be about: of caring and concern for one another rather than a ceaseless fight for higher wages where the strong win and the weak lose out. Yet the union movement did not embrace this new image; rather, it refused to incorporate WAPC into the movement and in so doing lost an opportunity to transform itself.

Conclusion

This chapter has moved from case studies of local branches to consider more extensive action initiated by women. A number of different types of action were considered. The issues they raised were wide-ranging. Prominent were women's right to work and the need to put a proper value, social and financial, on women's work. Respect and equal pay with white workers was demanded by Asian women. Men's right to work was an issue for the WAPC. Community issues were also of great importance: the proper provision and standard of public services within the community and the need to preserve the fabric of community life itself. Underlying these issues were democratic questions about who should be involved in decision making. Should not women have a direct voice in negotiating their pay and conditions of work? Should not community interests be involved in employment decisions which affect basic community life?

Except for men's right to work, all the issues had been neglected by the union movement. Some had been accepted onto the bargaining agenda but never given central importance. These included low pay, rights of part-timers, women's right to work, equal pay, and racial harassment. Others, conveniently regarded as political rather than industrial issues, had never reached the bargaining agenda. These included the provision and standard of public services and the need to keep communities alive. Cooperation between union and community interests was a question to which the unions had given little attention.

In the Introduction we suggested that women had access to a culture of femininity which reflected their interests and experiences as women in employment, at home and in the community. Here we suggest that the issues which emerged during the course of industrial action can be related to that culture. They express the culture of femininity in three ways. First, they give positive value to care and service for others, as shown in the night cleaners' and the hospital workers' campaigns. Second, they express the need for equal respect and value to be given to the different groups within the movement. This is illustrated by the Asian workers' claim for respect; in their and the Ford workers' claim for equal pay; and in the action in support of men's right to work. Third, and in some ways most significant, the issues reflect the much closer integration of women than men into the community, the web of relationships and institutions which make up social life outside the home and workplace. The importance women attach to community issues also reflects their greater knowledge of how different areas of life intersect and the fact that problems in one area tend to produce repercussions in another: how failure in public care provision affects the life of the home, how the loss of jobs may tear apart not only homes, but whole communities.

In initiating and running the various campaigns of industrial action the women showed considerable strength and energy; they acted as independent and articulate people rather than dependent and silent members. Their way of working, their insistence on keeping local control of local action and on cooperating with interested community groups reflects the concern within the culture of femininity for greater equality and democratic representation.

7 A pattern for the future? Case 8

We end Part 1 with a case which can be taken as a pattern for the future. Like some of the cases reported earlier, it documents a challenge to men's power and the culture of masculinity. But it differs in that it offers a strategy for deliberate change, rather than an ad hoc challenge reacting to a particular set of circumstances. It has been introduced by women, its aims are to empower ordinary members - with special reference to women - and its methods are organizational change which begin at the branch but have effects up to the top. We refer to this strategy as developing a member-led union. We report the well documented case of one particular branch, from NUPE's N. Ireland division. But the strategy has been applied in this division more widely.

A member-led and women-led branch

In the seventies, a health service branch in Belfast consisting mainly of low-paid, part-time and often temporary women workers set out to make trade unionism more relevant to ordinary women members. This meant challenging conventionally accepted masculine union values and ways of doing things. It resulted in a new branch organization, different forms of struggle, greater participation of women, and better representation for them. They were led by a woman officer; feminist values lay behind the initiative (Cockburn, 1991:134; Roundtable, 1988).

The NUPE N. Ireland branch improved the representation of women in a number of different ways which we recount below. Our main sources are a television programme (Channel 4, 1988) and the report of a roundtable discussion between an academic and four paid officers (Roundtable, 1988). Reference is also made to other published material (Cockburn, 1991).

Finding a voice

The women in the branch have found the confidence to speak on behalf of their own class and gender. A branch member put this forcefully:

> The working class don't need anybody to bleed for them, they're bleeding enough on their own......[They] have been patronised for years by people who claimed to talk for [them]......All they need is the confidence. If you constantly tell people that [you] understand......people start to get into......[a] defeatist attitude and think [they]......really don't understand. Everybody understands. Nobody is stupid......If you understand you can speak for yourself and I think that's where the change is coming, especially among women. (Channel 4, 1988)

For years union men have been speaking on behalf of women. For these women this is no longer acceptable.

Asserting the value of women's work

Women hold different values from men. According to a male NUPE paid officer, 'the mainstream issues' of union women 'are often completely different from those of men'. Many, he thought, revolved around 'relationships with children' (Roundtable, 1988:260). Highest on the N. Irish women's list however, came the proper recognition of the work women traditionally do - caring, cleaning and catering. This view was endorsed by NUPE women from other areas:

> We should bring it out that we do care, that we are proud of caring instead of apologising for it......We should get everybody to value women for it, rather than exploiting them. (CLCLC, 1985/6:13)

The women from this branch complained about being patronized by people who thought that 'just because you clean at home...... you don't need paying for it', and it's 'only a cleaning job......[done by] a poor little woman......' They not only asserted the social value of their work but claimed appropriate financial reward. They knew their work was essential to the hospital and asked how laboratory workers and others could carry out their tasks 'if the place was not clean'. 'Priorities' they insisted 'would have to change'.

> At one time it was a marvellous medical breakthrough when they realised that hygiene was important to medicine......People are going to have to realise that hygiene does matter and cleaning is of value. They will have to pay properly for having the job done properly. (Channel 4, 1988)

The social and physical conditions of work became of special importance to them in context of their 'double shift' at home (cf. Hunt, 1980). They claimed that

> work shouldn't be a place where you have to slog your heart out and go home exhausted......it should be a place where women can......do a fair day's work for a fair day's pay, but also be happy in the workplace and go home relaxed. (Channel 4, 1988)

Competitive tendering in the N. Ireland NHS provided an opportunity for the women to assert the value of their work in local union negotiations. They put together an in-house tender for the cleaning contract. They deliberately did not devalue their jobs by 'cutting everything back to the bone', by 'making [themselves] as cheap as possible' and speeding up the pace of work. Rather they insisted on valuing their jobs positively and giving them 'real worth', believing that this would guard against 'some fly-by-night organization' which could 'come in and take the jobs over' (Channel 4, 1988). They succeeded in retaining the contract despite demonstrating a need for *higher* costings than those proposed by the health authority (see also Chapter 13).

Ways of organizing that suit women

Informality and flexibility   Because women relate to people differently from men, branches run by women tend to be organized differently (Roundtable, 1988:266-7). The N. Ireland women favoured informality, mixing sociability with business. They ran meetings of different types: coffee mornings, meetings with speakers, small groups. For an AGM or an issue where everyone's opinion was needed, they accommodated shift workers by running a series of meetings at different times and venues. The stuffiness and formality of conventional branch meetings disappeared. A NUPE male officer described the new atmosphere:

When women have got control of the branch the whole system just falls away, and there is much more openness about trying to take the union to people, and to take on board issues which historically have not been the mainstream of the union, but may be the mainstream of what the women membership of the union want to take on board. (Roundtable, 1988:255)

Combined with childcare provision, such a style of organization transforms meetings from a regular 'dozen die-hards in a cold room' to quarterly gatherings, with cheese, drink and speakers, of between one and two hundred people (Roundtable, 1988:256).

Reaching out to people Recruitment blossomed as the women included and involved more and more members. During recent years, N. Ireland has been the only division of NUPE where membership has consistently increased. One of the organizers described the achievement:

What I've seen in the last [few] years is a tremendous influx of women who are prepared to be activists in your branch. I've seen it reshape your stewards' committees. I've seen it reshape the agenda and I've seen it produce a much more vigorous branch. I've also seen [that] vast numbers of people out on your picket lines are women. (Channel 4, 1988)

The value put on inclusion meant also that the women were anxious to cooperate with the men in the branch, a strong point of the strategy (Cockburn, 1991:135).

Shaping the structures to women's values Reaching out and articulating different values is not enough, structures need to be changed. As a male officer said:

We have to look at ways not of trying to get people involved in the structures, but of making the structure something very different. (Roundtable, 1988:260)

The NUPE women valued equality. They loosened the hold of bureaucracy and hierarchy, members and officers met on an equal footing. The mystique of office was dispelled. The role of branch officers at meetings was subordinated to that of ordinary members. Only then did women show any interest holding office (Roundtable, 1988:258). Further, branch offices were often shared and, when possible, rotated. Office-sharing was seen both as a democratic principle and a practice which made office-holding fit in better with part-time employment and with domestic commitments.

Representing the grass-roots at the top

For ordinary women to be truly represented their voices need to be audible at the top, informing and guiding the leadership. At present grass-roots voices are barely reflected at the top. In the words of McCormack:

> The hard reality is that the mainstream of the trade union movement at the grass roots level does not constitute the mainstream at the leadership level. And that is why the trade union movement is facing the question of change. (Roundtable, 1988:251)

Because of their energy and enthusiasm, coupled with the support of an active local constituency, some members of the branch were elected onto the union's NEC. These representatives spent a limited time on the NEC then resigned, thus giving other women a chance to take their place. The branch was also the source of the formal four-year limit on those NEC seats specially reserved for women (see Chapter 9) (Cockburn, 1991:134).

Limiting time in office is not enough; NEC members actively encourage and assist others to put themselves forward. As an ex-NEC member said:

> Now, I've gone up the structures to what they like to call the top......We in Northern Ireland do not call it the top. We like to say we've reached the *bottom* of the ladder when we get to the Executive Council. I have reached the bottom of that ladder. We believe, and I truthfully believe, having reached the bottom, you do what you can do, but you should only be there for a time and, if you really do believe in what you've been trying to do, then you must back away, you must then bring someone else along behind you to take your place......If we did that in all aspects I can see the trade union movement as a whole, both male and female,..... reaching out to hundreds and thousands of people to make the trade union a place for them, to make it [so that] they have a place in the union and their union has a place for them. (Channel 4, 1988)

Getting closer to the community

Family and community which constitute the setting for much of women's unpaid work also shapes the terms and conditions of their paid work. In consequence women are more able than men to identify links between family, community and trade union issues; these links can strengthen the union. The women from this branch were involved by the union in an oral history project about women's health and helped to produce a short book (NUPE N. Ireland Women's Committee, 1992).

Working on the project made members aware of the vast improvements in women's lives wrought by the public services. They began to see the relevance of trade unionism to defending not only their personal jobs but the whole public services area. A school meals worker described privatization and competitive tendering as a threat to 'the entire education system' with 'the absolute essentials crumbling.......no money for books, not enough teachers, [and] buildings in disrepair'. For her it was an attack on the working class and she looked to the union to repulse it (NUPE N. Ireland Women's Committee, 1992:113).

The organizer as facilitator

The union organizer pursuing a member-led strategy has a special role. she must create conditions where women can assert their own latent strength, take power from men, rebuild union organization from the grass-roots and develop ways of keeping the power there. This needs the skills of a facilitator, an ability to generate action without controlling it, a knack of putting knowledge about union procedures at the members' service, rather than using it to manipulate them.

For example, before union representatives can assert the value of women's work in negotiation, the organizer has to get women themselves to recognise and assert that value. In McCormack's words:

> You can't go in to represent the value of a woman cleaner without first of all, organisationally, taking on the task of making her assert her own value......But you can't get that confidence, that assertion of value, unless you perform the organisational task first. (Roundtable, 1988:259)

Organizers must work to an agenda defined by the members and this can be demanding. Even the NUPE divisional officer who instigated the strategy considered it so:

I'm finding that every time I move forward from things that are coming from the members, they demand a re-thinking of me, and that's a very unpleasant discipline. You think that you do really understand and then something hits you in the face. It's very tempting to think you do know best. (Roundtable, 1988:253)

Summary

The women from the N. Ireland branch now feel the union belongs to them; it has become a place to develop their opinions, to devise and implement policies in defence of their jobs. As McCormack reports, 'they love the space their union gives them to be together. Love is the right word. They enjoy the humour of it; they enjoy the challenge of it' (Roundtable, 1988:260). In this form of branch organization the authentic voice of women at the grass-roots has been able to emerge. The strategy has stood the test of time.

Applicability of a member-led strategy

NUPE N. Ireland women have shown that radical cultural change is possible at branch level. As a member-led strategy, it locates power at the grass-roots in a way which others do not. It has two main strengths. It involves all ordinary members not just union representatives and is highly democratic; and it is located at the grass-roots where policy initiatives often fail to penetrate. It brings the challenge to masculinity into workplace and branch where the mass membership is to be found.

In N. Ireland where the predominance of women in a close-knit occupational culture gave immediate access to a culture of femininity, the women succeeded in feminizing their branch. For unions like NUPE, with a high proportion of low status and low-paid women, it seems to us a powerful strategy. One male officer at least sees it as a strategy for feminizing and reinvigorating whole unions:

> At some stage.......a particular union would have an identity where it was seen to be presenting the interests of women......then women would flock to that organization in very large numbers (Roundtable, 1988).

Without making quite such optimistic claims we believe that low-paid women service workers are so poorly represented by their unions that any strategy which significantly increases their activity and involvement should be given encouragement.

Different types of unions

How applicable is a member-led strategy as a means of challenging the culture of masculinity in other situations? It may be less useful to unions catering for white-collar career women because of the way professional identity tends to weaken (though not eradicate) gender identity.

The strategy might be very effective in unions and branches with a high proportion of black women. Assessing the TGWU's unsuccessful efforts to recruit black women cleaners at Heathrow, Virdee made various recommendations. High on his list was self-organization at branch level, calling for the same member and officer involvement as in the N. Ireland case (Virdee, 1992, 1993). A member-led strategy of this nature would probably help recruitment wherever there are concentrations of workers, women and men, from groups currently subordinated within the movement.

Where men predominate, a member-led union might, however, actually reinforce masculine values, for instance the family wage, traditional prop to the wage claims of low-paid men. It should, however, enable more women to speak out. It would also give more power to the relatively powerless men at the grass-roots.

Finding the organizers

Finding paid officers with the commitment, energy and flexibility to develop a member-led organization, might be difficult. Most paid officers are male, with a reputation for controlling rather than facilitating. Recent research has indicated they are more responsive to members' views than had been thought (Heery and Kelly, 1990). However, responding in the sense of routinely allowing grass-roots members to define their own agenda, is a radical requirement not often made of paid officers. Officers might well find themselves more than usually pressured between the claims of their members and those of the leadership. This has already happened in NUPE: for example the branch insisted on taking an equal pay claim to tribunal in the face of the leadership's wish to use collective bargaining.

Women, rather than men, might be attracted to the work. Those with children might find difficulty because the need for flexibility, including working unsocial hours. Job-sharing might be a solution. Those undertaking this kind of organizational strategy would benefit from special training and support networks common among women officers.

Conclusions

The influence of masculinity in grass-roots culture is so all-pervasive that any way of contesting it should get careful consideration. A member-led union, as exemplified by NUPE N. Ireland, seems to us to be a development of great potential, especially in the many areas where women outnumber men. In those circumstances it should be seriously considered as a pattern for the future. Even where men outnumber women, the fact that attention is paid to *all* members should bring an improvement for women.

Part Two
UNION POLICIES TOWARDS WOMEN

8 Attraction, encouragement and education

In Parts 2 and 3 our focus changes from the grass-roots to a more comprehensive view of the trade union movement looking at recent developments and how they have helped to advance women's interests. In Part 2 we look particularly at policies designed to improve the representation of women, both as a group and in their diversity.

Four policies for increasing women's participation

These policies can be considered under four main headings. Policies of attraction attempt to bring new people into membership and secure existing members. Policies of encouragement offer women an advisory role, but no formal vote in decision making. Educational policies increase their knowledge, skills and confidence. Policies of empowerment are designed to assure women positions of influence and power. The first three are discussed in this chapter, policies of empowerment, a key way forward, in Chapter 9.

Policies of attraction

Recruitment

Recruitment into trade union membership is essential if unions are to carry out their basic function, of representing the interests of working people. This applies to women as to men. But it is only one aspect of recruitment. Keeping up membership numbers is also a financial imperative, particularly acute in recent years. These two imperatives are closely intertwined. The promotion by the unions in the 1980s of a woman-friendly image brings them together.

The proportion of women joining unions has always been lower than that of men, except for black women where the reverse is true (Lee, 1987). They have always been seen as presenting special problems. In the eighties almost one in two employed men was a union member, but only one in three women. As unemployment rose, unions failed to attract even those who found jobs and by the early nineties only one in four employed women were members (LRD, 1991). In these circumstances recruitment has become a priority.

Union interest in recruiting women has been growing since the end of the Second World War, concurrently with the increase of the number of women in paid employment. The big public service unions like NUPE and COHSE led the way. In 1969 NUPE introduced a Nurses' Charter and in 1974 appointed a special officer to run a nurses' recruitment campaign. In the early 1970s it campaigned to recruit school dinner ladies; in 1975 and 1977 it co-operated with other unions, NALGO, ASTMS, NUT, NUS and FBU, in campaigns against government-imposed local authority cuts. Significant pay increases were obtained for dinner ladies in 1972-3 and nurses in 1974. In some white-collar unions such as ACTT and ASTMS, women's campaigns began in the early seventies (Hunt, 1976); ACTT later produced a TUC publication about women in the media (TUC, 1984). In the eighties NALGO produced the first pamphlet attacking the sexism of union language. But it was 1990 before women got a resolution against sexist language passed by the TUC. Even then the reports in the media treated the subject as a joke (BBC Radio 4, 1990; Heffer, 1990).

A woman-friendly image

The desire to represent women (both members and those not yet in membership) and the need for membership subscriptions, in combination, have led the unions to cultivate an image that attracts women. From the mid-eighties there was a large increase in the number of women's issues covered by union publications: maternity and paternity leave, equal value, unfair dismissal, sexual harassment, women's health, VDUs (visual display units) and safety, childcare, problems of unpaid carers etc. The unions vied with one another to show how greatly they cared about the interests of women.

Falling membership and the Thatcher government's attacks on trade unions at this time resulted in a general reassessment of union policy. Two very different responses emerged. Firstly right-wing unions like EETPU pioneered single union agreements and consumer services such as credit and holiday facilities (all later taken up by other unions); this was known as the New Realism. Secondly, some of the larger general and service unions revived traditional concern with the most exploited and lowest-paid groups in society, groups which consist largely of women.

Notable among the champions of working women was the union now known as GMB. The policy statements of their newly appointed General Secretary, John Edmonds, were widely reported. In 1986, for example, he called on unions to tackle the poverty pay of the 'new servant' class, mainly women, working in the private sector (*Guardian* 26.5.86). The TGWU intention to target 'temporary, part-time and women workers, young people and ethnic minorities who have been......neglected in the past' was reported in the media (*Guardian* 27.2.87). NUPE was already representing part-timers forced into the private sector through privatization of public services (*Guardian* 6.1.86). It also publicized a range of other policies affecting women: equal opportunities, union democracy, union education and low pay.

Unions claimed interest in wider issues like the arts and environment and a wider constituency than their own members. In 1986 Edmonds stated that 'a union should not simply represent its own members, or even the 10 million in the trade union movement; its real constituency was all working people in Britain'. He urged the GMB to become 'central' to popular culture......[and to] 'enter territory inhabited by Bob Geldof, Greenpeace and the animal rights organizations' (*Guardian* 4.6.86 and 26.5.86).

In 1987, in preparation for an amalgamation and name change, the then GMBATU employed the services of the advertising firm Lamborghini. A new slogan, 'Working Together', replaced 'Unity is Strength'; there was a new logo. Edmonds aimed to make the new GMB 'the foremost organization in Britain in the struggle for women's rights'. These changes of image, what we have termed policies of attraction, were followed by policies of encouragement and empowerment. Ten seats were reserved for women on the enlarged national executive (*Guardian* 23.6.87) raising their representation from six to 32 per cent, and making it almost exactly proportional to their number in the membership. In 1987 the influential GMB pamphlet *Winning a Fair Deal for Women* was published, confronting the way in which collective bargaining discriminates against women. We refer to this later when discussing policies of empowerment.

A trade union journal   NUPE's changing policy towards women can be illustrated by analysing material published in the union journal, *Public*

Employees. Between 1966 and 1976 there was a radical change, pictorial and textual, from an almost exclusively male image to one that included women. In 1966 women's issues were segregated in a Woman's Column; women were patronised ('She wept in my advice bureau' was the title of an article by Frank Allaun MP); the family wage reigned - low pay was discussed in terms of low-pay families and the problem of fatherlessness. Women did sometimes protest. In 1966, when women had just become a majority in the union, an article challenged the conventional classification of workers into three categories, 'skilled', 'unskilled' and 'women', calling it a 'national disgrace'.

In the early sixties there were few photographs; most were of men, union officers. Women who appeared were in the role of wife or secretary, giving or receiving flowers. An exception, in 1967, was the Birmingham School Meals Women's branch outing; the trip catered for 725 women and children.

1968 marked a turning point. A new column entitled 'Women's Talk' reported 'Suddenly everyone's talking about women'. Noting that 'women are at work as well as in the home' the journal asked: 'Will a man's place be at the kitchen sink?' The general secretary wrote of his 'gratification' when three women were elected to the union's sixteen-strong TUC Conference delegation. A Nurses' Charter was announced. Women began to write letters to the journal. But the older image - the female pin-up - persisted. In January 1969 the union's 'Miss UK', a school meals supervisor, appeared in a bathing costume. A long correspondence ensued on the pros and cons of the pin-up, mostly among men, concluded in August by the editor with the directive 'Last Word on Our Birds'!

In 1971 the union proclaimed itself 'probably' the largest women's union. However, features were still written by men; letters from men were protective or patronising, talking about 'championing' women and 'speaking for' them. Yet women became more visible. Retirement photographs showed women as well as men. A note of thanks to two long-serving women 'collectors' (of subscriptions) reported that: 'Ladies like those are the unsung heroines of NUPE's recent history'. Pictures of nurses appeared on the front page - pretty, young and white. In 1973 the Albert Armstrong trophy, for the best achievement by women branch members, was founded in memory of an old member. There were nine applicants in the first year, seventy in 1975. In that year the first suggestions about reserving seats on the NEC specially for women were published. The ensuing correspondence, mostly from men, included the claim of 'tokenism'. But it was a woman who suggested that as 'a women's union......we would be the laughing stock of the TUC movement', illustrating how deeply ingrained in women's minds is the association between men, power and authority.

In 1975, the year the Equal Pay Act was implemented and the Sex Discrimination Act passed. A Woman's Page was introduced; it reported the first day-release course for part-time school meals stewards in London. By 1976 the 'campaign against the cuts', stressing their disproportionate effect on women, was highly publicized. Issues such as childcare and the connections between low pay and women were being aired. An article on taxation which failed to mention married women provoked an indignant letter saying, ironically, that all members should have been included, 'even the two-thirds majority' of married women! By 1976 photographs of action - demos and marches - had overtaken presentations for faithful service and awards of union benefits. Women were included, as workers in their own right.

By the late eighties the image had entered the age of equal opportunity. Pictures balanced images of gender, race, age and youth. Six people appeared on the front page of the 1988 conference issue: three black people and three white. Four of the six were adults, two could be clearly identified as women. Inside were photographs of speakers and of people who attended conference but did not speak. There were just under three women to every four men among the former, just over among the latter. Although this was well below the proportion of women in the membership, it undoubtedly over-represented their contribution to the conference. Such a display was a declaration about the equal importance of individuals to the union, regardless of gender, race or age.

An equal opportunity image was also apparent in other unions' and in TUC publicity. A black woman was the first of ten union members profiled in GMB's recruitment pamphlet *Voices*, affirming gender and race (GMB, c. 1987). The remainder of the pamphlet gave equal representation by gender and race. The 1991 edition of *Working Women* a TUC educational booklet, adds disability. On the front cover a young black woman in a 'hard hat' replaced the middle-aged white woman kitchen worker of the 1983 edition (TUC, 1983, 1991d). On the back cover a large photograph of a white woman in a wheelchair, affirming disability, was combined with an inset of two white women catering workers.

Changing image and changing culture   Social images change through a complex combination of factors, their importance differing with unions and through time. NUPE, for example, was originally a male union, largely made up of roadworkers. In the fifties and sixties it deliberately built up its female membership. Rumblings of dissatisfaction were heard from women who felt their interests were being ignored. By the seventies the gender gap between membership and leadership began to cause the leadership concern: the promotion of a woman-friendly image was one means of bridging it. The main motivation however, was increasing the membership. John Edmonds asserts this explicitly in a comment about organizing or in other words recruiting members:

> In future the success of a union official should be measured by his (*sic*) ability to organise workers not by his ability to negotiate on behalf of existing members. (*Guardian* 21.8.87)

And behind numbers was finance. Inez McCormack (NUPE) endorses this latter view in relation to part-time workers:

> Recognition of the need to organise part-time workers is a managerial market force reaction......I have yet to hear a voice speaking for the representation of women's needs themselves, and for the movement to be at the service of women, rather than of the movement's need to survive. (Roundtable, 1988:251)

In one sense, however, why the unions were courting women was not too important. What was important was the creation of a climate where women felt included rather than excluded. The non-unionised public as well as members were made aware that trade unionism should belong to women as much as to men.

How effective are such exercises in changing the way men actually behave, in opening up the stifling white, male narrowness of trade union culture? Union literature sets guidelines and publicizes policy in a fairly graphic way. Though it tends to reach only the activists, they are arguably the most influential people. Media publicity has a wider influence. Personal commitment by leaders can be important. GMB's John Edmonds is believed to be committed and impatient of delay or evasion on the part of officers (Colling and Dickens, 1989:35).

However, there are grounds for disquiet; changes initiated from the top may prove superficial and power structures resistant to them. Men may continue to manipulate in a movement which remains fundamentally concerned with men's interests. As a man from NUCPS's Ethnic Advisory Committee put it:

> We now have......a much higher profile for 'women's issues'......a change in the union's policies, but not a change in its structures, its

priorities, its orders or its culture......[these policies] are operating within a framework of a male culture......they carry male values......So this whole issue of policies, by itself, is actually a con. (Roundtable, 1988:255)

Changing images from the top does not, of itself, change culture. But it may help. A practical consideration is that unions appear more willing to commit resources to image promotion than to other pro-women policies. Even in image promotion some unions have a long way to go. ASLEF's motto, 'Brothers in Unity for Mutual Help', is described in a 1983 report by TSSA as 'a motto to be proud of!' (quoted in Robbins, 1986:53). Either ASLEF is gender-blind or it must want to put women off.

In October 1987 trade unions reached their highest level of popularity since 1954: 71 per cent of Gallup respondents saw them as a 'good thing' (*Guardian* 9.10.87). Perhaps the new less self-centred, more inclusive and woman-friendly image had increased their popularity.

New recruitment initiatives

A recent LRD study of 37 unions found few with comprehensive recruitment policies. A mass of literature has been produced, but it has reached activists rather potential new members (LRD, 1991:26). Examples are: GMB-APEX's on career breaks for women and maternity leave, NUPE's on women's health and NALGO's and USDAW's on low pay and equal pay. The N. Ireland division of NUPE has had success recruiting, but this is the spin-off from a new method of organizing which involves grass-roots members (see Chapter 7).

Since the eighties new patterns of employment have emerged. Developments in information technology have given rise to a new group of homeworkers, white collar, often skilled and freelance. NUJ and ACTT have produced useful models for recruiting these professional homeworkers (Huws, 1984:67).

However, the biggest increase in workers is among low-skilled or unskilled women in the new servant or 'under'-class, a group without a traditional voice in the union movement. Recruitment is needed in all areas of employment, but the need is greatest in this difficult and growing low-status, low-paid and unorganized workforce. Some unions have made efforts. In 1991 MSF National Women's Sub-Committee published comprehensive recruitment guidelines, listing - under branch, workplace, regional and national levels - twenty-five different measures for recruiting women. Drawing attention to groups marginalized by the movement, it pleaded for each MSF member to personally recruit another woman. Angela Coyle made a similar suggestion in her pamphlet on contract cleaning (Coyle, 1986). Women do not seem to have responded. Other unions have targeted specific groups: USDAW part-timers, RMT catering workers and TGWU workers in hairdressing.

In 1987 TGWU launched its Link-up recruitment campaign directed at low-paid workers including women and ethnic minorities. The intention was 'to change TGWU culture to make it more welcoming'. One way of doing this was by liaising with local community groups (LRD, 1991). Others included the use of recruitment teams drawn from local branches and of women-only teams - on the principle that like should be used to recruit like. Recruitment teams were to be trained and literature for targeted groups produced in their own languages. It has been used by the Leicester Outworkers Group; their information packs for homeworkers are produced in several languages. This device has been used infrequently by UK unions, the TGWU Link-up attempt to recruit contract cleaners at Heathrow being one example (see Chapter 12). However, in Australia it is routinely used to recruit immigrant homeworkers (West Yorkshire Low Pay Unit, 1990:126). The Heathrow recruitment initiative also put into practice the policy of liaising with community groups.

Policies of encouragement

We look next at policies to get women's issues onto the trade union agenda and to involve women themselves in the structures.

Women's issues

Issues and the trade union agenda It has been argued that if women see issues which interest them on the agenda of trade unions they are more likely to join and to become involved. But it is questionable whether progressive policies for women do have this result. Unions like IRSF have found that they lead only to a 'relatively slight' increase in women's involvement (IRSF, 1987:25)

If they are to become involved in union organization, women need to see these policies implemented. But implementing policy is far more difficult, time-consuming and expensive than publicizing it. Cooperation has to be gained from a range of people, members, officers, employers and legislators. Equal pay was part of formal TUC policy for nearly a hundred years before the Equal Pay Act was passed. It is a prime example of the unions' failure to get their policies on women's issues implemented.

Another difficulty with the argument that putting women's issues in policy increases their participation is that issues which reach the agenda (often through the efforts of activists) are not necessarily those which most concern the majority (Elliot, 1984:69,70). Unions must be seen to address issues of significance to the majority of ordinary women before more will become involved. Some are now highlighting issues of topical appeal - for example TGWU campaigns on equal pay and on carers - but selected on the hunch of the minority rather than at the request of the majority. Nevertheless, putting women's issues into policy goes further than image-changing. It is a public acknowledgement of a shift in values. To that degree, it undermines the culture of masculinity.

Consulting the grass-roots More convincing is the move towards consulting members directly about policy matters. In the seventies, using membership surveys, several unions asked women what issues they thought important. NALGO was one of the first (Rees, 1990). IPMS and USDAW both explored the different priorities of women and men. USDAW additionally examined the differences between part and full-timers, and sought views from potential as well as actual members (LRD, 1991; Rees, 1990; USDAW, 1987, 1990). By giving ordinary members an opportunity to express their opinions about policy, the unions hope to convince women of the relevance. Then women can be expected to become more active.

In 1993 COHSE, NALGO and NUPE merged into UNISON. In making their new constitution they used a new method of tapping the views of all members, including women. Members of the three unions were asked to get together in groups - at workplaces, branches, trade union schools, or informally. Clearly set out discussion documents, with response booklets, were distributed through trade union branches. Groups were asked to ensure that women, black people, disabled people, lesbians and gays were all included. The fair representation of each of these categories was to be discussed in turn. Members were asked to locate barriers to involvement, define bargaining priorities and suggest how representation could be improved. The results of the consultation went to the working committees drawing up the constitution. It was an ambitious exercise, but the response was disappointing. Nevertheless, the principle of consulting members outside as well as inside formal union structures is an advance.

In the eighties unions were criticized for being undemocratic, with particular allegations that leaders were more militant than their members. The Thatcher government generated and used fears about union power and militancy to introduce a series of laws curtailing the rights and powers of the unions (Elias, 1990). These included a requirement to conduct secret postal ballots of all members for the election of officers to the NEC and before taking industrial action. The need to set up postal ballots may have encouraged the unions' use of surveys rather than branch meetings to consult their members over policy.

In allowing people to speak for themselves, and in its inclusive and anti-hierarchical character, the attempt to consult members directly is consistent with the culture of femininity. In practice it will help to enfranchise more women.

Special structures and an advisory voice

Special structures for women, within the constitutional framework of both the TUC and individual unions, were the first means used to improve women's representation in the movement. The structures gave women an advisory voice but no voting rights. The assumption was made that experience in special structures would increase women's confidence and skills, leading them automatically into mainstream activity. It was further assumed that special structures would give women a new status which would persuade men in decision making to listen to their advice. The assumptions were ill-founded. Neither of these things happened.

Women's Advisory Conference Special structures go back to 1920 when the women's NFWW merged with the mixed-sex Workers' Union. Special representational measures for women were built into the resultant NUGW, but most survived only a short time. The most important, however, has been the annual TUC Women's Advisory Conference which has met regularly since 1931. This had considerable limitations. The first was men's power. The Conference and its organizing committee NWAC, were for many years in the control of men. The few women on NWAC were closely integrated into traditional trade union culture, a tough bureaucratic male union world. They succumbed to the culture of masculinity and failed to confront the men (Elliot, 1984:69-70; McGwire, 1986).

The NWAC was accountable to the TUC General Council rather than to the Women's Advisory Conference; and it thus controlled rather than served that Conference. Conference tried to bring NWAC under its own control, demanding that more of its members be elected directly from the Conference, fewer from the TUC General Council. The Conference won this battle. By the 1980s women were in a majority on the NWAC: in 1987 they held sixteen out of twenty-four seats. Of the twenty-four, ten (all women) were elected from the Conference, fourteen (six of them women) from the TUC General Council. To make the NWAC further accountable, Conference asked that the Chair be rotated annually. In 1987, after many years of insistence, the rotating Chair was established.

The Women's Conference (its current title) has had a reputation for being a bland affair. In part this derived from its lack of constitutional power. In part it came from being a gathering of like-minded people, a 'celebratory' occasion, marked by a mood of 'harmony, goodwill and even self-congratulation' (Shaw, 1984:59). Most motions seem to be passed overwhelmingly, often without dissent or even discussion. One reason for this is the virtual absence of the people who would disagree - the men. Another is that the women are in agreement about the nature of their long-standing grievances (Cunnison, 1988). A few issues have aroused deep feelings: these include reforms supported from the floor but opposed by the organizing Committee, and the question of whether the Conference itself should continue to meet.

As a representational forum, the Women's Advisory Conference had severe limitations. Some of these still exist. It has no direct voice in top policy making. Although a few selected resolutions from the Conference go forward to the TUC Annual Conference, they have to be passed first by the organizing Committee and second by the TUC General Council, a male-dominated body. By 1992 the number of resolutions allowed increased to five. However, Conference is still demanding that resolutions be allowed to proceed straight to the TUC Conference as of right. They have also requested that a number of seats on the TUC General Council be reserved for Conference delegates.

In 1986, both Conference and organizing Committee were allowed to drop the term 'advisory' from their titles. This term had become an irritant, indicating a lower status than that of a 'full committee'. In 1992, after a fierce debate and narrowly-won vote, men were excluded from future participation (*Everywoman*, May 1992). Unions had had the option of sending men or women and a small number of men had always been delegated.

Women's officers and other advisory structures The 1979 TUC Charter for women (Appendix 1) recommended unions to set up Women's Advisory Committees at national, regional, divisional and district level, and to appoint special National and Regional Women's (or Equal Rights) Officers. The advisory committees were intended to liaise with elected decision-making bodies at appropriate levels, and up and down their own hierarchies. But they carried no voting rights. The recommendations were adopted slowly and partially. In 1982 Hunt reported that eight major unions had special committees to advise on policy, some with special responsibility for organizing women (Hunt, 1982:168).

The NUT first appointed a national officer, the 'Woman Official', in 1971. ASTMS set up an advisory structure in the mid-seventies (Harrison, n.d.). In NUPE demands for a national women's officer were resisted in 1937, 1947, and 1953. In 1973 a motion called for 'lady organizer to represent school meals nationally'; and an amendment to it demanded that a national 'woman organizer be appointed forthwith'. The amendment was passed, but no action taken (Nelson, 1977/8). A National Women's Officer was finally appointed in 1982.

A survey in 1989 reported special national officers in thirty-one out of forty-three unions (SERTUC, 1989:4-5). By 1990, according to the results of a postal questionnaire (outlined in Appendix 4), National Women's or Equal Rights Officers had been appointed in nine of the ten unions with the largest number of women; and the AEU, an erstwhile male bastion, had a Women's Officer and positive policies for women. LRD reported, for 1988, that five unions (AEU, COHSE, GMB, TGWU and USDAW) also had special officers at regional level (LRD, 1988a); the postal questionnaire in 1990 revealed two more, MSF and NUPE.

National women's officers are at the top of the union hierarchy. Their effectiveness however, depends on adequate resourcing and their acceptance by other national (male) officers. There are subtle ways of devaluing their work. For their first few years in office the two highest women's officers in NUPE were paid less than men of equivalent rank. Moreover, a lower rank is usually assigned to National Women's and Equal Rights posts than to other national posts. The Women's Officer of the TGWU is unusual in having been appointed in 1990 to the highest rank, that of national secretary. There are very few black women paid officers. In 1987 the first to hold a national office was appointed National Equal Rights Officer of NUPE.

Some unions' advisory structures, with sufficient resources, have been very active. Some have become points of initiation for further structures relating to race, disability and sexuality. NUCPS, basically a management union, was formed in 1988 by a merger of SCPS and CSU. It inherited from SCPS a set of advisory committees (Drake et al., 1980). After the merger NUCPS set up it own structures. A National Women's Advisory Committee met regularly, advised NUCPS on education and organized each year a Women's Seminar and a meeting for women delegates to the NUCPS Conference. Policy called for all 'Groups, Branches and Districts' to set up women's advisory committees (NUCPS, 1988).

At the same time NUCPS set up a National and Regional Ethnic Minorities Advisory Committee to give a direct voice to black people; no specific arrangements were made for black *women*. A People with Disabilities Working Group was set up and an informal Lesbian and Gay Group. In the early nineties some NUCPS advisory committees achieved direct representation on decision-making committees. We refer to this in Chapter 9 when discussing the 'corporate voice'.

The TGWU too has advisory structures for both women and black people. Black women are poorly represented on the TGWU Women's National Advisory Committee: in 1991 only one of twenty-three members was black. There were proportionally more women on the mixed-sex black workers' National Race Equality Committee. The reason is largely structural; half of black people are women but in the UK only five per cent of women are black. But white ethnocentrism is also a factor (*Feminist Review*, 1984).

Black women tend to be more active trade unionists than black men so that, in unions where women predominate, special structures give them quite a powerful voice. In 1992 the proportion of women in NUPE's National Race Advisory Committee, elected in open contest, was 73 per cent.

Branch and workplace structures NUPE in 1984 and GMB in 1987 recommended that women's committees or groups be set up at workplace or branch (GMB, 1987; NUPE, 1984). Since then several unions, among them ACTT, GMB, NUJ, NUT, FDA and IPMS, have established Branch Equality Officers, the first four within the rulebook (Colling and Dickens, 1989; SERTUC, 1989:45). The appointment of informal women's officers has also been suggested as a means of counteracting male domination at that level. Such measures would strengthen the link between members and the advisory structures. But according to LRD (1991) they are not being put into practice; branch attendance is often too small to form a women's group; women who find enthusiasm through women-only education lose it when confronted by old hands who have 'heard it all before'; and activists are often over-stretched by multiple commitments. Groups formed to address topical issues may wither once the crisis passes; groups which depend on one person's dedication and enthusiasm may fold if that person moves on.

However some experiments have succeeded. USDAW reports that their branch 'women and health get-togethers', discussing issues such as cancer screening and the menopause, have proved popular. 'Harassment officers' have been appointed by an NUT and a NALGO branch. But suggestions for safe transport or escorts for women attending evening meetings seem not to have been put into practice (LRD, 1991).

Equal Rights Department The demand for a TUC Women's Department to give central and symbolic importance to the role of women, is old; the demand for an Equal Rights Department recent. The issue was argued at the 1987 TUC Conference. Rose Lambie of COHSE proposed the establishment of a Women's Department, 'properly funded and staffed by women'. An NUT amendment called instead for an Equal Rights Department. NUJ and TASS women supported the Equal Rights amendment, at the same time expressing concern that such a department could be used to 'exclude women from the male-dominated corridors of power' (*Guardian,* 11.9.87). The amendment was passed and an Equal Rights Department established. It was headed by Kay Carberry, Secretary to the National Women's Committee, who became the first woman to head a TUC Department.

Its brief was to coordinate women's interests throughout the movement. It saw itself as a facilitator, responding to the needs of activists. But it has taken initiatives, for example in running seminars and conferences on equal pay (TUC, 1990k). It has produced policy statements and negotiators' guidelines on a wide variety of women's issues (TUC, 1990a-j).

A 1991 negotiators' pack *More Than You Bargained For* clearly signified the department's intention to influence national and grass-roots negotiation. It looked at a series of eleven issues from wages to pensions, raising for each questions about 'how to identify discrimination, the interests of women members and what to aim for in negotiation' (TUC, 1991b). In 1992 under financial pressure the TUC merged the Equal Rights Department with that of Social Policy; additional responsibilities include health, health and safety, environmental protection, disability, social security, benefits and pensions.

The effectiveness of advisory structures There are difficulties in assessing the effectiveness of special advisory structures. The contribution of the TUC Women's Conference stands out. Its longevity attests to its value. Its supportive, consciousness-raising and confidence-building functions have all been important in allowing women to find their own voice. However, some have felt that the Conference marginalized women's issues and this was too high a price to pay. More women now, particularly in the white-collar unions, know what they want and are prepared to speak out. Some would prefer women to put all their energies into the mainstream structures, rather than support a system of indirect representation such as the Women's Conference.

Assessment within individual unions is more difficult. Major problems have been reported: committee members were frequently not elected but appointed by the (male) hierarchy; places were often filled by men who then dominated them; committees were accountable to no one; they had no finance, no power and often no guidelines. Hence they were often ignored by those in the main structures (CLCLC, 1985/6:24). These must be set against successes like that of NUCPS. Further, research suggests that where unions have put resources into special structures, overall participation by women has increased (Hunt, 1982:170). That is not always the experience of the individual. In 1985 an activist from SCPS reported:

> Even though there is a really thorough women's structure inside the union, there is no real change in the power structure in that the men are doing the important jobs, and they discuss the important issues down in the pub, when there are few women around. (CLCLC, 1985/6:20)

This suggests a need for empowerment rather than mere encouragement.

Educational policies

Trade unions have a long tradition of support for education. Though the movement has fostered a class analysis of society, it has always put a high a value on free discussion and the pursuit of knowledge. It has recognised in education a powerful agent of social change, for both individuals and the working class.

Individuals have been awarded scholarships to attend institutions of further and higher education, such as Ruskin, Northern and Fircroft Colleges. Many then go on to serve the union movement as paid officers; others enter politics and work for the broader labour movement; some leave the union and labour movements altogether. Far more men than women have taken advantage of this facility. Trade unions have also traditionally provided evening courses on subjects such as politics, economics, labour history and international affairs, funding teachers and paying student fees. Domestic responsibilities have limited women's attendance.

In the 1970s unions transferred their resources to a programme of basic training for shop stewards and health and safety representatives. The government agreed to provide paid leave of absence from work for members to attend. Women, free to attend during work hours, have benefitted. A recent initiative likely to help both sexes is the provision of basic literacy courses at the workplace, again with paid time off to attend. Here, NUPE has been a pioneer.

An ILO convention entitles workers to paid educational leave. The UK government and TUC have agreed that shop steward training fulfils this entitlement. Other European countries have different interpretations. For example, in Italy, some unions have negotiated 150 hours paid leave a year, to enable workers to reach school-leaving standards. Take-up has been high among women, courses have been organized around women's issues and feminist teachers recruited (Caldwell, 1983).

In **Case 4** we noted the value of trade union education in sustaining and developing women's trade union and gender consciousness. 'Women-only' courses were of particular importance, aiming to release women's confidence in their personal abilities and their social and cultural resources. They do this by establishing mutual understanding, respect for individual experience and networks of support. Women thus feel able to represent themselves. A minority of women have criticized these courses. For example, Walton reported that twelve out of sixteen NALGO social workers would not want to repeat their experience of women-only education. Her explanation is that 'women who excel either as employees or as trade unionists are less likely to be sympathetic to the forms of oppression which less successful women experience' (Walton, 1991:168): a bleak outlook.

In 1978 the TUC Education Service reviewed its service for women. Out of this emerged the short 'bridging course'. This had two aims: to persuade women who already showed interest to take on the office of shop steward; to prepare them for the mixed-sex basic training expected of all stewards. Paid leave was negotiated for ordinary members as well as stewards. Bridging courses thus reached women not normally exposed to trade union education. Women tutors were provided.

Individual unions also introduced women-only education. NUPE was among the first to run residential courses for women; several others including MSF have followed suit. A work-based scheme begun by GMBATU (now GMB) was introduced with an ordinary member, rather than formal tutor, acting as co-ordinator. It was still running in 1993. In 1990, our postal survey of twenty-three unions with national women's or equal opportunity officers reported two-thirds with some form of special education for women. NUPE has recently introduced women-only training for members of national and regional committees. Since the late seventies women's committees of trades councils have also held women-only functions on varied issues.

Women-only education persuaded many women to undertake further trade union education: in some localities up to 60 per cent have done so (Beale, 1982). Networks of information and support established on TUC courses have helped activists in their work. Special education for women may, however, divorce women's issues from the mainstream movement; providers and tutors are aware of this danger.

In the early eighties the TUC tried to make basic mixed-sex shop steward courses more relevant to women. They set out to challenge the sexism engrained in TUC education. McIlroy gives the flavour of the problem when writing about

> the sexist comments and jokes in the bars at tutor briefings, the John Wayne virility antics of some tutors and Education Officers, the sexual predatoriness that emerges in relation to female students. (McIlroy, 1982:16)

Tutors were advised to make changes. First, casework should include issues of relevance to women, presented as routine union business. Second, language should refer to both sexes, for example 'she' and 'he' used alternately to refer to shop stewards. Third, tutors should be prepared to confront sexism in the classroom. Fourth, women-friendly techniques like single sex and small group discussions should be used. Course material was rewritten. All students of the basic course were provided with a copy of the TUC Equal Opportunity Policy Statement. Efforts to increase the number of women tutors were only partly successful because of cutbacks in TUC spending.

The move to feminize basic shop steward education was very promising. The course became a much less threatening experience. Women learned more about issues directly related to women's jobs, and men began to accept women's issues as normal union business. Men also learned about sexism and how it disadvantages, controls and offends women. Unfortunately, again partly because of TUC cutbacks, feminization of trade union education was not carried forward in the late eighties.

Relatively few unions have incorporated women's issues into their own educational programmes. Only half those responding to our 1990 postal questionnaire had done so. Three of the twenty-three (AUT, NUT, and USDAW) raised women's issues in all courses. Ten more ran awareness courses, on equal opportunities, sexism or racism.

Conclusions

In this chapter we have considered three types of policy used to improve women's representation in the unions, those of attraction, encouragement and education. These policies have had limited success. The woman-friendly image is in many respects a public relations exercise, nevertheless it begins to chip away at the culture of masculinity. Consultation of grass-roots members begins to enable women to speak for themselves. In theory, the advisory voice gives women a platform within the movement thought in practice they can be ignored. It does not ensure an input into decision making. Innovations in union education especially women-only courses have, however, been important in equipping a minority to challenge male power and the culture of masculinity. In the next chapter we discuss the fourth policy, that of empowering women through structural change.

9 Union democracy and empowerment

The failure to represent women

The failure of the policies discussed in the last chapter to secure fair representation for women suggests a fundamental problem in the democratic structures and procedures by which trade unions are governed. A number of unions have acknowledged the need for basic change and have devised new structures to enable full participation by women and minority groups. We have termed these policies of empowerment. Before discussing them we look at how union democracy short-changes women.

Democracy is a historic tenet of the movement held with pride. Nevertheless it has failed women, as it has in other major institutions. Critics have alleged that structures and practices of trade union government do not always follow democratic principles. Allegations of voting irregularities appear periodically in the media. Charges are made that the structures encourage apathy with the result that the leadership tends to ignore the views of the membership. We are concerned here with the appropriateness of these structures for the representation of women. They rest on the notion that each member has an equal opportunity to take part in union government, indirectly through the vote and directly through standing for office, starting at the bottom and moving up to the top.

The union movement is made up of individuals who belong to different groups which, in addition to common aims, have divergent and often conflicting interests. The differing interests of occupational and industrial groups are widely recognised and built into most of their representational structures. In addition unions are generally organized by locality. There are groups, however, which occupy a distinctive role in the productive process but whose basic identity is unrelated to it. Women comprise the largest of these; black people and those from minority ethnic groups, immigrants, disabled people, and lesbians and gay men comprise others. Most are discriminated against in the labour market and in society generally. Unions themselves have no tradition of providing for their representation.

Memberships of these groups cut across one another to create smaller groups, each with a particular experience, identity and set of interests. They give rise to the diversity of voice contained within the collective identity of women. They are the site of multiple discrimination - for example, black, disabled women suffer from a different and greater discrimination than white, disabled women. Individuals from them are disadvantaged if not disenfranchised within the union movement, women more so than men; few are elected to office, decision-making committees or delegate conferences; very few become paid officers.

Writing on democracy and trade unions Fosh and Cohen discuss the representation of minority groups. They introduce the notion of 'participatory democracy' which involves incorporating effective mechanisms of accountability into union rules and procedures. They suggest that a strongly participative element in local union organization, together with a 'commitment to collectivism', may bridge the gap between different groups, ensuring that articulate members of one group will speak for inarticulate members of another (Fosh and Cohen, 1990:117, 125-6). This may happen. But the evidence is that women, black workers and others find their interests overlooked (Cunnison, 1983a, 1989; Munro, 1990; Rees, 1990:199-200).

A different approach is to identify the under-represented groups and then devise special measures for their adequate representation on all decision-making bodies. This approach, known as 'proportionality', is currently favoured by the union movement. A clause in the updated TUC Charter for Women at Work called for unions to

> set targets for women's representation on union executives - with the aim of representation proportionate to membership. (TUC 1990a)

The updated TUC *Charter for Equality for Women within Trade Unions* went further. The principle of proportionality is also written into the rules of the new union UNISON, and its NEC is empowered to implement it (UNISON, 1992:14-15).

Proportionality is currently also in vogue in the Labour Party and in business. For example in March 1991 the BBC introduced targets for women in senior and middle management (*Guardian*, 13.3.91). In October, the business community, backed by the EOC and TUC, launched

Opportunity 2000. Fourteen of the largest UK firms set ten-year targets for improving the position of women in management (*Guardian*, 28.10.91). However, before we discuss proportionality and other policies to empower women, we assess the current numerical representation of women in the movement and how it is changing.

Numerical representation of women

In 1992 women constituted about a third of TUC-affiliated union membership. In some unions they formed a clear majority. With few exceptions, they were under-represented at all levels, from shop stewards and convenors to national executive councils. Their involvement in decision making was minimal. It is no surprise that women members generally do not feel their unions really belong to them, nor that their leaders are accountable to them.

The local leadership

Local leadership is the crucial level, the springboard for participation in regional and national decision making. A union must represent the interests of its members here if it is to be truly democratic. Branch and workplace are where the concerns of ordinary members are taken up or are pushed aside as irrelevant.

Local representation of women has improved over the past two decades, but patchily. Documenting this is difficult. Not all unions collect or publish the information; records are not always reliable. Gender is a recent preoccupation; even where information is currently available past records may not be. It is therefore possible only to give some examples.

Shop stewards COHSE, NALGO and NUPE reported on the position of women shop stewards in the lead-up to the merger into UNISON (C/N/N, 1990). We give the figures below (figures bracketed with 'f.' are the proportion of females in the total membership). In 1990 they were: COHSE 52% (79%f.), NALGO 42% (51%f.), and NUPE 39% (74%f.). Although progress has been made, no figure is yet near parity. In 1979 COHSE (then 75%f.) reported a figure of only 24%, ranging from 15% in Wales to 37% in the Northwest (COHSE, 1979).

In 1974 NUPE (then 63%f.) reported only 28% (Fryer et al., 1974:12). After that year NUPE began to encourage women stewards; in 1979 a local study of NUPE in Humberside reported a figure of 33% (Cunnison,

1983a); in 1984-5 local study of NUPE in the West Midlands reported a much higher figure of 60% - though still less than parity (Munro, 1990:139, 143). Among unions without policies for promoting women stewards, representation is probably much poorer. For example, in 1989, a figure of only 5% was reported for the AEU (14%f.) (Colling and Dickens, 1989:17).

Branch secretaries Shop stewards are the front line of the movement, but the branch is the basis of its organization. The secretary, concerned with negotiations and casework, is usually the most influential branch officer. It is there that women's involvement begins to be 'filtered out' (Fosh and Cohen, 1990:195; Ledwith et al., 1985).

Women achieve nowhere near parity in the post of secretary. In 1990 the percentages reported by COHSE, NALGO and NUPE respectively were 32% (79%f.), 27% (51%f.) and 27% (74%f.) markedly lower than for shop stewards (C/N/N, 1990). Figures from 1986 for other unions show similar under-representation, CPSA 43% (70%f.), APEX 38% (54%f.), USDAW 27% (61%f.) and IRSF 23% (62%f.) (IRSF, 1987:11). Rees's research in NALGO confirms these findings. She reports that women and men became active and held office in equal numbers, but that far more men became branch secretaries or other key officers; women became thrift or welfare secretaries (Rees, 1990:143). One study suggested that the proportion of women in a branch had to be well over 80% for a woman to be elected branch secretary (COHSE, 1979). In 1989 CPSA reported the proportion of women branch secretaries attained parity with the membership in only two out of twenty-one 'sections', British Nuclear Fuels and British Airways (personal communication). Overall only 42% of CPSA (71%f.) branch secretaries were women (LRD, 1991:20).

As with shop stewards, there has been progress, notably among the white-collar unions. In the NUT for example, the proportion of women secretaries in 1975 was 20% (66%f.) but by 1990, following a promotion campaign, it was 50% (71%f.) (LRD, 1991:20; NUT Annual Reports). In NATFHE (36%f.) women have been very active and the proportion, c. 32%, was reaching parity (LRD, 1991:20). In 1990 FDA (18%f.) the higher civil servants' union, reported parity (postal questionnaire).

Some unions, however, have not progressed. SOGAT (31%f.) reported a figure of only 4.3% for women secretaries, and substantial under-representation in all branch offices except trustee and treasurer (Ledwith et al., 1985:18-21). In 1986 in the NUR (5.5%f in 1979) only two of the 595 branches reported women secretaries (Robbins, 1986:45).

Overall, women's representation in local union leadership is very poor. Only in exceptional cases has parity been reached or exceeded. Even in the public service unions where special efforts have been made, there are only around half as many women as there should be. In unions where no special efforts have been made, the situation is worse.

The national leadership

National executive committees National executive committees (NECs) are powerful bodies responsible for day-to-day interpretation and implementation of policies decided at delegate conferences, and for policy decisions in between conferences. The proportion of women on them has exceeded parity only exceptionally: in 1985 the figure for TASS (12%f.) was 13% (Meade-King, 1986). In 1990 an LRD survey of 37 unions found that women formed 20% (TUC-affiliated union membership 34%f.) of NEC members. In eight unions there were none. In a further twenty-one, women were significantly under-represented. Only in another eight (GMB, MSF, IPMS, NATFHE, FBU, EMA, AUT and FDA) did the proportion reach parity; six of these were white-collar unions (LRD, 1991:4-6; Appendix 3). Three of the eight had reserved seats for women. Over the past few years LRD has identified improvement in fifteen unions, but regression in five (LRD, 1991:7).

Over the longer period, there has been undoubted improvement. For example in 1975 the NUTGW (90%f.) had only three women (20%) among the NEC members. In 1986 women obtained eleven out of fourteen seats. For the first time in the union's long history women were in a majority; they included the first black woman NEC member (*Tribune*: 17.1.86). The position in NUT had also improved. In 1985 (NUT 66%f.) the figure was only 17%; but by 1990 (NUT 72%f.) it had reached 29% (LRD, 1991:8-9). In the FDA in 1992 it had reached parity.

Union conference delegates Delegate conferences, elected by branches, are generally the supreme policy-making bodies of trade unions. Again there is gross under-representation of women. The LRD survey reported figures at or near parity in only 9 unions (AEU, MSF, UCW, RMT, NATFHE, FBU, EMA, AUT and ASLEF); none had many women members; none were predominately female; four were white-collar (LRD, 1991:6).

Similar results were produced by our 1990 postal questionnaire. Parity was exceeded only by RMT (5%f.); both AEU (14%f.) and MSF (21%f.) closely approached parity. The ten unions with the largest female memberships fell far behind. In three, GMB, NUPE, and USDAW, the figure reached around two-thirds of parity. NUT, ACTT, BIFU, NALGO and HVA did not keep appropriate records.

Delegates to the TUC   The LRD study shows slightly more progress in respect of TUC delegates:

> Ten unions (TGWU, MSF, RMT, IPMS, NATFHE, NUJ, NULMW, FDA, NAPO, and AUT) had TUC delegations with women represented in similar or greater proportions than in their membership. Only the TGWU reserved places for women (12), resulting in a 20% female delegation compared with 17% women in [the] membership. Compared to the position in 1985, women did better in 17 unions and worse in only five. (LRD, 1991:7)

This brief review shows uneven but undoubted progress, accelerating in recent years. But women remain seriously under-represented.

Black women in the structures

Black people, it is estimated, constitute 4.7% of the population of working age in the UK (TUC, 1991c:7). They are concentrated in the Midlands, Yorkshire and, particularly, London and the south-east, but with substantial communities elsewhere. Black people are also concentrated in certain jobs, notably low-paid service work and in certain unions, for example NUPE and TGWU, which is thought to organize around 23% of all unionized black workers (TGWU, 1989a). The proportion of black people in trade unions is not known, but we know that they join in greater proportion than white workers, that this is especially true of black women and that black people have been willing to take action in support of white workers as well as on their own behalf (Lee, 1987; Wrench, 1987:162).

Nevertheless black people, women in particular, are very poorly represented. Since unions have only recently acknowledged the need to monitor the position of black workers, precise information is unavailable (LRD, 1988b). Few unions systematically collect the statistics. TGWU does, and has published figures for 1988 and 1991. Black women made up around one per cent of its trade groups committee membership (3 out of 400 in 1988, 4 in 1991). They were represented on only a quarter of its regional committees (3 out of 11 in 1988, 4 in 1991). Lower down, things improved. They were represented on just over half the district trade group committees (6 out of 11 in 1988, 7 in 1991). The highest proportional

proportional representation on any committee was only around six per cent, and that was in the south-east where black workers are most concentrated (TGWU, 1991a:8-10). Though these figures indicate very poor representation, their publication shows that TGWU is addressing the problem.

Self-representation

Before discussing the unions' empowerment policies we look at women's need for self-representation. In contrast to the trade union movement, women put a high value on the role of personal and subjective experience in the construction of knowledge. If this value is to be accepted by the movement, women must be enabled to speak for themselves, and that entails organizational change, modifying the structures of representation. Because unions are large organizations self-representation cannot mean that every woman is entitled to speak for herself, but it can mean that women are entitled, wherever possible, to representation by women.

This brings a number of problems the first of which is potential conflict over values such as trust and empathy. These are of fundamental importance to the union movement's attempt to represent a very varied constituency. They help to create solidarity out of diversity. They underpin mechanisms of accountability, enabling the stronger to speak on behalf of the weaker. However, trust and empathy have not been strong enough for women to feel fairly represented. In claiming the right to self-representation they do not intend to undermine these values but to prevent their use to legitimize women's subordination.

Second, sheer size means that unions must operate by representative democracy, electing officers and legitimating them to speak on behalf of the membership. Office generally brings power in the form of information, money and status. Democracy thus legitimates the more powerful to speak on behalf of the less powerful, in practice men on behalf of women. In the past this was considered an important means of progressive social change. But, while some men have used their office to make life fairer for women (**Case 4**; Cunnison, 1991), others have not, but have used the power of office to colonise women's minds, to patronise and misinterpret them (cf. Morris, 1991:22; Chapter 7).

Men speaking on behalf of women are handicapped by lack of personal experience. In saying this we do not intend to undervalue the human capacity for empathy which has an important role in the union movement and should be fostered through training in the skills of listening and

We consider it to be of crucial importance in securing fair representation for women in the policy-making structures of the movement. With respect to negotiation the situation is somewhat different. We discuss this in Part 3.

Now we consider how to identify the groups most in need of special representation. We have argued that women constitute a group with shared identity, common experiences of subordination and a common culture of femininity. Their experience of subordination is worldwide. According to a UN report of 1980 'women constitute half the world's population, perform nearly two-thirds of its work-hours, receive one-tenth of the world's income and own less than one-hundredth of the world's property'. UK women are better off than many. Yet though they make up nearly half the workforce and a third of union membership, their voice in union government is nowhere near proportionate. The need to empower them is now recognised by the majority of the movement.

However, women's diversity raises problems about which groups should be empowered, and in what way. Women may define themselves in many ways. For example among self-defined black women, some may define themselves additionally as Asian, Indian, Afro-Caribbean, as young, as lesbian or any combination, each of which could claim particularity of experience, of identity and of multiple oppression. In theory fair representation requires that each group be enabled to articulate its own particularity. To empower all on an equal footing would be a task of enormous complexity and expense. There has to be selection.

Representation is most rationally organized along lines of subordination, but which groups should be recognized as the key ones? This problem may be approached from an analytical or experiential standpoint. In the Introduction, taking an analytical standpoint, we proposed gender and capitalism as the two most significant principles ordering society. Since trade unionism is itself an organizational response to capitalism this indicates women as a key group in need of special representation, one within which other women's voices could be empowered.

In discussing other subordinated groups, we identified race or ethnicity as the most significant source of discrimination, more so than sexuality and disability. Though not numerous within the UK, black people (using the term politically) form the greater part of world population. Located mainly in the 'southern' or 'third' world, they suffer - with some exceptions - far more oppression than the predominantly white 'northern' or 'first' world. Black people in the UK identify with the deprivation of black people of the third world and this strengthens their own identity. This analytical approach leads to identifying women and black people as the key groups most in need of structural empowerment within the unions.

leads to identifying women and black people as the key groups most in need of structural empowerment within the unions.

This accords with history and practice within the TUC. The TUC's first national women's conference was held in the 1930s and its first Charter for women produced in 1975. TUC recognition of black people came later. The first *Black Workers' Charter* was published in 1981 and reissued in 1988. In 1984 Congress recognised the right of black workers to self-organization. In 1989 a TUC negotiators' checklist for black women was produced (TUC, 1989b). Other groups have yet to achieve this degree of recognition, though some unions have moved towards their equal structural empowerment. However within the TUC gender and race have a higher profile; they are the only groups in the Equal Rights Department with their own National Committees which include directly elected representatives. A third Committee, made up solely of members of General Council, deals with all other groups.

In putting special emphasis on gender and race we are not trying to establish a 'hierarchy of oppressions' (Adams, 1989; Briskin, 1990). We accept that the experiences of oppression, from whatever source, may be equal. An experiential approach might seek self-definitions and select those groups which have made the greatest impression on public consciousness. These are women, black and ethnic minority people, people with disabilities and lesbians and gay men. All now have public voices and self-organized structures in the wider society. All have become accepted within the equal opportunity movement and drawn strength from it. Other marginalized groups, old people, young people, carers, the unemployed, children, homeless people, immigrants and asylum seekers have established less firm public voices. But they too could also be said to need special representation.

Proportionality and reserved seats

Proportionality and reserved seats both aim to guarantee women a role in major decision-making bodies. Proportionality is a more powerful policy in that its ultimate goal is the full numerical enfranchisement of women. But in practice it is usually implemented through a series of intermediate and lower targets. It is a complicated and expensive process.

Proportionality

The TUC *Charter for Equality for Women in the Trade Union Movement* (1990b) defines the movement's policy of proportionality:

> Unions should aim to have women represented on decision-making bodies in proportion to their numbers in membership. Targets should be set, with a timetable for achievement. Failure to meet targets should mean that quotas are adopted. (TUC, 1990b)

It is easy to set proportionality as a goal. To achieve it is more difficult since it depends, *inter alia,* on making an accurate assessment of the numbers in the membership and the structures. For women this can be relatively easily done. Parity cannot be achieved in one operation: realistic interim targets need to be set and progress towards them regularly monitored. Proportionality thus involves administrative expense. It is slowly being introduced. MSF and UNISON have already adopted it.

An alternative to implementing it throughout is to set targets for particular committees and delegations. Out of nineteen unions who responded to our 1990 questionnaire only two were using or considering targets: ACTT (27%f.) for the NEC; AEU (14%f.) for TUC delegations. Monitoring was more popular; six were monitoring their TUC delegations and six more were considering doing so. APEX had monitored the gender of branch secretaries and conference delegates between 1976 and 1986 (IRSF, 1987).

Introducing proportionality in respect of black or disabled workers, whether women or men, is more difficult. There are data-collecting difficulties connected with problems of definition; definition by management is likely to be unacceptable; self-definition may result in significant non-cooperation. Again, a partial rather than full policy of proportionality is an easier option. Some respondents to the 1990 survey had set targets for black members; more were engaged in monitoring. MSF (21%f.) was monitoring the composition of its National Advisory Committee in respect of women, black members and people with disabilities; NUJ (29%f.), was monitoring black and disabled people within the membership. NUCPS (37%f.) was about to set up a monitoring scheme for all four groups. None of the nineteen however had set targets or were monitoring black *women*, nor disabled women. However, the fact that some unions target and monitor shows that the exercise is possible.

Targeting and monitoring do not automatically result in increased representation. Women must be motivated to participate and practical obstacles minimized. Times and venues of meetings need to fit with domestic commitments; help is needed with childcare; TGWU for example offers financial assistance. Unions have been working along these lines for some years. In 1983 the TUC surveyed women's representation; 49 unions replied. Seventeen had examined their internal structures to identify impediments and a further five were doing so (Ellis, 1987). The LRD survey of 37 unions found 27 with creches at their annual conferences, 24 at union training. With its 1978 Charter for the under-fives (updated in 1989) the TUC began seriously supporting childcare provision (TUC, 1978a, 1989b). In 1990 a TUC childcare resource pack reviewed provision, outlined union policies and campaigns, and gave reading and contact lists (TUC, 1990g). A negotiators' guide to childcare was produced in 1992 (TUC, 1992).

Reserved seats

In its immediate aims the policy of reserving seats on decision-making committees is more limited than proportionality, empowering only a small number of women, but it is relatively easily put into practice. Seats were first reserved for women in 1921 on the merger of the NFWW with the Workers' Union, to compensate women for loss of control over the Federation. Two seats were reserved on the TUC General Council. In 1981 the number was increased to five, in 1990 to twelve. In 1991 women had gained a further five in open contest, thereby holding seventeen out of a total of fifty-six seats.

NUPE was the first individual union to succeed in improving women's representation through using reserved seats. They were brought onto the NEC for the first time in 1975 by the addition of five extra women's seats. In 1976 the first five women were joined by another who won her seat in open competition. By 1990 there were twelve women out of twenty-six members, or 46% (72%f.). Occupation of reserved seats is limited to four years after which women must compete in open contest. The seats are seen as a temporary measure, to be used only until parity is reached.

The 1979 TUC Women's Charter recommended unions with large female memberships to ensure women's representation on NECs by reserved seats or co-option. However, reserved seats have not been popular with the unions (CLCLC, 1985/6:19). A recent study found them in only five: NUPE, GMB, MSF, NATFHE and NAPO (LRD, 1991)). The Tobacco Workers, BIFU and APEX have all had seats reserved for women on their NECs, but abolished them in the mid-seventies (CLCLC, 1985/6:19).

Seats may also be reserved for women on other committees or delegations. Labour Research mentions reserved seats on regional or district councils for GMB, AEU, NUPE, COHSE and NAPO (LRD, 1991). Responding to our postal questionnaire ACTT, TGWU, AEU and UCATT reported reserved seats for women on their TUC delegations.

Reserved seats at NEC level appear to be more appropriate for some unions than others. Predominance of women in the membership is one point in their favour. Where negotiations are carried out nationally it has been suggested reserved seats give women some influence on them (Harrison, n.d.). What then accounts for their unpopularity? One problem is that they lack a territorial constituency and their links with the membership are therefore tenuous (Hunt, 1982:170). In contrast NEC members elected to ordinary seats have clear links through territorially based structures. It is also argued that the system gives women an unfair advantage, but this ignores the disadvantaged position from which they start. Could it be that men find it too difficult to relinquish power voluntarily?

Proportionality and reserved seats would undeniably advance the position of women, although reserved seats affect limited numbers. However, because neither provide for access to office - where most power resides - they cannot guarantee fair representation. If proportionality were achieved women would still have to face men's formal and informal power, their control over bargaining agendas, and the ever-present culture of masculinity.

Self-organization

Self-organization is another dimension to representation. It refers to groups which are run by members, independently or semi-independently of other union structures, but resourced and facilitated by the union.

Special structures - committees and their officers, conferences, and seminars - are created to resolve problems of under-representation which have been acknowledged by conference. Pressure may come from paid officers, the TUC or outside bodies, but union activists are usually the main source. Some groups selected for special representation begin with a modicum of self-organization. However many do not; new structures are generally decided by men at the top, rarely by members of under-represented groups. With time, demands for self-organization tend to appear. Some groups develop a high degree of self-organization. The Women's Conference, set up and controlled for many years by the central (male) structures of the TUC, has recently been moving towards self-organization. Some groups, like the NUCPS Lesbian and Gay Group, begin as informal self-organized groups only later getting formal union recognition.

Self-organized groups may be formed at any level. NALGO, for example, has recommended that all its branches set up self-organizing equal-opportunity groups. A research report has suggested that branch-based self-organized groups might be particularly useful in unions with a high percentage of black women (TUC, 1991c:51; Virdee, 1992:20). Some self-organized groups have improved representation by new ways of running meetings. NALGO's Lesbian and Gay Conference split into workshops which discussed and formulated motions, then put them before the full Conference. The NALGO Women's Conference has considered following suit.

A corporate voice

A corporate voice may be defined as the collective voice of a group which has been formally guaranteed the right, uncensored, to take part at all levels in constructing the agenda, debating and voting in the union's decision-making bodies. The structures needed to support a corporate voice are the same as those that support the advisory voice. Indeed a corporate voice may be thought of as an advisory voice 'come of age'.

Women need self-representation and self-organization. They also need guaranteed influence in union government. While reserved seats guarantee this for a limited few and proportionality promises it - in the future - for the many, the creation of a corporate voice would allow the majority a voice in trade union government now.

There are other cogent reasons for supporting the idea of a corporate voice. Men have dominated the movement for so long that a strong collective voice is needed to counteract their power and influence. It would be more effective than the fragmented efforts of individual women. Further, because of long experience of subordination women lack confidence and experience in public life. A collective voice, developed in their own space would enable many more to make a contribution and so would enfranchise greater numbers. It is clearly desirable, wherever possible, that those speaking for a corporate voice should be elected.

Examples from the unions

No systematic study has been made of special representational structures. But information has been collected in respect of the different groups and this indicates quite extensive provision. Women's or Equal Opportunity Conferences have been reported in twenty-six out of thirty-seven unions questioned by LRD (1991:17). A study of ten unions (FBU, GMB, IRSF, MSF, NALGO, NCU, NUCPS, NUPE, TGWU and USDAW) reported seven with specialist national committees for black members or race relations, six of them 'advisory', and a further one at the planning stage (TUC, 1991c:15). Another study reported fourteen unions with informal lesbian or gay groups (LRD, 1992a:3).

Individual unions can provide more detailed information about the changing character and status of representational structures in the different groups, which may combine different aspects of self-representation, self-organization and a guaranteed role in decision making. We look at the situation in three unions, NUCPS, NALGO and UNISON.

NUCPS

Within its advisory system (see last chapter), NUCPS has special representational arrangements for four groups: women, and black, disabled, and lesbian and gay workers. Each has a National Committee and an Annual Seminar (less formal than a conference). Since 1988 when the system was set up, women and black members have both tried to achieve a degree of self-organization, but black people have been far more determined. Asserting their independence, they changed the name given to them by the white NEC - the National Ethnic Minorities' Advisory Committee - to the Black Members' Committee (dropping the irritant term 'advisory') (TUC, 1991c:15). Constitutionally, this Committee still has only advisory status. Nevertheless it has won the right to reserved seats on the NEC, placing black workers there for the first time. The Black Members' Committee thus has moved towards the status of a corporate voice. The Women's Advisory Committee also made a proposal for reserved seats, but after several women (including members of the NEC) spoke against the proposal, it was defeated. From their own choice, disabled workers, and lesbians and gay men in NUCPS, remain in a different role. The former remain an informal group still largely run by the NEC, the latter is more of a self-organized group with advisory status.

NALGO (since 1993, part of UNISON)

NALGO went further than NUCPS in developing both self-organization and a corporate voice, but the development was gradual. The same four groups were recognised. The first National Women's Conference was held in 1975. Following this a National Committee on Discrimination was set up, with women in the majority. In 1979 it became the National Equal Opportunities Committee. Women's issues were always its main concern. In 1989 it was reconstituted as a self-organized group.

The NALGO Black Members' Group emerged through struggle. A Race Equality Working Party, set up by the NEC in 1982, was predominantly white. Resenting white control, black workers boycotted the conferences it arranged in 1983 and 1984, and held alternative meetings. In 1986 after a rapprochement between black and white, NALGO agreed to grant black members the right to self-organization. It funded the first self-organized National Black Members' Conference and from this a National Black Members' Committee emerged. The Lesbian and Gay group grew out of an NEC initiative in 1984; the Members with Disabilities Group began in 1989. All four groups are self-organized and have a corporate input into policy making. Each has a National Committee and an officer attached to it who works to the group's remit; for each, NALGO funds an annual conference which has the right to put two motions on the agenda to the annual conference.

UNISON (1993 merger of COHSE, NALGO and NUPE)

Unlike the others, UNISON began life with a new constitution. Even so the issue of representation is not without problems. Some stem from the different character of the constituent unions, NUPE being basically blue-collar and working class, NALGO basically white-collar and middle class, and with a stronger and more structured tradition of women's activism, with COHSE somewhere in between.

Fair representation is listed as one of UNISON's aims, and defined as

> the broad balance of representation of members of the electorate, taking into account such factors as the balance between part-time and full-time workers, manual and non-manual workers, different occupations, skills, qualifications, responsibilities, race, sexuality and disability. (UNISON, 1992:15)

In practice, the same four groups are recognised as with NUCPS and NALGO. All four are given corporate status with the right to elect representatives to speak on their behalf at branch, regional and national level, and to formulate motions and initiate action at such meetings (UNISON, 1992:20). Close links have been established between UNISON's NEC and the National Women's Committee. The National Women's Committee, who already have right of representation on the NEC, have extended a reciprocal right to NEC women to attend the National Women's Committee and Conference.

UNISON women are further empowered through a policy of proportionality which applies at all levels of union government. There are no arrangements for achieving proportional representation of black, disabled or lesbian women. But there is an important innovation, the use of reserved seats at regional level for low-paid women - 'female members earning less than the maximum of the lowest subscription band'. This applies to regional committees only (UNISON, 1992:12). This measure will ensure that the most exploited women - who also have least union experience - have a chance to put their view and exercise their vote.

The system of special representation which UNISON has constructed differs from that of NUCPS and NALGO. It has three main traits. First it acknowledges the need for fair representation of a whole variety of groups, including those defined by the labour process as well as ethnic and other minorities. Second it gives the four most commonly acknowledged groups the status of corporate voices. Finally, it places women highest on its equality agenda and introduces specific measures for the low-paid among them. This is partly a matter of justice, partly a matter of recognising that UNISON is largely a women's union and if it is to be strong and successful women must be integrated into its governing processes.

Representing multiple oppression

Finally we consider women's multiple oppression. Union representation has so far been concerned with groups subordinated according to a single criterion, not with multiple oppression. No attempt has been made to develop self-organized groups, advisory or corporate voices, for black *women*, disabled *women* or lesbians.

These women must find representation through the National Women's or appropriate Minority Members' Committees. These Committees, which are structurally focused on a single form of oppression, need to be made aware of the problems of multiple oppression. There are two main ways of fostering this awareness. The first is liaison between National Committees so that each becomes more aware of the dimensions of the others' problems. In NUCPS the Black Members' Committee has two seats reserved for members of the Women's Advisory Committee, and vice versa. The Women's Advisory Committee has one seat reserved for a lesbian from the Lesbian and Gay Men's Committee. Within each Committee there are also informal caucuses, for example a strong black women's caucus has recently emerged in the National Women's Committee. In NALGO each of the four National Committees has the right to co-opt a member from the other three groups. The UNISON rules printed before its 1993 launch did not include such arrangements: they were to be made later in collaboration with the groups concerned.

National and Regional Equal Rights Officers are another means of raising awareness. They generally have a responsibility for integrating the work of Women's and Minority Committees. A recent TUC study reports that Regional Equal Rights Officers in TGWU were able to formulate negotiating proposals on behalf of black women by collating information from both the Women's and the Black Members' Committees (TUC, 1991c:22). Women's Officers too have a responsibility for promoting the interests of women with multiple oppressions, but they are not so well placed structurally as Equal Rights Officers to do so.

Apart from these two general principles, we note some particular innovations. In NALGO and NUCPS Black Members' Groups have tried to introduce gender equality. NALGO required equality of delegations to the Black Members' Conference, on one occasion reducing an all-male delegations have been reduced to 'observer status'. In NUCPS the Black Members' Committee set up a Working Group for Black Women. It adopted a goal of sex equality on its own Committee. By 1992 women comprised around one third. But the existence of single member constituencies made it difficult to move further without directing some to put up women candidates only. UNISON has resolved the problem of single member constituencies by allowing the appointment of both a woman and a man, and then requiring them to 'share the delegation' (UNISON, 1992:12). It is notable in both NUCPS and NALGO that black women have received more support from Black Members' than Women's Groups, probably an indication of white ethnocentrism. Some NUCPS black women have complained that white women do not perceive them as women, only as black. Similar evidence has been reported, of black women feeling ignored by largely-white women's advisory structures (Virdee, 1992:21).

Women's networking

At all levels of the union movement there are men who find it necessary to put women down, to try and make them feel out of place. This applies particularly to women who hold office. So in order to attain fair representation women need the support of other women. Networking, as a method of mutual support, is a product of the feminist movement. It consciously draws on one of the strengths of men's ways of organizing, the 'old boys' network, and uses this way of linking people to bring structure to the diffuse notion of 'sisterhood'.

Women's networks within the union movement tend to be based on activists within an occupation or industry (for example 'Women in British Telecom'), activists within a territorial area, or paid officers within the same or different unions (CLCLC, 1985/6). Networks may be based on the same grade of work, or formed to bridge gaps between different grades and levels within the union.

Although most are informally organized, there is a move towards their formal recognition and integration into mainstream structures. NUPE has formally recognised the network existing among its full-time women officers. NUT reported formal support for networking among its local association equal opportunity officers, and IPMS among women members (postal questionnaire). Not everyone agrees, a member of SCPS thought unofficial status gave them the 'vital' freedom to span different unions (CLCLC, 1985/6:27). Some unions, however, have rules which discourage or even bar all unofficial groupings.

Networks sometimes extend beyond the union into the community. In the seventies' struggle against competitive tendering NUPE women worked closely with community groups. Networks may extend internationally for example within Europe. They may extend into women's organizations concerned with trans-national manufacture and its disastrous consequences for women workers in the third world. An example is the organization Women Working Worldwide, a group which focuses specifically on the international division of labour in industries employing women, active in the new technology, textiles and clothing industries (WWW, 1983, 1992). Sometimes women's networks reach across long distances as when NUTGW workers from the UK supported striking union women garment workers in the Philippines (LRD, 1986). Nearer to home a study of black workers in ten trade unions in the UK recommends networking as a means of addressing problems which too easily 'disappear' between the women's and black workers' committees, and urges officers to facilitate black women's networking - if this does not 'fall foul of the union's rulebook' (TUC, 1991c:23).

Another area where networking has proved valuable is among women paid officers. Very few in number, they are particularly vulnerable to harassment from men. Reports reveal that their sexuality is constantly questioned. Some women say they have only been able to do such jobs because they were single, divorced, or without children, or because they had very supportive husbands (CLCLC, 1985/6:27). Furthermore, women 'at the top', just like men, have a tendency to become isolated from ordinary members, thus compounding rather than solving the difficulties of women at the grass-roots. One solution to this kind of problem is to limit the time in office. Networking up and down the hierarchies provides another, enabling top women to keep in touch with and better represent the interests of those at the bottom (CLCLC, 1985/6:27).

Conclusion: representation, social division and male culture

This chapter has discussed various policies for improving women's representation. All involve some modification or addition to union structures. They are: self-organization, reserved seats, proportionality, a corporate voice, and women's networking. Of these the corporate voice seems to us the most promising, guaranteeing women space to develop their collective ideas and a platform from which to make themselves heard. All the policies, however, have strong merits and all have limitations, indicating that they might best be used in combination with one another, and also with those referred to in the last chapter.

We have also raised the problem of representing women from diverse groups, black, disabled and lesbian women. No special structures exist for them. They have to find representation either through women's structures or the mixed-sex structures for other subordinated groups. Several of the latter are based on self-organization and in close touch with their grass-roots membership. However, leadership from the top may be needed to ensure the representation of seriously marginalized and under-represented groups such as homeworkers, migrant and and refugee workers. Historically, most self-organized groups have had such support. But if self-organization were widely adopted, union culture itself would probably become more 'friendly' to the emergence of special groups.

The policies of the corporate voice and of self-organization entail recognising social divisions. Though this might seem damaging to union solidarity, the reverse is the case. Divisions exist, reflections of the way society is ordered. They are likely to be destructive only if they remain unrecognised. Strength will come from openly confronting differences, establishing ways of working together and creating a web of cross-cutting ties.

Though policies of empowerment have resulted in more women on decision-making committees and more holding union office, proportionality of representation, with a very few exceptions, is a long way off. But as we pointed out earlier, even if achieved it would still leave women with many problems. Perhaps the biggest of these is the pervasive hold of male culture, the underpinning of formal and informal male power. In Part 3 we look at the possibilities of challenging the culture of masculinity and promoting one of femininity by means of giving priority to women's issues, many of which have been neglected in the past, and including more women in the negotiating process.

Part Three
NEGOTIATION, MASCULINITY AND FEMININITY

10 The trade union as a negotiator: Case 9

Focussing now on negotiation, we examine how far recent initiatives contest the prevailing culture of masculinity and positively respond to a culture of femininity. But first we take a general look at the negotiating role of the union and its importance for women.

The scope of negotiation

The traditional negotiating role of trade unions may be defined as the duty to act on behalf of members, as individuals or collective groups, in pursuit or defence of their rights and interests as paid employees. The emphasis is mainly on dialogue with employers and on contractual rights, but the defence of statutory employment rights is becoming increasingly important. Unions may also act on behalf of their members in respect of rights which do not arise directly out of employment, for example on matters of personal hardship or on issues of social justice such as deportation.

The processes of negotiation thus include collective bargaining on behalf of specific groups of workers, and individual casework in pursuit of contractual and statutory rights infringed by employers. Contractual rights may be based on statutory law, on oral or written contractual agreements, on custom and practice, on works' or company rules. Another highly important side to the negotiating role, and one which underlies these processes is constructing the negotiating or policy agenda: that is identifying the range of issues on which unions are prepared to negotiate, both collectively and individually. The negotiating agenda includes the narrower bargaining agenda which refers to issues that unions intend to bring to the bargaining table and the priorities to be given to those issues.

Statutory rights

Recent years have brought change in the field of statutory rights. Defending individual rights at work has become more important. An LRD guide, *The Law at Work* (1990a) lists seven major statutes between 1970 and 1977 bearing on such rights, and a further eleven between 1978 and 1990 - mostly amendments. Britain's entry into the European Community brought her under the jurisdiction of European law thus making the European Court of Justice the highest court of appeal for UK citizens in pursuit of certain legal rights. It has also influenced the content of recent UK statutes.

Collective bargaining

Traditionally the role of the trade union as negotiator has been in collective bargaining, fixing the pay and conditions of workers, including the creation of the bargaining agenda. Collective bargaining in the UK has a complex structure. There are two main levels: first multi-employer bargaining which may be national, regional or industry-wide; second single-employer bargaining at the level of company, division, workplace, or sections within workplaces. National paid officers usually represent workers at the first level, regional or divisional paid officers at the second. At plant level or below, branch secretaries or shop stewards may act for workers. Workers are often covered by both levels of bargaining, with multi-employer or national bargaining usually determining hours, shift pay and holidays, while single-employer bargaining covers basic, incentive and sick pay, and work arrangements (Colling and Dickens, 1989:5). Some bargaining in Europe is transnational (TUC, 1991a:33).

Formal and informal agendas

Formal bargaining agendas are guided by union policies decided at national conferences. They are drawn up by special negotiating bodies in consultation with the workers concerned or their standing representative committees. At national level there is consultation between national negotiating committees and the national executive committee of the union. At the workplace, the paid officer, branch secretary or shop steward may liaise with the branch committee and with workers concerned.

Negotiation means flexibility and even a formal agenda cannot be rigid. The question arises: at the point of negotiation who and what determine what is fought for, what conceded? Here the idea of a pre-existing informal bargaining agenda comes into play. This agenda can be thought of as a set of implicitly agreed issues and priorities which the movement has developed over the years, issues which revolve around pay and the interests of men and skilled workers (Cockburn, 1983; Roundtable, 1988; Walby, 1986). In dialogue with employers, negotiators - it is argued - are strongly influenced by the informal agenda. It has a powerful though implicit effect on the outcome of bargaining.

The informal agenda has another role, before bargaining begins, in the selection of issues to be included in the formal agenda. Even more important, it identifies the issues to be excluded - often those which most concern women (Colling and Dickens, 1989; Cunnison, 1983a; Munro, 1990; Roundtable, 1988).

Reshaping the formal agenda

Traditional union interests are those of white, working class men, but recently their focus has shifted. Major changes in social awareness in relation to gender, race and minority status, increased multinational and transnational manufacture and the development of the European market have all played a part. The unions have looked within themselves to women and to minority groups - black people, lesbians, gays, the young and old and others whose special interests are often ignored. They have looked to groups outside, homeworkers, the unemployed, government trainees and voluntary workers. In this context of varied group interests, establishing and prioritizing a bargaining agenda becomes a more problematic activity. The role of the traditional informal agenda in shaping the formal and bargaining agenda becomes open to challenge.

Paid officers can have an important role in reshaping the formal agenda. Part 1, especially the N. Ireland study (**Case 8**), has illustrated their importance in responding to women at branch and workplace. Within the local authorities many officers have helped to reshape the bargaining agenda through the negotiating equal opportunity policies (Cockburn, 1991). Networks of officers at national level have been involved in lobbying within the European Community.

Accommodating union conflicts

In collective bargaining, conflicts of interest between different groups of workers are addressed during the shaping of the bargaining agenda. When rights are pursued via the law, unions need to develop procedures for dealing with potential conflicts within and between unions (Huws, 1989).

Equal-value and sex discrimination cases may both cause friction between union members. Equal-value claims challenge the superior status customarily given to jobs done by men. Sex discrimination cases may involve public censure of union members.

A shopfloor negotiation in the fifties - Case 9

How are women disadvantaged in collective bargaining and other forms of union negotiation? What are the social processes by which this comes about? We have already touched on these questions in **Case 2**. We approach them now by examining a shopfloor negotiation of the late 1950s and drawing out basic structural and cultural themes linking gender and negotiation. The case has been selected as a worst possible scenario of trade union negotiation: from the viewpoint of the women involved it was almost wholly negative. It describes a negotiated settlement concerning one small group of women. It shows a negotiating process controlled by men, a lack of trust between the women and their male shop steward, collusion between management and officers, and a determination by men to preserve gender differentials, even to the point of imposing a price and wage cut upon the women. There have been changes since this case took place, but the central fact of men's power over the negotiating process remains. Research in the seventies and eighties has documented the continued exclusion of women from negotiation (Colling and Dickens, 1989; Cunnison, 1991; Ledwith, 1991; Ledwith et al., 1990; Purcell, 1989; Westwood, 1984).

The story

Following a change in their job, a group of women machinists struggled together to win an increase in their piece-rate price only to have this taken away from them some months later, with the full consent of the union who had represented them. The reason given was that their earnings had risen too high and some of them were making more money than the men (Cunnison, 1989). The episode took place in a multiple tailoring firm.

The structure of negotiation

National negotiation   The NUTGW (National Union of Tailors and Garment Workers) is over 90 per cent female. Although it was the first mixed-sex industrial union to appoint a woman as General Secretary, national negotiations until very recently have been dominated by men.

Small-scale manufacture and cyclical trade characterise the clothing industry making trade union organization difficult. In multiple tailoring, however, where mass production methods led to large manufacturing units unions were able to establish themselves. They were aided by the welfarist and paternalist views of some large employers.

Because it was strongest in multiple tailoring the NUTGW opened yearly wage negotiations with the employers' association from that sector of the trade. Differential rates for the different categories of workers had been nationally agreed. Jobs were ranked in a traditional hierarchy where men's jobs were valued more highly than women's.

Top of the job hierarchy was cutting; tailoring came second, and pressing (of the finished garment) a rather poor third. These were all men's jobs. Below these three came the women's jobs: machining, preparing work for machinists, hand-sewing and under-pressing. Most women worked at machining. Their skills were undervalued, the stress involved in their work unappreciated. The workforce was predominantly female.

Local negotiation Payment was by piece rates negotiated locally between the union and factory management. Power on both sides of the negotiating table lay with men. Shop steward representation was partly occupational, partly departmental. The result was that women, who predominated in the workforce, were proportionally under-represented. A chief steward was elected by the shop stewards. He was a cutter.

The chief steward was allowed paid time of work for union business. No other steward had this concession; he therefore took charge of most union negotiations. Therein lay his power. The paid officer was only called on in difficult cases; most matters were left to the chief steward. The chief steward and production manager had developed an 'understanding' and negotiations were often carried on in the manager's office behind closed doors (cf. Ledwith et al., 1990:25). Women sometimes complained that their opinions had not been sought. The understanding included the paid officer. Like the chief steward, he often went to management before consulting with members involved in a dispute. This all smacked of collusion. This closeness between union and management is an example of 'sweet talk and soft deals' and the marginalizing of women rather than of a good working relationship between lay and paid officers (Heery and Kelly, 1990; Ledwith, 1991). It recalls the union-management relationship of **Case 2**.

No woman had ever been chief steward; with one exception they had all been cutters. The most experienced steward however, was a woman. By careful negotiation over the years she had raised the earnings of the women she represented above those of other machinists. Ironically, male stewards held this against her: in their eyes she had raised wages out of the accepted hierarchy and it made her unsuitable to become chief steward. As a machinist, they claimed she could not understand the problems of cutters, tailors and pressers. No questions were raised about the appropriateness of cutters representing machinists. Further, her lifestyle, which contradicted male stereotypes of working class women, made the men uneasy. She was a spinster of fifty who regularly spent her holidays at adult education courses. The male stewards were determined she would not become their chief steward.

Process of negotiation

The job in question, sewing flies onto trouser fronts, was complex varying slightly according to trouser style. A change in style had necessitated the negotiation of a new piecerate price. The women were represented by the chief steward. Because the case proved difficult the paid officer also became involved.

On the shop floor two negotiating processes took place, the one explicit, the other implicit. First, the explicit. Management offered a new price. The women said that this was too low; the job was hard and they could not make 'their wages' - the amount they earned on the old job. Negotiations took several weeks. During this time the women were paid, by agreement, the average of their previous earnings. They did not attempt to explain their position, merely reiterating that the job was too hard. They left management to suggest a solution.

At the same time the women were engaged in an implicit strategy of holding back on output. They took no one into their confidence, certainly not the chief steward of whom they were deeply distrustful. They stated emphatically to one another - in tones that were easily overheard - that it was quite impossible to work any faster than they were doing. Occasionally, only, one heard a whisper 'we musn't let *him* know.....' - while they discussed the output totals they had reached. ('Him' served for chief steward, departmental manager or husband, as appropriate.)

The outcome

Low output combined with constant repetition that the price was too low, created uncertainty in the mind of management who finally removed part of the job and offered a slight increase in the price. The matter was settled.

Later, however, the women felt they need no longer hold back. Gradually they returned to their normal rapid pace. Their wages rose, and some months later someone in management noticed. The union was told; they investigated and found some women 'earning more than the men'. The ultimate sin. This was the nineteen-fifties, before the idea of equal pay had become common currency (see for example Friedman and Meredeen, 1980:194-5). The union made no attempt to defend the women. In the chief steward's view they 'hadn't a leg to stand on'. The price was cut. The women did not complain. It was obviously what they expected of a union which they did not trust.

Persistent structures of gender and negotiation

In this case a man negotiated with other men on behalf of women. Today this is still the rule rather than the exception. In **Case 9**, women's exclusion from negotiation is linked to patterns of job segregation sanctioned by national negotiations. The men's occupations were all represented by shop stewards, but among the women's jobs, only machining was. Proportionally more men presented themselves or were persuaded to act as shop stewards and thus become involved in negotiation (see **Cases 1, 5,** and **6**). Women's responsibility for domestic chores no doubt emphasised this pattern. The fact that the chief steward came from the highest status job in the factory echoes current research findings that negotiators and officers are drawn from high rather than low status jobs, another factor in women's exclusion (Rees, 1990).

Women were absent from the management negotiators, also a result of job segregation. There was only one woman in management, a personnel manager but without any responsibility for industrial relations. Since men sat at both sides of the bargaining table they were able to pursue their own interests at the expense of women. Working men defended their privileged earnings and status; management kept down costs.

Paid officers generally play a greater part in local negotiations than in this case. At a regional and national level, they are more important. Most national negotiating teams are composed largely of paid officers, acting on the advice of lay committees. Women's representation among the paid officers, particularly at the top, is even worse than among the lay organization (Heery and Kelly, 1988a). This points to a further gender bias against women, but also to a promising channel for change.

Persistent cultural themes

Four cultural themes are evident in **Case 9**. One is the low value placed on women's jobs compared to men's, regardless of complexity, a judgement explicitly reinforced by union agreements. A linked notion is that women should earn less than men who need a higher 'family' wage. These ideas were part of the conventional wisdom. Women did not fully accept them as their behaviour showed. But they did not articulate their disagreement. Men's greater power enabled them to impose their views.

A second theme is the double standard that ran throughout the union. This was linked to the different valuation of women's and men's work. It meant that raising men's earnings was given positive value, but raising women's was not. Thus the cut in the piece-rate price could be agreed to, and the experienced steward was criticized for having improved her members' wages. So also the life-style of a woman was judged relevant to her performance as a steward.

Finally there was the alienation of the women from their union. These were not acquiescent women; they were fighters (cf. Purcell, 1979). They were suspicious of men negotiating behind closed doors, men who shared certain values, for example about the impropriety of women earning more than men. They might, as part of the conventional wisdom, support the abstract idea of a family wage, but in practice they wanted to earn more money when the opportunity arose. The job change was introduced to benefit management; they were determined to benefit. They could not trust the union, but they could try to use it.

Despite the persistent structures and themes, the industrial relations scene has changed. The behaviour of the union seemed shocking at the time, now it would seem indefensible. The notion of equal pay is widely accepted and the need to revalue women's work is gaining ground. The NUTGW has begun to re-assess the relative value of the work of machinists and cutters (SERTUC, 1989).

Why is negotiation so important to women?

Righting the wrongs of a male-dominated movement

Women and collective bargaining Free collective bargaining, as it has worked in the past, stands indicted by feminists and pro-feminist men within the trade union movement (Campbell, 1980; Cockburn, 1988; Roundtable, 1988; Weir and McIntosh, 1982). Managed by men on their own behalf, it has operated to privilege them. It has been and remains an important influence on how the rewards of work are shared out between different categories of workers. Through consistent support of pay and skill differentials the collective bargaining process has sanctioned and supported job segregation, one of the main pillars on which women's subordination rests (Colling and Dickens, 1989:3).

Things could be different. The trade union movement has always been formally committed to democratic government. Recently it has begun to admit the extent to which it has failed women, particularly in respect of equal pay. Following a survey of 636 workplaces and 100,000 workers carried out by his union, John Edmonds of GMB claimed that women were being 'robbed' to the extent of £15 billion a year (GMB, 1987; Harper, 1987). In the future, by getting negotiation to work for instead of against them, women can use collective bargaining to remove instead of impose injustice.

Collective bargaining is an efficient medium for change because of the numbers agreements apply to. It also acts as a reference point for workers outside the movement. In 1984, 56 per cent of establishments in private manufacturing bargained with trade unions on behalf of at least some of their workers (Milward and Stevens, 1986, quoted in Colling and Dickens, 1989:48). Trade union recognition is higher in the public sector where women form a majority of the workforce.

Women's officers are keen to make constructive use of collective bargaining. Pat Turner, National Equal Rights Officer of the GMB has called it 'the tool for making change' saying 'it has to be used on behalf of women' who are 'fed up' with being 'lowest down on the priority of collective bargaining issues' (BBC Radio 4, 1988a). This will mean a struggle. In the words of long-time feminist Barbara Castle, 'It's time that women picked up the battle. You don't deserve to win unless you fight' (BBC Radio 4, 1988a). The struggle must not be blind. If women are to use collective bargaining to deliver more just rewards, they must understand how it has disadvantaged them in the past.

Equal pay and statutory rights   Until very recently, trade union use of equal pay legislation has been at best half-hearted. The original legislation (1970 Equal Pay Act), was very costly and extremely user-unfriendly; the amended legislation (1983 Equal Value Act) is an improvement but has still been described by Anthony Lester QC as 'almost incomprehensible, almost totally unusable' (BBC Radio 4, 1988a). However, some officers have been able to use it to notable effect and this raises the question why others have not (Campbell, 1990; Cunnison, 1991).

Excessive cost is one reason given by the unions for their reluctance to use the legislation. However, expensive litigation has been used on behalf of men for example when the TGWU defended London dockers dismissed during the 1989 national dock strike. They won over £1 million for the men (TGWU, 1992:11). Taken together equal pay, and sex and race discrimination cases still make up only a tiny proportion of unions' legal work.

Trade unions have also disliked the legislation's individualistic nature. Cases claiming equal pay have to be taken individually; judgements apply only to named individuals who have filed applications, regardless of how many others may be in similar situations. As a matter of policy, several unions have decided to pursue the collective bargaining route to equal pay rather than that of litigation. Collective bargaining has also been preferred as a 'real commonsense way, rather than [a] stressful, costly legal' route (Margaret Prosser, in BBC Radio 4, 1988b). Recently however, the unions have found how to exploit equal-value legislation to persuade employers to come to the bargaining table and negotiate about equal pay (see Chapter 11).

Direct and indirect sex discrimination   Sex discrimination, or sexism, takes direct and indirect forms. Direct sexism exists wherever women are treated differently from men explicitly because of their sex, indirect or institutionalized sexism wherever expectations are implicitly built around a male model. Sex discrimination at work, direct or indirect, is now illegal; it is also against the declared policy of most trade unions.

Negotiation can be used in two ways, to combat sexism and control it. First, unions can encourage and support individuals willing to take cases under the Sex Discrimination Act. Second, non-discrimination agreements can be negotiated with employers, focusing either on particular aspects of discrimination such as access to training and promotion, or - as in the case of equal opportunity agreements - covering discrimination over a wide area.

Conclusion: new agendas, priorities and practices

The absence of women from negotiating teams has not only trapped them in low-pay and low-status jobs, but also rendered them relatively powerless to shape a working world which would cater for their own needs, those of their children and others for whom they care. By influencing the negotiating process women would be able to put a new value on women's work, extend the negotiating agenda to include individual, employment and community issues of importance to them and introduce new, woman-friendly practices in the running of the union organization.

Trade union negotiation will not work in women's interests until fundamental changes are made: 'It is not' as Cockburn puts it 'just a question of an addition of committees and reserved seats' but of a 'profound change in the negotiating life of the union' (Roundtable, 1988:253). Among the changes we regard as necessary are the following. First, women's interests, issues and judgements about priorities must be included in a new bargaining agenda to be set before employers. Second, representation of women, especially low-paid women must be improved among the conferences and committees that shape and implement the agenda. This is the only way of making sure that the goals and priorities are determined by the grass-roots membership and it is why UNISON's pioneering policy of reserved seats for low-paid women is so important. Third, there must be an explicit challenge to the old informal agenda which is a product of the culture of white, male, working class masculinity; the reshaping of the formal agenda, the proportional representation of women, the pursuit of equal opportunity policies can do much to bring this about. Fourth, it is particularly important to effect an increase in the numbers of women negotiators, lay as well as paid. The importance of this as we argue later is that women bring with them a different style and method of negotiation. The N. Ireland experience shows that involving grass-roots women in branch organization can bring changes to the culture of masculinity in the unions. Drawing in women as negotiators from the grass-roots and at succeeding levels can draw upon the strengths of the working class culture of femininity to effect similar changes.

In the final chapters we have selected major initiatives in trade union negotiation which seem to us to be working towards a fairer deal for women. We have put them in two groups according to whether their main effects seem to be to challenge the existing culture of masculinity, its values and practices, or to draw upon the alternative culture of femininity. Chapter 11 deals with the challenge to masculinity.

In these various ways negotiation can be used to bring into being a more just and a fairer society. It is often argued that men have nothing to lose by this. Indeed, things can be so arranged that men do not lose money. But this slides over the fact that men stand to lose power over women, power in the negotiating process, power in over the distribution of financial rewards and social status. There may well be advantages for men especially for low-paid men at the grass-roots (Cockburn, 1988:253). There may be advantages for men too in the emergence of a less stressful working life and a family life where they can play a greater part. If women take their full place in the union movement, the movement itself though changed, will be stronger. But we cannot evade the fact that men will have to yield some of their power to women.

11 Challenging masculinity through negotiation

Positive changes in the negotiating context

The eighties were a mainly negative period for the unions, when attacks by the government and economic recession forced them to retrench. For women, however the decade was positive. Britain's entry into Europe, the popular acceptance of equal opportunities and changes within the union movement itself combined to create a favourable negotiating context.

Legal background and European context

Entry into Europe widened UK women's statutory rights and introduced a new final court of appeal, the European Court of Justice. It thus increased the trade union opportunities for the pursuit of rights through legal means. The improvement in rights also provided a new benchmark to which unions could refer when negotiating with employers.

The UK 1970 Equal Pay Act had proved almost unusable. It allowed comparisons to be made only between women and men doing 'like' work, which was interpreted legally to mean virtually the same work. Yet, widespread job segregation means that, except for the professions and the civil service - which had already achieved equal pay in 1961 - women and men rarely do the same work.

European law takes a more liberal stand on women's rights than UK law. After Britain's entry in 1973 into the European Community, European law took precedence over UK law in certain respects: 'directives' passed in Europe became legally binding on member states.

The right to equal pay for 'equal work' was introduced by the Equal Pay Directive (under articles 110 and 119 of the Treaty of Rome), equal pay for 'work of equal value' under two later Directives (75/117 & 76/207) (Sweet and Maxwell, 1991:1050). Deficiencies in the 1970 UK Equal Pay Act led the European Commission to threaten to take the UK before the European Court. As a result, the 1983 UK Equal Value Regulations were passed, enabling comparisons between women and men employed by the same organization but doing different types of work. The Regulations made UK equal pay legislation workable, but it remained complex and expensive.

The Equal Treatment Directive (based on article 235) aimed to diminish job segregation. The 1975 Sex Discrimination Act failed to comply with this Directive. Another EC protest resulted in the 1986 UK Sex Discrimination Act which made employers' use of sex-discriminatory grading schemes illegal (Dickens et al., 1988). However, procedures for implementing it were not introduced until 1993. The Trade Union Reform and Employment Rights Bill of that year allows remedy to be sought at Industrial Tribunals (EOR, 1993).

Most Directives have to be passed unanimously. Several, including one on part-time, temporary and contract work, have been blocked by the UK on grounds of interference with the free market. Directives under the health and safety heading require only majority approval. Thus a 1991 Directive on maternity rights was introduced despite UK and Italian abstention. It entitled all women to at least fourteen weeks' paid maternity leave, regardless of length of employment. Payment is at statutory sick-pay rates only, but women have the right to return to their jobs. This is a big improvement for the UK where, in 1990 it was estimated that only 60 per cent of women had the right to return (Phillips, 1991).

The UK is the only EC member which refused to sign the 1989 Social Charter setting out the fundamental social rights of workers. It specifically mentions equal treatment for women and men and its planned application revives the directives on part-time and temporary work and adds fourteen new ones. However, since unanimous voting is required, the Social Chapter as it is now known, is stalled.

Claiming rights under statutory law is costly, complex, time-consuming and emotionally draining. Women pursuing claims need support. In the trade unions this supporting job has fallen to paid officers, predominantly men. They have been slow and reluctant to give their support. The EOC has been more active, within the constraints of its budget; so have many law centres.

Unions have been more active in campaigning and lobbying about the effect of prospective European legislation on UK women. But this work has been in the hands of women activists including women research officers. The major body is the Women's Lobby of the European Trade Union Congress, formed in 1990 (CREW, 1990a).

Among the equality issues which trade unions were actively promoting within the European Community in the early nineties were black women, sexual harassment, job evaluation schemes, pensions, shifting the burden of proof in equal pay cases from employees to employers, the position of women in the newly established European market, and 'atypical' workers (those not on permanent full-time contracts; most are women) (CREW, 1990b:14; TUC, 1990i:24).

Improvements in the negotiating context

Women's negotiating position has improved over the past two decades. A new range of issues has entered collective bargaining. They include childcare, special leave for domestic responsibility, women's health issues, sexual harassment, sexuality, and maternity, paternity and parental leave. (Parental leave agreements give mothers the right to nominate for leave 'the person of her choice' - spouse, partner, grandmother, sibling or any other.) The TUC and individual unions have produced publicity setting out guidelines for negotiating and implementing these new measures.

The numbers of women and their influence on union decision-making bodies have grown significantly, as has their ability to push women's issues forward into the negotiating arena. Women's influence has also increased in the advisory structures and through local, national and European networking. The expansion of women-only education has played a crucial part in increasing women's confidence and their negotiating skills.

Changes have taken place in the culture of the movement, from the top through the new image-making, and from the bottom through new forms of grass-roots organization (**Case 8**). A significant change here is that some union men now openly question the culture of masculinity and its consequences for the unions (Roundtable, 1988). This is part of a growing interest in masculinity (Hearn and Morgan, 1990) and it marks an important step forward in building a union movement where women and men are equal.

Equal opportunities as a bargaining issue

The equal opportunity and anti-discrimination legislation was in part a product of the social movements of the sixties - student, left-wing, libertarian and feminist. It marked a shift in public thinking about equal rights. Equal opportunities became an acceptable goal. In the eighties an equal opportunity 'movement' emerged challenging discrimination against women, black people, people from ethnic minorities, disabled people, and lesbians and gay men. The movement was active in employment, education and housing. It became accepted by employers as well as by trade unions, and negotiators devised equal opportunity policies setting out comprehensive ways for removing discrimination (Huws, 1982). The negotiation of an equal opportunity policy became a mark of a progressive employer. However, many such policy agreements were merely statements of intent (Ledwith, 1991:52). Research indicates that intentions far outran achievements, and that traditions of masculinity have impeded implementation (Colling and Dickens, 1989; Dickens et al., 1988; Ledwith et al., 1990; Ledwith, 1991; Leonard, 1987).

Although employers as well as unions support the idea of equal opportunities, most employers incline towards initiatives which cost little and increase efficiency. In selecting issues, popular options include sexism-awareness training and women-into-management programmes. The former may improve industrial relations, the latter makes women's skills more accessible to management. Neither benefit the majority of working class women. Unions are mainly concerned with issues which affect the majority but these are expensive to employers, who resist them. Even local authorities, the least resistant, but they too have been reluctant to consider equal pay (see the equality audit below) (London Bridge, 1987).

Working for equal pay

Drawing a line between negotiating processes which challenge the culture of masculinity and those which draw on a culture of femininity is difficult. We have distinguished between initiatives which are basically redressive, aiming to give women the same rights which men enjoy, and initiatives which are basically forward- and outward-looking, introducing new issues and new priorities. To the latter we add initiatives which seek to revive some of the traditional but almost forgotten goals of the past.

Claiming equal rights for women questions basic cultural assumptions held - almost as articles of faith - by male trade union negotiators. These assumptions go as follows. Women should earn less than men and be financially dependent upon them, leaving to men a higher 'family wage'. Men should receive more opportunities for training and promotion. Different jobs are appropriate for each sex. Men's jobs are inherently more skilled and central to the economy and therefore warrant higher pay and status. Women's sex and family roles are not only primary, but relevant to extra-familial situations including paid employment.

Claiming rights challenges another basic assumption of many (male) negotiators, that women outside the home should remain silent and unseen. Inez McCormack sees equal value claims as a way of 'bringing [women] into vision, because negotiators don't usually see them' (McCormack quoted in Campbell, 1986b).

Equal pay legislation

Under the 1983 Equal Value Regulations a woman making a claim must show, according to standard job evaluation practices, that her job is equal to that of a named male comparator. Employers have no responsibility to show equal payment, only to refute the claimant's case. Claims go through a complicated system of industrial tribunals. Judgements may be appealed in higher courts - the Court of Appeal, the House of Lords and the European Court. For these, employers invariably use barristers. The unions try to do likewise but legal aid is not available. The process lasts a long time: in Julie Hayward's case, the first to be filed after the 1983 regulations, it lasted seven years.

Employers fight, and can buy expensive legal representation. Although the judgement applies only to the individual who filed the case, a lot may be at stake. A claim was made by six secretaries and a typist against Lloyds Bank. If the women women won, the 'knock-on' cost to the firm was estimated to be around £6 million (NPEC, 1992b). Bea Campbell estimated the underpayment to women in the banking industry as a whole to be in the region of £17 billion (Campbell, 1989). This makes employers determined to fight such cases. Costs run into hundreds of thousands of pounds, so women need institutional support. The EOC only takes cases which are likely to set precedents. Run-of-the-mill claimants must look elsewhere.

Considering the scale of women's underpayment, very few claims have been made. Only 25 cases per annum were filed between 1984 and 1988. The EOC has argued that under-use is due to complexity, and has made detailed recommendations for changes in the law (EOC, 1990:1-2). The fact that the burden of proof is on claimants creates difficulties for them. The European Community is drafting a Directive to shift the burden of proof to employers; in 1990 this move was being blocked by the UK (TUC, 1990i:22).

Even women who win their cases pay a price. Levels of compensation tend to be low and payments delayed. The process itself is stressful and several women have also suffered subsequently at work and had to change jobs (Leonard, 1987). Nevertheless the law has brought significant victories. The Belfast women hospital cleaners were able to draw public attention to the low value ascribed to essential cleaning. Success increased the self-respect and self-confidence of all involved.

UK law limits judgements to the named applicant and disallows 'class actions' such as those allowed in USA law. Nevertheless, unions have found ways of making claims apply to more than the original claimant. Prior agreements are made between union and employer that a named woman is claiming on behalf of a category of similarly placed workers. Thirteen women canteen workers from the NUM filed claims on behalf of 1559 other women (*Guardian* 8.7.86); one woman speech therapist, supported by ASTMS, filed on behalf of 1330 others (Campbell, 1989). In 1992 when the last case reached the House of Lords, the decision went against the claimant; differences between the bargaining structures of claimant and comparator were accepted as a 'material factor' in the defence; this meant the 60 per cent difference in pay was not examined (Gregory, 1992:467). That decision was then appealed.

Successful claims by employees of large companies may be extended to other women in the organization and, through union action, to other enterprises. Following a claim by checkout operatives at Sainsbury, USDAW persuaded several other firms to review their wage-payment systems (LRD, 1990b:4). However, research suggests that potential benefits to other women of successful claims remain largely undeveloped (Chambers and Horton, 1990).

Unions could give claimants much more support. A paid officer from northern England provides an example. He took the first case to be successfully concluded under the 1983 Regulations and was responsible for eight of the 120 cases taken in the UK between January 1984 and June 1988 (Cunnison, 1991). His technique was to proceed under the tribunal system, but when it became appropriate, to settle by negotiation. Between 1984 and 1988 he was responsible for three of the 29 cases settled in the UK by negotiation rather than tribunal. The TGWU who did not at first take his work seriously later became enthusiastic.

Equal pay bargaining

So high is the cost of litigation that threat of it may be sufficient to persuade employers to negotiate at least some way towards equal pay. Several unions have used this technique. In 1985 after an equal value claim was proposed, SOGAT reached a national agreement bringing 25,000 women bookbinders and collators up to equal pay with male machine assistants. In 1991, when the TGWU set out to negotiate equal value for women employed in the car industry (one eighth of the workforce), it began with an equal value claim on behalf of 130 Vauxhall sewing machinists (TGWU, 1991a:14-15). BIFU proposed supporting claims of thousands of employees with secretarial skills (mainly women) and comparing them to men in computing jobs; the RCN has considered claims for company-employed occupational health nurses (Gregory, 1987). The health service unions threatened to bring 4,000 cases to persuade the employers to agree to a regrading exercise involving 180,000 ancillary workers (Sulaiman, 1991). Thus equal value law, though framed in terms of individual rights, can be used with collective bargaining to challenge women's subordination within grading structures and thus job segregation itself.

Skill and regrading Under UK equal value legislation the presumption is that negotiated job evaluation systems are non-discriminatory: the claimant must prove otherwise. Unions have come to acknowledge that grading and job evaluation schemes which they themselves have negotiated are strongly discriminatory. Regrading through collective bargaining has become an important means of redress. It has a disproportionate effect on black women who are crowded into the lowliest jobs (Cockburn, 1991:217).

The first big regrading exercise was the 1986 re-evaluation of manual workers' jobs carried out jointly by local authority unions and employers. The unions concerned were GMB, NUPE, and TGWU. Women and men were equally represented on the union and employer panels who carried out the exercise. Ten panels were set up, each evaluating over 80 jobs. Eleven core jobs were evaluated by all ten panels and no job by less than four. A national coordinating panel compiled the results.

Changes in the method of evaluation took account of the qualities women bring to their jobs. Under the old method, factors used in assessment included requirements for skill, supervisory responsibility, initiative, mental and physical effort and the conditions under which the job was performed. Firstly, a new factor 'responsibility for people' was added to cover requirements found more often in women's than men's jobs. Secondly, in assessing manual work less emphasis or 'weighting' was given to physical effort and skills acquired through training (common requirements of men's jobs), and more to mental effort and tacit skills learned at home (common requirements of women's jobs). Further, the method of assessing physical effort was changed from focusing on sharp bursts of strength (as needed in lifting heavy objects) to sustained physical effort (continual bending, kneeling, stretching, lifting and carrying as needed in jobs like that of the home help).

The re-evaluation improved the grading position of a number of women's jobs. The old system used grades, from one for the lowest and five for the highest, according to customary judgement. The new one assigned them points, rating them according to an agreed list of factors; under this system the lowest job scored 158, the highest 630. The new evaluation raised the rating of the home help from grade three to 630 points, making it second from the top, exceeded only by the school caretaker. Some jobs were downgraded; one of the biggest drops was refuse collector which went down from grade four to 272 points. The two jobs with the lowest ratings, domestic assistant and school cleaner, were still both 'women's jobs'.

All job evaluation remains a matter of judgement. Old prejudices about the value of women's work die hard. That is why it is so important to involve women with experience of the work, as was done in the local authority regrading.

In 1986 the health service unions began negotiating a similar re-evaluation of NHS jobs (White, 1986). The concentration of NHS women employees in low-grade jobs makes a strong argument for re-evaluation. In 1985 approximately 70 per cent of women ancillary staff were in bottom grades one and two, while 70 per cent of men were in top grades three to five (figures from NUPE). Equal value cases taken by Belfast hospital workers had prepared the ground, but progress was slow until 1991 when the unions threatened large-scale tribunal litigation. Serious negotiations then began. National regrading has been interrupted in some areas by the introduction of hospital trusts and reversion to local bargaining. Guidelines issued to local officers now responsible for negotiations cover equality bargaining.

Higher grading for women's work means recognition of its social value. Recognising tacit skills curbs the exploitation of women as 'natural' carers. Basic pay is also improved. But because many extra payments are attached to men's jobs, the increase in the pay packet does not match the increase in grading. Regrading does not mean equal pay. After the re-evaluation, a refuse collector-driver (with 588 points) and a home help (630 points) were both on a basic pay of around £113 for a 39-hour week. He earned £170, the home help only £113. His pay was augmented by bonus, overtime, and payments for bad weather and special collections (BBC Radio 4, 1988a).

An equality audit Following the local government regrading an 'equality audit' was set up. GMB and TGWU were involved, NUPE having withdrawn because of the UNISON merger. The equality audit had a wider remit than regrading. The aim was 'an end to all forms of discrimination', between blue- and white-collar workers and between part- and full-timers.

'Common grading structure(s) and single-table bargaining' were to be established (TGWU press release, 15.7.91). A joint equality audit with employers was proposed. Meanwhile negotiations were to proceed on individual issues.

The regrading exercises of local government and health service employees are on a different plane; they demonstrate the unions' radical commitment to the principle of equal pay. They are part of the 'long term strategy for reducing the earnings gap' which Gregory has identified as a requirement for progress (Gregory, 1992:466, 471).

Re-evaluating women's work does not have to be on a national scale. Local initiatives can bring change. NALGO nursery nurses in Bradford placed a wage claim in 1984-5; there was no response and in 1987 they decided to act. With support from parents and community groups they threatened industrial action. Just before the action was due to start management agreed to re-evaluate their jobs. Those on top grades gained an extra £561 a year, those at the bottom £900 (Somerton et al., 1988:36-42).

A minimum not a family wage

Low pay is a massive and growing problem for women workers, especially those in manual work. In 1987, according to the New Earnings Survey, 80 per cent of manual and 44 per cent of non-manual women workers were low-paid. Around 66 per cent of the workers who fall below the Council of Europe's 'decency threshhold' are women (Somerton et al., 1988:10-12).

For years unions pushed up the wages of low-paid men by appealing to the family wage. Only recently have unions recognised low pay as a woman's problem. An early solution proposed by some unions was a minimum statutory wage, a legally enforceable figure, to be fixed independently of collective bargaining. However, powerful craft unions such as the AEU and EETPU, which have used collective bargaining very successfully on behalf of their skilled male membership, were strongly opposed. Some general unions such as GMBATU and TGWU also opposed the idea. In 1967 the TGWU put forward an alternative proposal for a voluntary minimum wage. It was accepted by the TUC but proved ineffective: the proportion of low-paid workers continued to increase. Support for a statutory minimum wage revived. Proposals were passed in 1981 at the Women's Conference and again in 1984 at a special TUC Conference. In 1986 a statutory minimum wage became part of TUC policy. The AEU and EETPU continued to express reservations (*Guardian* 4.6.91).

Several unions such as TGWU have explicitly abandoned the 'family wage approach' (TGWU, 1988). This marks a significant departure from traditional union masculinist policy. NUPE and GMB policy of routinely negotiating higher percentage increases for lower grades, marks another.

Extra payments

Earnings are made up of basic pay, overtime earnings, shift pay, bonus earnings and various allowances. Over the years unions have negotiated extra payments whenever the opportunity arose. Men have consistently been the greater beneficiaries. GMB research into the difference between women's and men's average earnings suggests that low grading is the biggest single explanatory factor, accounting for 65 per cent of the difference. Second in importance comes the fewer hours worked by women, accounting for 25 per cent. Bonus, shift and premium pay and other extras come only third but accounts for 10 per cent of the difference (GMB, 1987). In the case of low-paid workers the percentage tends to be much higher.

The attachment of extra payments to men's jobs has been part of the movement's policy to raise the earnings of low-paid men. Some types of extra payment however are inappropriate for the kinds of jobs which women do. Bonus schemes, which depend on increased speed of working, are a case in point. They became popular in the 1970s as public spending cuts led employers to search for increased productivity. But they do not suit caring jobs, most of which contain a discretionary element where carers must judge clients' needs and how to respond to them. In this context speeding up makes little sense. Further, in some manual jobs, women habitually work at too great an effort for speeding up to be practicable.

Some unions now explicitly recognise that extra payments are a source of discrimination against women. The GMB was the first to suggest tackling this problem systematically through collective bargaining. It proposes that the discriminatory element in shift pay and bonus should be considered routinely in all negotiation, together with grading and other issues (GMB, 1987). From the point of view of fairness to women, much can said for playing down extra payments and stressing instead as GMB and NUPE are doing, the need to raise the wages of the low-paid and re-evalutate women's jobs.

Although extras remain important, evidence shows that greater priority is being given to other issues, including those that specially concern women (LRD, 1989). LRD recently surveyed thirty workplaces, twenty-one manual and nine non-manual. It examined the range and frequency of issues appearing on the bargaining agenda (LRD, 1990b). Shift payments headed a list of sixteen items; bonus, shift patterns and overtime were well up in the lead. However, paternity leave came second. When manual and non-manual bargains were looked at separately different patterns emerged. Shift pay and shift patterns were still among the three most popular in a fourteen-item list for manual workers. But for non-manual workers paternity leave topped the list, while childcare, overtime and redundancy procedures tied for second place.

Challenging the culture

Access, training and promotion

Among the factors which account for women's continuing low pay are job segregation by sex, women's relative lack of training opportunities and failure to achieve promotion. Trade unions can help to remedy this situation by negotiating access and training for women in traditional men's jobs, and in new jobs emerging through changing technology, and by negotiating positive promotion programmes. GMB has produced a negotiating guide suggesting how such issues might be raised with employers (GMB, 1992a).

In seeking access to skilled craft apprenticeships women face resistance from both male trade unionists and employers. Local authorities have been less reluctant than private employers: access clauses have often been included in equal opportunity agreements. Some individual unions have been active in the private sector. In 1991, after studying obstacles faced by women in the transport industry, TGWU approached bus companies to develop job-sharing schemes and to encourage employers to recruit women through career fairs; and it gave support to organizations such as the Lady Truckers Club (TGWU, 1991a:12). A general negotiating guide on women's training at the workplace and a model training agreement were produced, both with sections on equality.

Discrimination in promotion has been accepted as a union issue. The media has drawn attention to the 'glass ceiling', the transparent barrier which prevents high-fliers from reaching top jobs. Women in all types of work, from blue collar to top managers, have their glass ceilings. The trade union movement itself stands indicted for its failure to promote women to top jobs (Heery and Kelly, 1988a).

But the problem of discrimination in promotion arises at all levels. Some equal opportunity policy agreements have introduced positive action programmes for women, but opinion is divided as to their desirability and efficacy. Specific clauses relating to promotion have been reached between white-collar unions and local authority employers. For example discrimination-free procedures have been drawn up for job and training applications and interviews. Assessing applications and interviews, however, raises difficult questions about criteria for appointments and also the need for monitoring and targeting (Huws, 1982). Less has been achieved in private employment.

Some promotion ceilings are highly visible, for example the barrier between blue and white collar work where workers are unable to pass from one grading structure to another. This affects more women than men simply because more are on the lowest grades. The GMB/TGWU equality audit is hoping to solve this problem by instituting a single grading structure. The monitoring exercise of the equality audit will show exactly where different groups, women and men, are blocked. Action can then be taken.

Negotiation can help minority groups such as black women by opening access to areas of employment traditionally kept for white people, and other ways. GMB for example has negotiated training in English as a second language for workers in the hotel and catering industry; many Asian women have used this opportunity. The Women's Committee of the European TUC is particularly supportive of initiatives in this area.

Union initiatives on behalf of black workers have been very few; some are reported in Chapter 12. The proposed GMB/TGWU equality audit which included minority groups was never set up. However, in 1992 the CRE, which had been interested in the project, began a three year study into the position of black workers in local authority employment. Over forty authorities which have both large workforces and high ethnic populations will be monitored. Although gender is not formally a focus of the study, data on black women will be collected where possible (Gribbin, 1992). The results will enable unions to locate blockages to black women's promotion and provide a basis for negotiation.

Sexism and sexual harassment

With sexism and sexual harassment we confront the heart of the culture of masculinity. Sexism is a deep-seated force in our society, very much part of normal behaviour (Wise and Stanley, 1987). It refers to all types of formal and informal discrimination on grounds of sex, and includes both personal and institutional discrimination. Institutionalized sexism in employment is embodied in rules and customs about hours of work, promotion, training, and eligibility for different types of jobs. All are subject to trade union negotiation.

At the end of the 1986 TUC Women's Conference a woman train driver and member of ASLEF called for union men to relinquish some of their power to women. Earlier she reported how the men she worked with had used their power to harass her. While driving a train at 50 mph she had been sexually assaulted by a fellow trade unionist. She lodged a complaint against the harasser and he was sacked, whereupon she was persecuted by her fellow trade unionists. They sent her to Coventry; they thrust hard-core pornography in front of her as she ate and tried in various ways to humiliate her so that she would leave (Cunnison, 1988).

Sexual harassment is a particular form of sexism defined as unwanted sexual attention ranging from 'jokes' to physical abuse. It is widely used by men to control and intimidate women and exclude them from posts which men wish to keep for themselves. It is also used by men with power and authority over women to exact sexual favours. Often hidden from view, it can be extremely distressing and injurious to health.

Until the 1980s most union men treated sexual harassment as a joke. It became a serious union issue when the TUC made its opposition a matter of policy, drawing up a working definition and issuing guidelines for women wishing to take legal action. Several unions took a stand earlier. Recently unions and local authorities have made explicit reference to sexual harassment in equal opportunity agreements. And it is reaching the bargaining agenda in the private sector. Agreements have been made between TGWU and ICI, and NALGO and the gas and electricity companies. In 1991 AEEU advised that it be considered in annual wage negotiations. In 1993 MSF published a booklet urging all employers to make it a disciplinary matter (*Guardian*, 19.1.93).

In a recent pamphlet NALGO has suggested tackling the problem at branch level through incorporating protection from sexual harassment into the contract of employment. It has also given advice on ways of supporting victims and on whether to represent harassers. It suggests standing arrangements for dealing with harassment cases (NALGO, 1992a). Several unions have procedures for dealing with harassment in their own organizations. COHSE has disclosed the dismissal of one officer on these grounds (Harper, 1992).

Since the 1975 Sex Discrimination Act women can take harassment cases to industrial tribunals. Few have done so. In addition to the usual problems surrounding tribunals, women face embarrassment at speaking publicly about sexual matters and difficulty in proving events which have taken place in private. Unions have given women little help with the practicalities of fighting cases. That has been forthcoming more from the EOC and law centres.

The unions now treat sexual harassment seriously. That is evident from the financial support given to a film about a woman sacked for supporting a victim. It tells how the union (mostly men) won back her job in a high street shop, with public support raised through mass picketing and demonstrations. Based on real life, *Business as Usual*, with Glenda Jackson as the sacked women, was released to the general public in 1987. The Cannon film company financed the film in its later stages of production. Earlier, several trade unions (TGWU, ASLEF, ASTMS, NALGO, FBU, TWU and the Seamen's Union) provided critical financial support (*Monthly Film Bulletin*, 1987). The action of the union in the film shows men using their power as 'capacity' (Haraway, 1988) to support, not to subordinate.

In making sexual harassment a negotiating issue, women have changed it from a private into a public issue (Mills, 1970:14-15). The behaviour of men both as individuals and as part of an institutional pattern comes under scrutiny. Men can be publicly challenged and brought to account, a first step to getting them to change (Segal, 1990:295). The routine incorporation of sexism awareness into all basic trade union education would assist that change. A similar argument could be put forward in relation to racism-awareness training and the need to educate white people, particularly paid officers and branch representatives (Virdee, 1992:20). Black women face complex problems. Their constant need to defend themselves from racial harassment may divert their attention from sexual harassment. Unions therefore need to be specially diligent in providing them with sexism-awareness training. Although both sexism-awareness and racism-awareness training can be useful, they must be approached sensitively (Simmons, 1989; Wrench, 1987:172).

Removing the penalties of caring

Maternity agreements Recently the unions have tried to negotiate a better deal for women as mothers and carers. This is bound up with women's right to work outside the home and to economic independence. Although they think men should do more, most women still see themselves the more appropriate carers. Yet, they insist that caring should not penalize them in paid employment. They have pressed trade unions to assert the social value of unpaid care and to address the financial and other problems of combining paid and unpaid work.

As more women work during pregnancy, and for a longer periods, maternity provision becomes more important (EOC, 1992). The 1974 Employment Protection Act was a milestone in maternity rights, lessening the economic burden of maternity by introducing the right to specified periods of paid and unpaid leave and to return to work after giving birth. It was not inclusive. Those in most need, in casual employment or on low hours, were excluded.

During the eighties, despite union campaigns, women lost out on statutory maternity rights. Government legislation attenuated the 1974 Act and fewer women qualified for its maternity and other benefits. However the 1991 EC Maternity Directive, mentioned earlier, recently brought UK women the first improvements for fifteen years. Even so UK maternity agreements are among the worst in the EC in respect of paid leave. On the other hand the total period of leave allowed is the longest (EOC, 1992:17, 18).

Statutory provision is the benchmark. In the seventies and eighties several unions negotiated better maternity rights than those of 1974. In 1991 UK statutory maternity pay, for those who qualified, was 90 per cent of average weekly earnings for the first six weeks, followed by a lower rate for the next twelve (TUC: 1991b). In 1992 NALGO reached improved agreements with some large companies including Asda, British Gas and Nestlé. NALGO's Camberwell branch negotiated 26 weeks leave on full pay and 13 on half pay, with leave entitlement up to 65 weeks.

More recently unions have also negotiated leave for fathers, partners, nominated carers (specially important for one-parent families), leave for adoption and for special circumstances. TGWU have reached agreements for paternity or nominated carer leave (TGWU, 1990). GMB, NALGO and NUPE's agreement with Leeds City Council allows women up to 63 weeks maternity leave, during 30 of which they receive some level of payment. Fathers, partners or nominated carers are entitled to eleven days' leave. Women must be permanent employees, with at least six months service completed before the baby is due, and must undertake to return to work for at least three months after maternity leave.

New agreements have been negotiated. GMB and British Gas have agreed a 'returner's bonus' for women who return and stay for three months after the birth. In addition to normal maternity pay, they get fifteen weeks maternity at half pay. Those who return and stay for a year receive a lump sum. A combined maternity career-break scheme grants unpaid leave of three months to two years, taken at any time, with the right to return to a similar job. Both depend on a prior period of employment. Agreements have been reached giving carers special leave in times of particular stress such as illness of children, old or disabled dependants.

Lost promotion   Too often maternity means lost promotion. Women who take time out for birth and childcare lose experience and confidence; they often return at lower grades and pay (Martin and Roberts, 1984). When considered for promotion they are often compared with men of the same age and found wanting. This is a big problem for women in white-collar and professional jobs. Within the civil service staff were not allowed to apply for promotion from administrative to executive grade. Women and their unions complained of discrimination and an agreement was negotiated allowing then to apply at a later age than men.

When men enter teaching from other occupations, their skills and experience are regarded positively and rewarded accordingly. Women teachers and their unions complained that the skills which women acquire in the course of childrearing were, when they returned to work, given a negative value. In the seventies, however, the teaching unions negotiated limited recognition of women's childcare experience. Returning teachers were credited with salary increases for their years in childcare, but at half the rate of teachers in employment.

The unions have also tackled the problem of losing experience and confidence. A career-break scheme negotiated by the banking unions enables women to keep abreast of developments by arranging short spells at work during the period of maternity leave. This and other schemes to encourage women's promotion within banking have lead to more women entering management (Crompton and Le Feuve, 1992) but not in reaching top management postions (Savage, 1992). Career breaks and special arrangements for women returners have also been agreed between NALGO and the NHS.

Childcare Looking after young children is a responsibility that nearly all women carry at some point. Several different forms of childcare are provided outside the home, privately or publicly funded. The diversity of provision makes comparison difficult. However, EC figures covering the years 1986 to 1989 show that public provision for childcare in the UK is among the worst in Europe. Provision for very young children is poor throughout the EC; at two per cent the UK is among the lowest. For children between three and compulsory school age (from five to seven) provision is more extensive. Some countries like France and Belgium provide over 95 per cent. The UK with 35-40 per cent is again among the lowest (Crawley, 1991; Commission for the European Communities, 1990).

Public provision of childcare has a chequered history. Nursery education has been seen as a means of releasing women for the labour market. Government support has blown hot and cold depending on the perceived need for women's labour. Support given during the second world war was withdrawn shortly afterwards. Union support has followed a similar pattern.

Since the 1970s however, the TUC has supported public childcare unequivocally. It is seen as giving women the right to paid work and young children an educational headstart. Public spending cuts, however, have prevented any expansion in provision. Unions have looked to private childcare including workplace nurseries, funded jointly by employers and employees. The problem here is that women who need nurseries most can rarely afford to pay the contributions. Individual unions have run campaigns on childcare and produced information for members. A comprehensive NALGO pamphlet included advice on setting up a workplace nursery (NALGO, 1991). TGWU (*Putting Kids in the Picture*) and GMB (*Who Cares for Kids?*) have both published on bargaining and childcare (TGWU, 1989b; GMB, 1992b).

Unions stress the need for childcare to be available at all working hours. Because many women work shifts the preference is for 24-hour nurseries. The TGWU and MSF have campaigned at Heathrow for a 24-hour nursery which would cater for the children both of the well paid and of those, mainly black and low-paid women, who work unsocial hours. Most women, however, have to rely on private childminders. Here the TUC has joined actively in campaigns to improve standards and pay.

The old and the sick Government policies have moved responsibility for the chronically sick from hospital care under the NHS to care in the community under Social Services. This, combined with the projected increase in the number of old people indicates an increasing burden on women. The physical and emotional stresses of caring are great. Carers' careers, earnings and pensions are often seriously curtailed (Glendinning, 1990). The value of unpaid care to society and the costs to carers need to be acknowledged publicly. Unions are getting involved in this area. TGWU recently carried out a survey of carers, in collaboration with the community group 'Opportunities for Women'. The resulting handbook *Carers at Work* has advice on bargaining for carers' rights (TGWU, 1990).

An equal right to work

Women have never had the same right to employment as men, but have been treated as a reserve army of labour, welcomed into the labour market when the economy is buoyant or in war, dispensed with in recession. Recession in the 1990s has brought new attacks on women's right to work. A TGWU delegate at the 1991 Women's Conference identified redundancy as a critical issue for women bringing about a change in negotiating priorities. 'Many of us' she said 'won't be negotiating career break schemes, childcare and job sharing agreements over the next few months. We'll be arguing over redundancies, retaining jobs and improving conditions for part-time workers and......increasing casualisation' (NATFHE, 1991). Equal opportunity policies negotiated before the recession often did not specify redundancy and retirement as areas of potential discrimination. Consequently they failed to protect women's right to work. Local authorities, forced to reduce staff, have discriminated against women. Absence and sickness have been used as criteria for redundancy and retirement (NALGO, personal communication). Both discriminate against women, many of whom take time off work to look after sick dependents. Unable to contest this discrimination, unions are now ensuring that redundancy and retirement are included alongside recruitment, training and promotion in their negotiating guides (for example GMB, 1992a).

Summary

This chapter has considered negotiation as a means of removing discrimination against women. Examples have been selected for the ways negotiation undermines received notions attached to the culture of masculinity. Issues about pay challenge the family wage and women's financial dependency on men. Issues about exclusion, access and promotion challenge horizontal and vertical job segregation, the idea that certain jobs are inappropriate for women and that women are not interested in career advancement. The issues of sexism and sexual harassment challenge common ways of subordinating women.

Negotiation assists in bringing issues from the private to the public arena. Bringing in sex discrimination and sexual harassment helps not only to call individual men and employers to account but undermines the general acceptability of discrimination and thus the foundations of the culture of masculinity. It provides an opportunity for men as a whole to make a reassessment, to try to change, to abandon features of the culture which oppress women while preserving those aspects of masculinity which, on reflection, are positive and supportive of others (Segal, 1990:289).

12 A culture of femininity: Attending to diversity

Negotiation informed by a culture of femininity

In this chapter and the next we conclude our discussion of negotiating initiatives, by relating them to the culture of femininity, beginning with the notion of diversity. Women come from different social and economic backgrounds, occupy different social and economic positions and have different interests and aspirations. One of the tenets of the women's movement is that diversity is to be publicly respected and valued. Feminist practice has not always measured up. UK feminism has been criticized for its ethnocentrism and middle-class bias (*Feminist Review*, 1984). In the unions white-dominated women's committees have done little to advance black women and their interests. Women are better represented in white-collar than blue-collar unions. Today trade union women are becoming more aware of diversity within their ranks and some marginalized members are beginning to assert their rights themselves. We examine how their interests are represented through the practice of negotiation.

Work fit for women: work fit for people

First however we raise three issues which bear on gender and negotiation over the whole range of women's employment. These are the need to value women's skills positively; women's need for flexibility in employment; and the consequences for them of the movement's traditional model worker, the full-time male.

Valuing women's work and skills

Feminists have long argued that women's unpaid domestic labour should be properly valued, socially and economically. Servicing the home - cooking, cleaning and shopping - particularly when there are children, constitutes a job in itself: paid employment is in reality a second job. Arguments have been advanced identifying the economic contribution of such labour (Creighton, 1985). The Wages for Housework Group has campaigned vigorously for two decades (James, 1976; *Guardian*, 15.6.93). While feminists have differed, all agree that such work should be publicly valued.

These debates have influenced trade union women who have provided the main impetus for union moves relating to domestic responsibilities. Moves discussed in Chapter 11 include: minimizing the economic and social cost of maternity for women; allowing greater choice about when to work and how children are cared for; sharing of care with men and partners; and acknowledging the skills that women acquire in the home. All imply that women's domestic work should be much more highly valued. Financing maternity leave and childcare from public funds is an indirect acknowledgement of social value. Caring roles are given added value by the suggestion that they are appropriate for men, whose time is traditionally rated more highly. But the clearest assertion comes from the recognition and reward of women's domestically-learned skills, equally with those learned at the workplace.

Practical and mental skills associated with caring and domestic management, which women learn in the normal course of their family lives, are made use of in paid employment, particularly in health, social services, catering and cleaning work. However, these skills have not been recognised as such, but perceived as abilities 'natural' to all women, and consequently not worthy of financial reward. Recent initiatives such as the regrading by GMB, NUPE and TGWU, discussed in the last chapter, value these 'tacit' skills, and guidelines suggest that they are included, as a matter of routine, in all job evaluations and negotiations.

The need for flexibility

For women to have the same chances as men, fundamental changes in work patterns are needed. To accommodate the daily demands of domestic responsibilities, work patterns need to be revised over the whole of paid employment, not just in jobs normally done by women. The trade union movement still holds as an ideal the model of the full-time worker. This ideal influences both the direction of its interests and the attention paid to different aspects of the employment contract. Far more energy and resources have been put into negotiating terms and conditions for full-time open contract workers than for part-time, temporary and casual workers, and especially homeworkers; similarly, more emphasis has been placed on full-time working, with overtime and extra payments, than on the varied contracts now becoming widespread. A full-time worker model is not applicable to most women; it is incompatible with their domestic lives and excludes them from certain jobs; it discriminates against them in respect of promotion and is wholly unjustifiable. In abandoning it unions would only be acknowledging the fact that

> the paradigmatic union member today [is] not the coalminer nor the railman but the female hospital ancillary worker......the old bargaining priorities [will] no longer work. (Cockburn, 1991:111)

Little progress has been made in dismantling the male model in jobs traditionally classified as men's work, although unemployment has resulted in some reduction of the working week. In other types of jobs the unions have faced a graver dilemma. Unions have not needed to persuade employers to introduce flexible working patterns; they have done so in their own interests. The increasing competitiveness of the market has caused them to seek lower costs through using part-time labour, short and temporary contract workers and homeworkers. Many women are attracted to such work, partly because unemployment diminishes choice, but also because they prefer flexible arrangements. However, flexibility comes at a price. By reducing weekly hours, employers can avoid national insurance payments. Statutory benefits, and others negotiated between unions and management, are often dependent on length of service and hours worked; so part-timers and those on temporary contracts may lose entitlement to unemployment and sickness pay and to pension money (Downs, 1988; Hurstfield, 1978; IRS, 1991).

'Policing' flexibility

It can be argued that unions would serve most women best by promoting a model of flexible working, because this is compatible with the reality of most women's lives. But it is vital that unions try to prevent employers using workers' need for flexibility as means of further exploiting them. The unions can do this only by paying more attention to the diverse groups of women in employment.

Several unions are trying to identify the problems which flexible working poses and find ways of maximizing gains and minimizing losses to employees. GMB, for example, has produced a *Negotiators' Guide to Flexible Working* (GMB, 1992d). Some items are particularly significant to women, for example career breaks, spells of work with reduced hours, flexi-time, job sharing, part-time working, temporary and short-term contracts. The guide includes a model training agreement directed to the needs of women returnees. It is intended to stimulate agreements such as that between between GMB and British Gas combining maternity leave and career breaks (Chapter 11).

Job sharing is a form of flexible working which some women find appropriate to their needs. It is the term used when two workers undertake together to fulfil the duties of a single full-time post. Usually each works just over half a standard week, with enough overlap to consult and compare notes about their job. Such an arrangement enables women to spend time both at home and in paid employment, and in spite of being on half pay, to retain entitlement to full contractual and state benefits. Arrangements negotiated with local authority employers by a number of unions (including NUT and NALGO) enable job sharers to remain in line for promotion, a big advantage over most part-timers who are customarily refused promotion. Employers generally benefit from job-share schemes: sharers tend to put in extra unpaid time in order to keep up with important events.

Attending to 'atypical' workers

In this section and the next we look at diversity from two different perspectives, first as defined in terms of the labour market and second as defined in terms of minority group status. We begin with 'atypical' workers, those who do not comply with the male-based model worker with whom unions have been traditionally involved: the part-time, short-term and temporary contract workers, casual workers and homeworkers. These are 'atypical' not in the sense of uncharacteristic: part-time workers for example comprise nearly a quarter of the UK labour force. They are only 'atypical' in not fitting a model which refers to times long gone. For this reason we use inverted commas. There are significant differences between and within the categories we have listed, and also in trade union activities on their behalf.

Until recently the union movement has done little to advance the interests of these workers even after recruiting them. But as their numbers have grown and those in full-time work have fallen, it is looking more seriously at problems of organizing and representing them. Most effort has been directed to part-time workers: they are now too significant a section of the labour force to be ignored.

Part-time workers

The large majority of part-timers are women. The percentage has been over 90, but is now 80 as more men work part-time. Any serious programme of advancing women's position must make the needs and interests of part-time members a priority.

For years unions ignored them: a NUCPS officer said of the sixties and seventies 'at that time.......my union.......didn't even recruit part-timers' (Roundtable, 1988:254). When they were recruited, it was usually on the basis of lower contributions and lesser rights and benefits so that according to a TGWU officer, they '......were not, effectively, part of the trade union organisation' (Roundtable, 1988:250). Their interests were often deliberately passed over in favour of full-timers. But times change. In the sixties NUPE saw the potential of part-timers for swelling the membership. With a recruitment campaign among school meals workers in the Midlands, it became the first big general union to actively seek them out.

In the seventies the feminist movement began to campaign for 'full-time rights for part-time workers' (Hurstfield, 1978; NCCL, 1989). In the eighties their recruitment became more general. But the movement still did not acknowledge the significance of the fact that they were predominantly women. This handicapped it in understanding the causes of discrimination against them and in devising remedial action. As Inez McCormack of NUPE has remarked: 'If you don't name *who* is low paid you disguise the issue' (Campbell, 1990).

Part-time workers' interests have been most successfully addressed in those unions like NUPE and USDAW where women predominate and where part-time working is the norm. These unions have begun assembling a bargaining agenda which gives importance to items selected by the workers themselves. They have thus begun the process of feminizing the agenda. They have also been able to make some negotiating gains on behalf of part-timers.

Both unions have tried to discover members' wishes, USDAW through surveys (USDAW, 1987, 1990) and NUPE's N. Ireland division through a member-led form of trade union organization (see Chapter 7). In 1991 NUPE launched a 'Positively Part-time Campaign' with a ten-point Charter; a main aim was to ensure that part-timers' interests were considered in all pay claims. NUPE N. Ireland put a motion to the TUC Women's

Conference calling for the minimum wage to be expressed in hourly rather than weekly terms, thus making the issue relevant to part-timers. The TGWU has explicitly committed itself to recruiting and representing their interests in its 1987 'Link-up' campaign, committing itself to 'change TGWU culture to make it more welcoming' (LRD, 1991:26; TGWU, 1989a).

In spite of the recession part-timers have made some negotiating gains. Examples are the equal value claim made by part-time workers from NUPE N. Ireland (Chapter 13), the raising of part-timers' issues in the equality audit programme of the TGWU (TGWU, 1991a:18), and the regrading of local authority and NHS manual workers (Chapter 11). More recently as a result of their negotiations, local authority part-timers have gained the right to sick pay. Agreement has also been obtained from some employers to pay overtime for work during hours when full-timers are normally on overtime rates, or work in excess of contracted hours. However, the recession has led others to withdraw overtime for work beyond contracted hours, and to allow only time off in lieu.

Public service to private contract

A problem facing public service unions has been the effect on members, most of them women, of compulsory competitive tendering. This has almost always resulted in a move to short, insecure contracts with poorer terms and conditions. The unions have tried to protect these workers, to prevent hours of work from falling below critical threshholds, and terms and conditions from deteriorating. And they have tried to keep them informed of their rights in their changed circumstances (Fairbrother, 1988; TGWU, 1989a:11-12). These problems have been occurring since the late seventies when competitive tendering first brought shorter hours, lost benefits and lower wages (see Chapter 6). Since it was made compulsory, in the health service in 1983 and in local government in 1986, the scale of the problem has grown.

Casual workers who are already part of a unionized workforce stand a better chance than those who are not. NUPE and other public service unions have continued to negotiate on behalf of members who have moved from public to private employment as a result of competitive tendering and thus been forced into temporary or casual work. The 1981 UK Transfer of Undertaking Regulations were brought in to comply with an EC directive aimed at protecting workers affected by takeovers and mergers. These Regulations, like the 1983 Equal Value Regulations, are complex and drawn up in a way which excludes many employees from that protection.

NUPE and TGWU are trying to use the Regulations, through the industrial tribunal system, to protect workers who have transferred employment as a result of compulsory tendering. NUPE has taken the case of school meals workers (*Guardian* 7.2.92), TGWU of refuse collectors. The cases are continuing (LRD, 1992b).

Other 'atypical' workers

Homeworkers The most vulnerable among 'atypical' workers are manual workers on temporary contracts, those in casual employment and - probably in the worst position of all - homeworkers. These are often pictured as a separate form of production, a home-based hangover from pre-industrial times. This is far from the truth. Homeworking (or outworking) is an integral part of modern industrial manufacture. Homeworkers are used by large and small organizations alike because of the extremely low wages they will accept, and also because of their convenience as a reserve army of labour to cope with erratic and seasonal demand, with swift fashion change and short orders. A high percentage of these workers are women. Union organization has always been weak among such workers, but unions are beginning to seek them out, identify their concerns and place their views on the negotiating agenda.

In commonsense terms, homeworkers can be considered as ordinary workers who perform their jobs in the home. In law, however, most do not have the status of employees but are technically defined as self-employed. They therefore fall outside the Employment Protection and Health and Safety Acts and have no redress for unfair dismissal and no entitlement to holidays, pensions, sick pay or benefits of any kind. In theory some homeworkers come under the protection of Wages Councils, but their rates are only very rarely enforced. Most earn very little money. They have to finance overhead costs of production such as electricity and the maintenance of tools and machinery. They are isolated from other workers. Many are members of minority ethnic groups and subject to discrimination. Others face discrimination as disabled workers. Fearful of losing their jobs, homeworkers are at the mercy of employers, who not only pay a very low wage but supply work erratically and at their convenience not that of their workforce. When work is needed in a hurry homeworkers may have to work through the night.

Early in the century the unions assisted in campaigning for legal wage protection for homeworkers. Aside from that unions ignored them (Allen and Wolkowitz, 1987:150-7). Policy changed in the seventies; working parties were set up leading to two TUC statements on homeworking, the latter incorporating a Homeworkers' Charter and a set of policy proposals (TUC, 1978b, 1985b). The proposals called for homeworkers to be given employee status with full legal employment rights and protection. They made recommendations about ways of organizing homeworkers and reminded unions of their obligations, under the 1979 Charter, to encourage members' full participation in union affairs. Little has come of these recommendations. A Select Committee of the House of Commons also recommended the granting of employee status, but Bills proposing this in 1979 and 1981 failed.

There has, however, been a great deal of activity among community groups supporting homeworkers. Since the seventies, local authorities have given funds to groups formed in London, Leicester, Nottingham, Dundee, Bradford and many other centres. Women working as volunteers and paid organizers have brought with them a feminist perspective and way of organizing, contacting homeworkers through local community networks, informing them of their legal rights, undertaking casework, providing general support and working jointly to create a strong organization (Allen and Wolkowitz, 1987). They have also gathered a certain amount of information regarding suppliers and the social and economic structure of homeworking. Where there are ethnic and immigrant minorities, information about workers' and citizens' rights has been translated into local languages. This has been a particularly important feature of the Leicester Outworkers Campaign.

Homeworking support groups have sought alliances with local trade unions. In Leicester, where homeworking in the hosiery trade has a long tradition, the NUHKW has worked consistently with the Outworkers Group. Union involvement has been increasing. In the early nineties GMB was trying to set up a homeworking branch in Leicester. The printworkers' union GPMU was organizing among homeworkers who make greetings cards, in collaboration with the Yorkshire and Humberside Low Pay Unit. More unions are becoming involved at a local level.

At national level however, the trade union movement has done little beyond campaigning for new legal protection. Tate has argued that paid officers have not been allowed the extra time and resources necessary to organize effectively in such difficult circumstances. She reports that more has been done in Canada by the International Ladies Garment Workers' Union where homeworkers have been included in a well funded strategic plan covering the industry as a whole (Tate, 1993). WWW report greater activity in Australia. In India SEWA (the Self-employed Women's Association) has built up a trade union of some ten thousand members among women homeworkers and casual labourers, from stonebreakers and sweepers to embroiderers and midwives. It shows that organization is quite possible (Allen and Wolkowitz, 1987:149; Lyon, 1991:190-2). Greater resources, a strategic plan and greater commitment on the part of the unions are all needed. But, following Allen and Wolkowitz, we suggest that it is also necessary to recognise explicitly the gender element in homeworking so that unions will, while negotiating to control exploitation, preserve those aspects of flexibility that many homeworkers find so valuable. The organization of homeworkers could be carried out by women paid officers. Their habit of networking across different industries and forms of employment would be useful in developing an industry wide strategy, as recommended by Tate.

Unions have been using techniques developed by homeworking groups to reach casual and short contract workers who cannot, perhaps because of employer hostility, be contacted on site. When a new shopping centre was planned in Glasgow's East End, USDAW cooperated with a local community group to leaflet the neighbourhood about union and welfare rights (Rowbotham, 1989b). The TGWU Link-up campaign has a policy of cooperation with community groups (TGWU, 1989a). But recruiting these groups is not easy and cooperation between community and union is not, in itself, a guarantee of success (Virdee, 1992).

Agricultural labourers An attempt in the early eighties in Humberside to recruit women casual agricultural labourers shows some of the difficulties and pitfalls of organizing casual workers. The women's committee of the local trades council was approached by the secretary of a local branch of the agricultural workers' union (NUAAW). A woman casual labourer had been unfairly dismissed and the secretary was seeking help in taking the case to an industrial tribunal. Substantial compensation was won. Following this the committee were asked for help in recruiting casual workers into the union. Two recruitment meetings were held. At the first, an open meeting, the women's employers turned up and left only under protest. At the second, over twenty women attended and a handful of men. Most were in casual agricultural employment. They were recruited into the existing branch of NUAAW but later formed their own branch with women as officers. The union brought Health and Safety Officers to the workplace and as a result some improvements were made in what had been substandard conditions. So far the initiative was successful. However, at the beginning of the next season the employers refused to rehire the women officers and other activists. Because of the nature of their casual contracts, they had no legal redress. They lost their jobs.

White-collar fixed contract workers   White-collar unions such as NUT, AUT and NATFHE have also tried to limit the damage which increased temporary and casual working brings to their members. But in a context of public spending cuts and high unemployment, they have had little success. AUT has just published a report on part-time and short-contract university teachers recording their continuing increase and the fact that they are usually paid by the hour, without allowance for time spent on preparation, marking and administration. It mentions a woman lecturer who taught for twenty-six years on fixed-term part-time contracts (*Guardian*, 23.1.93).

Workers on government schemes   A new group of workers to emerge in the eighties, and one in which the unions showed some interest, were those on government training and job creation schemes. Predominantly young, they were far more evenly balanced between the sexes than workers in most 'atypical' jobs. The unions may have seen them as future members but there were other reasons for union interest. The stated aim of such schemes was to train the unemployed, particularly the young, for jobs, and to fund the creation of new jobs. Their real function, it became apparent, was to keep the unemployment figures down. The workers' wages were, at least partially, funded by government bodies known successively as the YOP, JC, YTS, CP, Manpower Services and, in the nineties, TECs. The employers included private firms and public service and voluntary organizations. All the workers funded in this way were on shaky short-term contracts; there was never any guarantee that the employers' funding would be renewed. Union members tended to be hostile to this new low-wage workforce seeing it as a threat to their jobs and wage levels. Unions organized, both to protect their existing members and to fight a new form of exploitation. ASTMS (now MSF), TGWU and NUPE were among the first (Rowbotham, 1989b).

Diverse interests and minority group structures

We consider next the unions' representation and negotiation in relation to women from minority groups. Most women from minority groups are also 'atypical' workers, so their problems need to be addressed from both perspectives. This area has not been systematically researched but we report examples of trade union activity. Much work still has to be done to make the problems of these workers visible.

In Chapter 9 we noted how gender and racial differences are used to assign women and black people to particular types of low-status work, thus creating subordinate groups of workers with specific interests. We suggested that these interests could be articulated through the creation, for each, of a corporate voice within the debating and governing bodies of the unions. Such a corporate voice could effectively put the group's needs and interests onto the negotiating and then the bargaining agenda. Likewise differences in sexual orientation, in mental and physical ability and in age may be the basis for the creation of other advisory or corporate voices which articulate the interests of those minorities.

Black women

The unions' record of responding to the needs of black workers is poor, of black *women* even worse. The TUC itself did not give public support to black people's rights until the mid-seventies. For example, it did not publicly oppose the racism in the 1971 Immigration Act (Cockburn, 1991:177). But since 1976 when the Race Relations Act was passed, it has taken a firmly anti-racist stand, producing a series of pamphlets and negotiating guides. Even then individual unions were reluctant to comply with black workers' demands for a collective voice within their structures. In the late eighties NUPE, for example, repeatedly refused conference proposals for a formally constituted black workers' group, on grounds that it would fragment the membership. NALGO was more sympathetic, establishing a collective voice for black workers by 1986. By 1992 seven unions, including NUCPS, NALGO, NUPE and TGWU, had set up formal black structures. Individual black workers made their way to the top of the hierarchy: in 1991 Bill Morris became the first black General Secretary in the movement, in 1987 Gloria Mills the first black woman National Equal Rights Officer.

National Equal Rights Officers who are generally responsible for the minority structures and - where there is no separate Women's Officer - for gender, can help to advance the interests of women in black and other minority groups; as mentioned in Chapter 9, TGWU report that Regional Women's Officers are particularly useful in this respect. Where both National Women's and Equal Rights Officers exist, liaison between the two can draw attention to black women's issues on both the Women's and the Black Members' National Committee. The equal opportunities movement has improved the position of black women through the routine inclusion, in negotiation, of issues of particular relevance to them.

Although black women are still a relatively neglected group, more attention is being paid to their interests than ever before. There have been several types of negotiating initiatives. In Chapter 11 we referred to the union-initiated CRE study of the position of black workers within local authority grading structures, which has a built-in gender component. The location of blockages to black workers' promotion will help unions to identify discriminatory practices and bring them to the bargaining agenda.

Because they are disproportionately represented among low-paid local government and NHS manual workers, black women have benefited more than others from regrading. This has inspired one union, as a matter of deliberate strategy, to seek negotiated improvements in other areas where low-paid black women predominate (TUC, 1991c:42). In local government, TGWU, GMB and NUPE have tried to extend their equality audit into the area of black women's rights.

NUPE has recently addressed its attention to problems of racism, issuing publicity for members and guidelines for negotiators on racial harassment and indirect discrimination (NUPE, 1992, c. 1992a). Discrimination is a big problem for black women in nursing where they are directed and confined to low-paid low status work. In clinical nursing these discriminatory practices were actually reinforced by the recent NHS regrading, even though trade unions were part of the regrading agreements. Nurses were able to appeal against their grading, internally through NHS procedures or by taking their claims to an industrial tribunal. Between 1988 and 1993 NUPE supported a total of nineteen cases taken on grounds of racial discrimination. By 1993, it had lost only one, which was out of jurisdictional time. Twelve were won and eight were proceeding.

NUPE is active also in relation to immigrants. Like other unions it has joined in campaigning against the new Asylum Bill. It has published *Working for Just Immigration Laws* which gives a brief history of the law since 1971 and an explanation of why 'immigration law is a trade union issue'. An action plan for branches advises them: to assist members with immigration problems; discuss NUPE's proposals for immigration law reform; support local anti-deportation campaigns; affiliate to the Campaign Against Racist Laws; and involve other unions in joint campaigns (NUPE, c. 1992b). NUPE has recently supported two women members in their fight against deportation orders. The laws under which residential status are granted discriminate against women. For example those granted residential status as wives may be threatened with deportation if they divorce, even when marriage breakdown has been caused by the violence of the husband. NUPE is supporting the case of one woman from Mauritius in just such a position, a home care worker.

At a local level, several unions have also become involved with black women's and community campaigns on behalf of immigrant women. In the early eighties a Migrant Action Group was formed by Filipino women, who had come to work in hotels, hospitals and private families as resident domestics. Until 1979 government ignored its own ruling which barred women with children from obtaining permits to do resident domestic jobs. It allowed the children of some of the Filipino domestic workers to join their mothers in the UK. Thereafter it began to enforce the rule. It has also sought to deport women who have asked that their children be allowed to join them, even those who had entered before 1979, usually without knowledge of the rule's existence. In the eighties local trade unions assisted the Migrant Action Group in campaigns against deportations (Moreno et al., 1982:86, 88). From 1979 into the eighties NUPE campaigned on behalf of authorized immigrant hospital workers. From the late eighties TGWU has worked with Kalayaan, a London-based group which grew out of a Filipino organization, the Commission for Filipino Migrant Workers. Kalayaan is more inclusive than the Commission, campaigning on behalf of all unauthorized migrant domestic workers whatever their country of origin (Anderson, 1993). TGWU has joined in these campaigns and undertakes casework on behalf of members. Trade union membership is encouraged by the workers' organizations.

There are also trade unionists attached to community groups who work on black women's behalf, but as individuals rather than as local union representatives. An example is work done from the Employment Advice Centre funded by Hackney Borough Council. The borough has many Bangladeshi and Turkish women who work either as homeworkers or in small factories where their employers are often patriarchal relatives. Economic exploitation is often extreme. An added problem is that many work illegally without paying national insurance contributions, conniving with their employers in so doing. Sometimes this is because their residential status is not resolved. More often it is because wages are so low that if they pay contributions they cannot afford rent. In both circumstances they forfeit all rights and benefits. Another problem, which affects those working legally, is the numbers of small employers who fail to pay their own national insurance contributions or those they have deducted from workers. The result is their workers fail to qualify for benefits.

Immigrant workers' problems are compounded by the unfamiliarity with the English language; the language used in formal applications so necessary to obtain employment, welfare or citizens' rights, gives particular difficulties. Women are often at a greater disadvantage than men. At Hackney Advice Centre workers can learn about their rights in their own language, for example Turkish, Urdu, or Arabic, and are assisted in filling in forms. Leaflets written in local languages have informed workers of changes in laws which may affect them and their civil, employment and welfare rights. They are also informed about trade unions and advised of the advantages of joining. The Centre has organized leafleting campaigns at workplaces and in the community. But as with the homeworkers, the unions have devoted insufficient resources to face what is a massive and growing problem and centres have to rely largely on volunteers.

Negotiating initiatives on behalf of black women reported in Chapter 11 include TGWU's work on access to training and promotion, and its nursery initiative at Heathrow. This stemmed largely from childcare problems experienced by black women who, by choice or compulsion, usually work full-time (Stone, 1983). Childcare is sometimes resolved by couples working 'back-to-back' (the man by night and the woman by day) or by a grandmother taking responsibility thereby limiting her own employment opportunities. A 24-hour nursery as proposed by TGWU would solve the childcare problems of these women.

TGWU Link-up and the contract cleaners The attempt to recruit contract cleaners at Heathrow Airport was inspired by the local black community's concern about low pay and poor conditions among the women (80 per cent Asian) who made up this unorganized labour force (Virdee, 1992, 1993). They hoped the TGWU, as part of its Link-up Campaign (see Chapter 8), would recruit and negotiate on the women's behalf. Features of the Campaign included: literature drafted for minority groups, women-only recruitment teams, training for teams drawn from local branches and co-operation with local community groups (LRD, 1991).

Recruitment was difficult. As mentioned in connection with homeworkers, language and culture can form a barrier between ethnic minorities and unions. The main pamphlets in the contract cleaners' campaign were in English only, but some were produced in Punjabi, Gujerati and Urdu. In the case of women, familial control within a patriarchal culture can cause problems and did at Heathrow. (These are exacerbated with women employed by male relatives (Phizacklea, 1983.)) Another problem was that of illegal working by immigrants whose work permits had expired or who were waiting for legal right to residence.

The Link-up Campaign suggestion, that like should be employed to recruit like, was only partly followed. The recruiting officer, though black, was a man. In the publicity scant attention was paid to gender. One pamphlet carried a female image, a bold silhouette of a woman cleaner, but that apart, women's images rarely appeared. The main campaign pamphlet pictured only white men. However its text claimed to serve 'all sections of the workforce' and specifically mentioned 'male and female, black and white'.

Within the local community the Southall Trade Union Employment Advisory Service (STUEAS) and Indian Workers Association were involved. Local women's organizations however (for example the Southall Black Sisters), played no part. There was little involvement on the part of the largely male catering and baggage-handling staff at the site, due to cultural factors and employers' intransigence. The men had inherited a strong union membership and shop steward organization, built up by an earlier generation.

The campaign began with a cleaners' conference attended by community groups, and the local and national TGWU officers, including black men. No black women officers attended. After the conference, a recruitment drive began. A cleaners' branch was established and a paid officer appointed as secretary, a black man from STUEAS. He resigned after a few months having recruited only six workers. A woman could not be found for the post and a second man was appointed, this time with experience at Heathrow, in the union and community. In his year's contract he recruited only fifty out of the thousand cleaners. Conditions were difficult: the employers refused union recognition so everything was done through home visits; no branch meetings were ever held. The local TGWU office was all white and the women refused to use it. The women who were recruited did not get involved; they saw the union as a drain on their resources; many left, disillusioned. The TGWU, under growing financial pressure, closed the contract cleaners branch and transferred the remaining members to another.

The campaign failed to recruit and retain members and hence it failed to improve the pay and conditions of black women. In not appointing a black woman as recruiting officer it went against the Link-up policy on gender. However, it was successful in establishing ways of cooperative working with community groups.

Lesbians

Equal opportunity policies have been important in bringing lesbian interests, along with those of gay men, onto the movement's negotiating agenda. NALGO was the first union to take up the issue. In 1976 it adopted a resolution instructing all negotiators to attempt to 'add' sexual orientation to equal opportunity agreements. In 1985 the TUC passed a resolution calling for lesbian and gay issues to be integrated into the bargaining agenda of all affiliated unions. In 1991 an LRD study found that around half had done so. From its coverage of twenty-five unions with 5.5 million members (65 per cent of TUC membership), it reported that twenty-one included sexual orientation in equal opportunities statements, or had specific policies on lesbians and gay men (LRD, 1992a:17).

A campaign to gain for lesbian and gay partners the same rights and benefits as heterosexual couples has had some negotiating success. Agreements have been reached with NALGO for parental (covering both partners) rather than maternal or paternal leave, and with TGWU for nominated carers. CSU has obtained from the British Council and British Library, agreements for lesbian and gay partners to receive the same benefits on relocation as married couples do. NCU and British Telecom have negotiated similar relocation rights and also the right for pensioners to nominate their dependants. FDA and NCU have sought assurances that sexuality be not included in security vetting. The unions organizing in the health service have reached a joint agreement for sexuality to be included in equal opportunities programmes (LRD, 1992a). No policies or agreements, however, yet address interests and problems specific to lesbians. Fourteen unions have been reported as recently taking up cases of victimization on account of sexual orientation.

Disabled women

Disabled workers are recognised in much of the trade union movement as constituting a group in need of special representation, but distinctive interests of disabled women have not yet been acknowledged. A guide on the employment of disabled people was produced by the TUC in 1985 (TUC, 1985a). A 1991 TUC survey on the representation of disabled people received responses from twenty-three unions covering nearly two-thirds of its membership. Sixteen unions had negotiated equal opportunities agreements; sixteen provided training or advice for union officers; ten had committees dealing specifically with disability issues. The survey covered other matters including accessibility and communications. TUC guidelines for union officers were produced as a result of the survey (personal communication).

BECTU, BIFU, NALGO and MSF are among the unions with active disability committees which have produced their own policy statements; MSF has produced model policy agreements. GMB has produced a comprehensive document entitled *Ability 2000* which includes a negotiator's checklist covering registered and non-registered disabled people and employees who become disabled after appointment. It covers appointments, recruitment procedures, training and promotion, monitoring, access, facilities and health and safety, but not gender (GMB, 1992c).

Implementing policy has been, as usual, much more difficult, particularly so in the recession years of the early nineties. Most work still goes into persuading employers to fulfil their statutory obligation to employ 3 per cent disabled people (a figure which is well below the estimated proportion of disabled people in the UK), getting them to provide necessary equipment, and counteracting discrimination over promotion. There has been some success. BIFU for example has negotiated an agreement with the Bank of England to install 'minicoms', machines which enable deaf people to read telephone messages on screen. Unions, for example MSF, have taken individual cases of unfair dismissal because of disability. Up till now union policies and negotiated agreements are not gender specific; the particular problems of disabled women for instance as working mothers or wives have yet to be addressed.

Conclusions

This chapter began with a call for change in the character and focus of trade union negotiation. Only in this way can unions cope, on the one hand with women's difference from men, and on the other with the diversity which exists among different groups of women. Negotiation needs to become more flexible. Its traditional focus needs to move away from full-time work. More attention needs to be paid to the variety of groups which comprise the workforce, the part-timers, the homeworkers and the minorities. Their interests have been ignored for too long. The restructuring of employment is placing increasing numbers of workers, particularly women, in flexible employment contracts, making the need for a shift in negotiating priorities urgent.

In the remainder of the chapter we examined, with special reference to women, recent union responses to the challenge of diversity, describing efforts which unions have made on behalf of different groups and categories where women workers are disproportionately represented. We looked at the unions recruitment and publicity campaigns and the negotiated agreements which they have reached. We looked first at groups of 'atypical' workers, those who fall outside the traditional trade union negotiating model and then at members of minority groups.

These examples provide evidence that, in practice as well as policy, unions' negotiating priorities are indeed changing. However their motives have not always been the democratic empowerment of their members' diverse interests. The biggest shift has been in the attention paid to part-time workers where the moving force has been the unions' need for members and money. Nevertheless, the effect of bringing part-timers into negotiation will be a feminization of the bargaining agenda. The shift towards other groups, homeworkers, immigrants and different minority women, has been much less marked although there is evidence of union involvement in all these cases. Here the motivation more often has been the democratic right of diverse groups to union representation. Women, as paid union officers and members of community groups, have played a significant part in trying to get unions to negotiate on behalf of these. The role of women in union negotiation is discussed further in the next chapter.

13 Feminizing negotiation

Bringing back the 'sword of justice'

In this final chapter we look at the feminization of negotiation and how it would benefit the trade union movement. The culture of femininity directs women's interests both forward and backward. They point forward to new issues and new priorities, an agenda that includes childcare, community issues and the interests of minorities. They point back to the notion of trade unionism as a 'sword of justice' (Allan Flanders, quoted in MacInnes, 1990), to old themes such as fairness, responsibility for one another and for working class community life. A revival of these old themes coupled with a resolute attempt to adopt the new, would revitalise the movement in the 1990s.

Major problems face the unions today. Structural change, recession and government hostility have resulted in loss of membership and influence. Competitive pressures have eroded members' pay and conditions. The labour force has split into a core and a periphery, the former well organized and largely male, the latter poorly-organized and largely female. Workers' jobs and living standards are increasingly threatened by transnational manufacturing and commerce. In the public consciousness there lingers a seventies public image of trade unionism as greedy and self-interested. Negotiations directed towards women's interests cannot solve these problems, but they can be an important ingredient.

Feminizing the agenda

As members on an equal footing with men, women have a right to a part in defining the agenda. To achieve this it is necessary, in the words of Bernadette Hillon, USDAW organizer, to establish 'a climate in which all issues relevant to members are union issues' thus 'empowering women to bring to the union their own agenda' (Campbell 1990).

Women and men share common interests stemming from common needs for money, security of employment and tolerable conditions of work. But women also have distinctive needs and priorities. Feminizing the trade union agenda means extending it to include these needs and priorities. Using examples we look now at the process of feminization.

Women's working lives are home-based in a way which men's are not. Their lives cross to and fro between public and private arenas, between the collective and the individual. Compared with men, women place more importance on social than on economic value, on personal respect and dignity than on money. For women, trade union issues include workplace-based issues, but extend beyond the traditional goals of more pay and better conditions. More than men they emphasise issues such as community, quality of life and the rights of the underprivileged. We illustrate the implications of women's issues, by means of examples of negotiation relating to equal value, women's health and domestic violence.

Women's issues

Behind the fight for jobs: value and community Compulsory competitive tendering has led to many public service workers, mainly women, losing their jobs or having to accept lower pay and poorer conditions. When it was introduced in N. Ireland, NUPE cleaners from one of the Belfast hospitals decided to submit their own in-house tender (see Chapter 7). The women hoped to save their jobs. But their concerns went further. Cleanliness is a prerequisite of safe health care and they wanted to preserve the standard of cleanliness at the hospital, which they saw as an important community resource (cf. NUPE N. Ireland Women's Committee, 1992).

Cleaning services in six N. Ireland hospitals were put out to tender at the same time. All evidence showed that contract cleaning brought lower pay, harder work and job losses, and that it resulted in significantly lower standards of cleanliness. Although they badly wanted to keep their jobs, the cleaners were not prepared to lower the price of their labour in order to win the contract. They were determined that their jobs should be given due respect and value. At the same time they insisted that the cleaning should be done to the normal high standards of the hospital. They would not try to win the contract by skimping on standards (Channel 4, 1988). Their tender, prepared with professional advice, was based on NHS specifications. Using figures based on 1982 NHS contracts the women were able to show that the hours specified were insufficient to do the job to current standards - unless the pace of work was speeded up. They also showed that the materials specified were undervalued and that there was no allowance in the specifications for monitoring standards.

On August 31 1989 the cleaners from one hospital took action. Providing for emergency cover they marched to town together with six hundred supporters. A delegation put their case to the health authority. Backed up by the authority's own figures they argued for the introduction of new procedures and cleaning specifications. The outcome was that their in-house tender was accepted as, in due course, were those of five other hospitals. In two cases bids accepted were not the lowest (*PSA*, 1989).

Two important precedents were established: employers were no longer under so much pressure to accept the lowest bids regardless of likely standards of cleanliness; unions felt less need to recommend wage cuts in order to tender a low figure as they could argue, additionally, about standards. A way was opened for women to pursue fair payment and respect for their work without almost automatically inviting unemployment. The women's agenda in this instance was consciously directed to proclaiming the social value of cleaning work and to upholding standards in community hospitals.

New issues: women's health Among the issues women have placed on the union agenda are health, housing, unpaid care, abortion, domestic violence, child abuse and pornography, all of which bear more heavily on women than men. We take women's health in general, and cancer in particular, as an example of an issue which straddles workplace, community and home. Women have been disadvantaged in health matters partly because their illnesses have been less visible to the NHS than men's, partly because the NHS has served the working class less well than the middle class.

Between the ages of 35 and 59 far more women than men die of cancer. In 1989 the figures of cancer deaths per 1,000 deaths were: for women aged 35-44, 536.8; for men aged 35-44, 222.8 (*Social Trends*, 1991: 116). Women's excess deaths are due to breast, ovarian and cervical cancer. Yet until recently, cancers occurring in women received less attention and resources than those in men, and preventive measures for their containment were not promoted. Men cannot get these diseases, but the question arises, if men could, would not measures for their control and prevention have been taken much earlier?

NHS cancer screening services are available to all, but more use is made of them by middle then working class women. Cancer screening agreements negotiated by trade unions serve to redress both gender and class imbalances. Rights have been negotiated for women in employment for paid time off work to attend screening. Mobile clinics have been brought to the workplace. An agreement between Leeds City Council, GMB, NALGO and NUPE allowed women stewards time off to encourage other women to attend. TGWU and USDAW have both promoted agreements; USDAW reports that 75 per cent of its members are covered. Agreements mostly cover cervical but are being extended to breast cancer: NUTGW negotiated a breast screening agreement in 1988 (SERTUC, 1989). More generally, women's health has become a recruitment issue; in the mid-eighties for instance ASTMS and NUPE both produced packs covering stress, smoking, pre-menstrual tension, menopause, alcohol, sexual harassment and health and safety at work.

Though women's health is a new issue, the redressive nature of cancer screening revives traditional union concerns with equality and fairness. The programmes also save women - wives and mothers - from premature death thus benefitting families and community. Workplace health issues have not been neglected; possible hazards to pregnant women from VDUs have been publicized and agreements negotiated for the transfer of pregnant women to less hazardous work. Compensation claims have been pursued under health and safety legislation for disability caused by repetitive strain: AEEU recently won £60,000 for a disabled woman car worker.

New issues: domestic violence Domestic violence is another issue new to the union movement. NALGO's leaflet *You Are Not Alone: Domestic Violence is a Trade Union Issue* explains how it affects women's job performance, prospects and security, their health and lives. It mentions the specificity of domestic violence among minority women, disabled women and lesbians. It details ways in which branches can support members suffering domestic violence, gives information about possible legal action, and contact addresses for Women's Aid and other agencies. It suggests a negotiating agenda as a basis for agreements between branches and employers. Points listed include giving women time off and opportunity for redeployment, providing awareness-training for management and liaising with appropriate agencies (NALGO, 1992b). The acceptance of domestic violence as a negotiating issue implies union recognition that domestic relationships influence employment relationships. This is an important step towards understanding and trying to change the structural roots of women's subordination.

New issues: minority women Trade union efforts on behalf of black women have already been discussed in the last chapter, but they might equally have been dealt with here. They include addressing racial as well as sex discrimination in grading and pay, problems of deportation, developing ways of breaking down language and cultural barriers and trying to act on behalf of homeworkers and unauthorized workers. However, the scale of such effort is small; more resources and organization are needed.

Each of these examples has an impact beyond the workplace. The Belfast cleaners' fight for jobs raises issues about the quality of health care and community life. Cancer screening raises issues about the redistribution of resources. Acknowledging domestic violence as a public issue raises the question of mutual responsibility. Attention paid to minority women recognizes that we are now part of a multicultural society. These wider issues can help revitalize the union movement. They tap into a more comprehensive set of values than the sectional interests of the traditional 'brotherhood'. They turn the movement towards older values of fairness and justice.

Women's issues on the bargaining table

Many women's issues have entered trade union policy. Their routine inclusion in the current bargaining agenda must now be secured, and their place on the movement's long-term agenda safeguarded. In *Winning a Fair Deal for Women*, GMB introduces a strategy for the routine exclusion of sex bias from all workplace pay bargaining (GMB: 1987). Based on original research and written in simple language the booklet analyses the position of women in the labour market. Using tables and diagrams it shows the different ways in which sex bias influences workers' earnings. It then sets out a 'Bargaining Agenda' listing thirteen key issues where sex bias operates. Negotiators are advised to raise these issues in all workplace bargaining, covering all thirteen each time, as a matter of course. This strategy demonstrates to employers that sex bias is a serious issue. It also serves to educate employers (GMB, 1987:22-23). It is a strategy which unions could apply to other women's issues. However, not all women's issues are relevant to all bargaining situations so other approaches are needed.

The TGWU has aimed at widening the coverage of women's issues brought to negotiation. It has produced negotiators' guides in a range of areas including maternity and childcare, and race with specific reference to women (TGWU, 1989; 1991b). The guides set out the basic structures of disadvantage and suggest remedial action through collective bargaining. Examples are given of 'fair deals' negotiated by the TGWU.

Women's issues are now becoming a recognised part of the movement's current negotiating agenda. Their place in the short term is likely to be secured by the need for membership and by feminist pressure. Securing a place in the long term poses more problems. Cockburn and Gregory have argued that this will be achieved only with the redefinition of traditional union goals and priorities (Cockburn, 1991:216; Gregory, 1992:471). However, the adoption of a strategy like that of GMB, with precautions against sex bias incorporated in all negotiations about pay and conditions, must be a step in the right direction.

Feminizing negotiating practice

In Chapter 9 we suggested that fair representation of women in the governing structures of trade unions can only be achieved through representation by other women. Negotiation is different, and within negotiation casework and collective bargaining differ. In casework, representation by women - whether undertaken by shop stewards or paid officers - is generally desirable. The reasons lie in the fact of women's different life experiences and their tendency to do different jobs. NALGO have already given this right to their members. However, although representation by men as a matter of course is no longer acceptable, *in certain situations* it may be appropriate, necessary or even desirable. It is, in the end, the quality of the representation that counts. A woman paid officer, deeply concerned with empowering women, described a male branch secretary as 'one of the most democratic individuals I've ever met......the best negotiator I have ever been in with' (Roundtable, 1988:263).

Collective bargaining is usually undertaken by paid officers, often on behalf of mixed groups of women and men thus making self-representation in terms of sex impractical. Each sex must be able to trust the other to represent its interests. We argue here that, for equity in negotiation, women should play a far greater part in bargaining, and that if they were to do so, negotiation would be transformed to the benefit of all workers.

Women negotiators tend to have a particular style of negotiating practice. It arises out of their life experience and is a part of their culture of femininity. We term it a feminized practice. Nevertheless, it will be clear from the Introduction that this does not imply any female monopoly of such practice, nor that all women will invariably adopt it (Cockburn, 1991; Coyle and Skinner, 1988). Nor does it mean that similar practice is not associated with social movements other than the women's movement.

Links, alliances and networks

Among the characteristics which distinguish women's style of trade union organization, is a tendency to make links with community-based groups and individuals who share similar interests. This characteristic, which mirrors organizing practice within the women's movement, was important in the women-initiated campaigns and action of the seventies and eighties (Chapter 6). For example in Haringey there was cooperation between a branch of NUPE, a local women's group and a parents' group. A campaign began on the abolition of nutritional standards in school meals; it went on to oppose privatization and then rate-capping (ITV Yorkshire, 1988). The homeworkers' campaigns (Chapter 12) and the Bradford nursery nurses' campaign (Chapter 11) are other examples. On a different level women paid officers are involved in organizational alliances aimed at promoting women's issues. Many unions are affiliated to the Maternity Alliance and Childcare Now, both UK confederations of voluntary organizations. Such links enable the exchange of information and the coordination of activities such as lobbying in Europe.

Women trade unionists are influential in the new UK campaigning group, the National Pay Equity Campaign. Launched in 1991, NPEC is a 'broad based coalition of working women, trade unionists, academics and other supporters working for effective and accessible pay equity' (NPEC, 1992a). Women predominate, but men are also involved. Seminars and conferences have been held bringing together experts from the UK, Canada and Europe. NPEC has had funding from Europe and from the union movement: COHSE, NALGO, MSF and USDAW helped with a recent conference.

Women's networking has been active within the European Community (Hoskyns, 1991). The European Women's Lobby of the TUC (EWL) was formally constituted in 1990, before which it operated informally. It enables women to pool information on good practice with a view to getting it adopted in their own countries. It brings together a great deal of expertise. A 'Women Across Europe' Conference (organized in 1990 by the trade union section of the EWL and sponsored by the TUC) covered the issues of childcare, maternity, parental leave, sexual harassment, equality legislation, health and safety, pensions, training, lobbying, campaigning and race. It drew on women union officers and specialist staff, on lawyers, writers and journalists, and on representatives from voluntary organizations - the Scottish Child and Family Alliance, Childcare Now, the Maternity Alliance, the EC Equality Law Monitoring Network, and the Centre for Research on European Women - thus combining systematic attention to issues and links with a range of widely-based women-centred interest groups.

Staff at the Labour Research Department, an independent but trade-union financed research organization, are part of the network of European women trade unionists. LRD publishes *Labour Research,* a journal of news and reports about the trade union and labour movement, including regular statistical and qualitative information about women. It recently ran a pilot project compiling a database on collective bargaining and women's issues within the European Community. Organizations in each country asked their trade unions for examples of collective agreements on a list of thirty-five women's issues. Most countries were able to give examples of agreements on most: in the UK thirty-three out of the thirty-five issues were represented. No conclusions could be drawn about how extensively issues were covered, nor of the content of agreements. However, the database gives a wide range of examples which could be followed up and may serve to stimulate union negotiators (personal communication).

Grass-roots opinion and the agenda

Women near the top of the movement have been influential in prioritizing women's issues and getting them included in the bargaining agenda. Women at the grass-roots have had much less influence. Yet the outcome of the negotiating and bargaining process is just only if people can speak on their own behalf.

Recognising this, some unions have sought the views of women at the grass-roots. IPMS, NUCPS, NUPE, STE and USDAW have all recently used surveys, to ask members to place a series of bargaining issues in order of priority. IPMS found that women thought equal opportunities much more important than men did (75 per cent for women compared with 35 per cent for all members), but that both gave high priority to pay, pensions and job protection. IPMS women also placed more importance than men on working methods, short term and casual appointments, training, workloads and public policy issues (IPMS, personal communication). USDAW women gave a higher priority than men to part-time work and to problems of combining paid and domestic work, but overall USDAW reported 'no view or priority which is "typical" of women or of men'. For both women and men views were crucially associated with factors other than gender: with age, hours of work, dependent children and experience of trade union education (USDAW, 1987:27). The issue of equal opportunities was not listed by USDAW so women's views on this are not available.

In another survey of part-timers (90 per cent female) USDAW compared members and non-members. Differences emerged: members were satisfied with union services in relation to pay, conditions and individual problems; non-members were not aware of these services but would have liked them. Members were not satisfied with the way the union communicated with them; they thought it insufficiently committed to equality between part-timers and full-timers and to the physical conditions of work (USDAW, 1990:9-10). The union had difficulty making contacts and the rate of response was low.

A more promising way of finding out the views of grass-roots women is dialogue at the branch. A member-led strategy of organization as described in **Case 8** generates such dialogue. It releases confidence, particularly women's. Consciousness tends to be raised and more women are willing to speak out. A tactic used by NUPE N. Ireland during wage claims is to hold branch meetings where members examine their own wage slips to see the precise effects the current claim would have on them personally. In one such exercise, part-timers found that 'virtually every woman in the room who was working less than eighteen to twenty hours had, in fact, lost pay every time she'd got a pay rise'. This had come about either through a cut in hours or through moving into a poverty trap. The women began to question the way their union treated its part-timers (Roundtable, 1988:252). The strategy pursued in **Case 8** leads to a branch culture where women and men are viewed as equals. It would satisfy the women who took part in an IRSF survey who pleaded for a change in 'attitude' at all levels of the union (IRSF, 1987).

Feminizing the job of the paid officer

Men dominate the paid officer workforce which is responsible for most national and much local negotiation. This is a problem for women members who are unlikely to be well represented by people whose life experiences differ so markedly from their own. In the words of NUPE's National Women's Officer: 'It's very hard to argue what you don't experience yourself' (*Observer*, Living, 18.6.90). Research has shown that women officers do pay more attention than men to the interests of women members

(Heery and Kelly, 1988b). Sometimes this is forced upon them by senior men who try to off-load women's issues onto 'the woman' in the office. More often women's interests are attended to as a matter of principle. As one officer put it: 'Regardless of what the issue is, I've got a duty to look at the way in which that issue affects women'.

The number of women paid officers has been slowly increasing over recent years, but the percentage is far below parity with the membership. A recent study gave the figure for 1986 as only 10 per cent. Information collected from twenty-seven unions about the percentage of women paid officers in 1976 and 1986 showed an increase in fourteen, a decrease in nine and no change in the remaining four (Heery and Kelly, 1988a).

Most women paid officers work for unions with a large number or a large percentage of women or white-collar workers (Heery and Kelly, 1988a). FDA (20%f.), a small union for higher civil servants, is a case in point. In 1992 with two women out of a total of four paid officers, women were over-represented. Proportionally more women are employed towards the top of the hierarchy, yet few reach the top itself. In this the trade unions are no different from other large organizations (Savage and Witz, 1992). In 1992 only two of seventy-three TUC-affiliated unions had women general secretaries (FDA and NUHKW). In 1991 there were five, but shortly afterwards one (AUT) resigned, and two (HVA and SOGAT) vanished with mergers.

One area near the top where women are making progress is in appointments to national negotiating committees. In 1991 NUPE appointed women to two of their national negotiating teams. In the teams of some white-collar unions, such as NATFHE and AUT, women have a more prominent place. However, these are bright spots on a generally bleak landscape. Domination by men in national and local negotiation is still the general rule. In most unions national negotiating teams are made up mainly of paid officers. Thus increasing women's representation on national decision-making bodies is not a route into gaining them a place in the bargaining process.

By tradition paid officers are recruited from shopfloor activists. This does not work for women most of whom have come through higher education One reported she applied five times from the shopfloor for a job as a paid officer. Each time she was refused, but after taking a higher degree, she was immediately accepted. Although higher education is useful, the paid officer workforce is likely to represent ordinary women members better if more women officers are recruited from inside their own organizations. They can be recruited from research, administrative and clerical staff as well as from the shopfloor. NUPE and MSF have introduced 'trainee officer' schemes in order to tap such talent. The NUPE scheme combines formal education with work experience, 'shadowing' paid officers. Policies of positive advertising, education and assertiveness training can also encourage women from all parts of the union to join the ranks of paid officers.

To attract more women it is necessary to change the organizational culture of the paid officer job. Officers work very long hours; there is a high incidence of stress-related illness, alcoholism and premature death, all of which exact a toll on family life and personal relationships (Clegg et al., 1961; Donovan, 1968; Robertson and Sams, 1976; Watson, 1988). Heery and Kelly interpret the 'excessive and indeed, rather obsessive, concern with working long hours' reported by women officers as a symptom of the 'macho' organizational culture of the job (Heery and Kelly, 1988a:58). A new model is needed where full-time work, overtime and long hours on call are no longer routinely required. As a woman officer from BIFU put it: 'We need to deal with the causes as well as the symptoms of occupational stress and that means changing the traditional culture. It is quite obvious that the current macho variety wastes resources and makes people ill' (Cameron, 1989:36). Like other jobs, that of the paid officer should be reconstructed to fit domestic responsibilities, to match the reality of women's lives and encourage men to play a larger part in domestic life.

The unions have been hostile to women's efforts to change the paid officer job. In 1985 a positive action plan drawn up by NUPE's house union, the Society of Union Employees, was presented to their annual conference. Although attempts were made to remove it from the agenda, it was narrowly passed, but only after all references to job-sharing had been deleted. Men opposed it as 'elitist' because it demanded far better conditions than NUPE negotiates for its own members. The plan set a target of two women officers for each of eleven divisions and two officers of ethnic background in some divisions. At that time NUPE (66%f.) had twelve women officers, 180 men (*New Statesman*, 10.5.85). Attempts by men to thwart such initiatives indicate a wish to hold onto power, setting their own interests against those of the movement as a whole.

Prejudice against women is another characteristic of the macho paid officer culture which badly needs attention. A research study reported that more than 90 out of 101 women officers interviewed had experienced some form of sexual discrimination, half of them sexual harassment. Just under half felt disadvantaged in obtaining promotion and 80 per cent thought it harder for women than men to gain respect in the job (Heery and Kelly, 1988a). Inez McCormack spoke eloquently about this:

> The scars didn't come from the employers or the battles of organising - you know - driving forty miles to a meeting and finding two people and a dog and their dog was interested but the two people weren't. The scars came from the existing movement. The diminishing of you came from that movement. You were never diminished by the employer, by society or your members. You were diminished by a movement which could only deal with you by trying to put you down. (Channel 4, 1988)

Combatting this kind of prejudice is difficult. When necessary unions must use disciplinary procedures against their own workforces. Education also has a role to play: it can help people understand that sexism is not a personal failing but a socially engendered pattern of oppression. But in the end the most effective weapon against sexism may be more women officers proving themselves, by example, to be as capable as men.

If there is a significant increase in the number of women paid officers that will mean women doing jobs previously done by men. In the words of NUPE's National Women's Officer, it will mean 'pushing men off committees' (*Observer*, 18.6.90). A policy of proportionality applied to the officer workforce should have this effect. But its adoption might create a backlash from the men who presently run the unions. And without their practical consent it might grind to a halt. A policy of positive affirmation which increased numbers gradually might be more effective.

In unions as in management (Cockburn, 1991:72-2), women and men tend to have different styles of working, both when negotiating and when relating to members. Women officers' style tends to be less confrontational and more open. An officer explained:

> With men, it's the big ego thing. They like to see themselves as a permanent source of all knowledge; they never admit they don't know; they think on their feet, so often give wrong advice. With women, there is more emphasis on knowing where to go to find out, admitting they don't know, involving members in finding out, rather than developing the mystery of things. (Personal communication)

Further, many women officers bring to the trade union movement aims and values they have learned from the women's movement. They are for equality and against hierarchy, for sharing and against secrecy, for firmness and against confrontation. A woman officer explained her practice of sharing negotiation with lay members. When bargaining with management she always tried to have at least one lay member with her, usually the relevant steward (see also Roundtable, 1988:263). She kept to this practice even though managers complained about the changing composition of her teams. This style is very different from that of male paid officers who commonly work closely with lay officers, like branch secretaries, to the exclusion of shop stewards and other lay members (Heery and Kelly, 1990; see also **Cases 2 and 9**).

Involving the membership creates more work for paid officers, notably persuading managers to accept shop stewards as negotiators and training them in negotiating techniques. Woman officers would probably be prepared to undertake such work. One officer, who saw herself as representing a new, women-influenced culture of negotiation, had tried to introduce such training, but was prevented by her senior (male) officer. She saw evidence of more women and changed attitudes among industrial relations personnel in management (cf. Cockburn, 1991:72-2, 232-5; Coyle, 1988, 1989). Between the union and the management women, women's issues formed an area of common ground.

The accent on sharing makes women's style of negotiation more representative and thus more democratic than men's. The avoidance of confrontation may take some of the tension out of industrial relations and some of the pressure out of the officer job. But there are situations when confrontation is more appropriate. In this aspect of negotiation women have something to learn from men.

Using research staff

One new and important factor in negotiation is the increased complexity of the data on which collective bargaining is based. This is partly a consequence of new information technology which enables huge amounts of information to be stored, rapidly processed and instantly transmitted. It also results from greater organizational complexity among employers, due to multinational and transnational production and trading and the increasing prevalence of sub-contracting.

Negotiating is now said to take the form of an 'information war' between the parties involved. Negotiating officers therefore rely increasingly for back-up on specialist union staff, particularly research staff. The back-up role is particularly important in unions where officers have usually been drawn from the shop floor and the tradition of negotiation has been oral. Women tend to form a high percentage of research staff (much higher than among paid officers) and their influence in this area is correspondingly high. In 1992 women comprised approximately 60 per cent of the TGWU research section but were only 18 per cent of the membership. The actual number of research staff, however, is very small in comparison with paid officers, and financial problems currently facing unions puts research posts under threat. This is an example of a more general tendency for women in bureaucracies to be employed as 'specialist' rather than 'mainstream' managers and so be excluded from promotion to top posts where power resides (Savage, 1992).

In fact specialist research staff sometimes operate as negotiators in their own right. The early negotiations about regrading NHS ancillary staff were largely carried out by women research workers. In later negotiations, women were a minority on the union negotiating side, but a majority in the technical sub-group devising the new scheme. Thus the new complexity in negotiation increases the influence of women, both formally in constructing the detailed bargaining agendas of individual negotiations, and informally in the early stages of the bargaining process. A case can be argued for an explicit acknowledgement of researchers' new importance.

Women at the top table

Despite claims that issues of equality have a central place in the policy of the trade union movement, the reality is that at the bargaining table where deals are actually struck, women are usually absent. For the most part, men still bargain with men about women and white people bargain with white people about black people. The absence of women and black people is particularly evident at the national level although there are exceptions mainly among the white collar unions.

NATFHE is such an exception. It has two national negotiating teams, one for higher and one for further education. In 1992 in the higher education team, women were not only present at the national bargaining table, they were over-represented. Half the team were women (mainly lay representatives), yet women formed only around one fifth of NATFHE members in higher education. In the further education team women were less well represented. In recent years the higher education team has been more successful than the further education in defending the position of its (largely women) part-timers (personal communication).

National bargaining teams in the blue collar unions follow the traditional male-dominated pattern. Women at the top of the paid officer hierarchy usually occupy posts of National Women's or Equal Rights Officers whose remit is to advise, not to bargain, but who have no means of ensuring that their advice is taken. Pay is still the central concern of national bargaining. Pay and equality are still considered as separate issues. The systemic influence of gender and race on pay remains unacknowledged. If fairness and justice for women and black people are to be achieved, gender and race must be specifically addressed - as a matter of routine - in all national negotiations. And that is not enough. Their inter-relatedness must be acknowledged and the different positions of black women and black men also considered. At the present time, equality issues are regarded as central only in special circumstances, such as the regrading of local government and NHS ancillary staff.

A consequence of this is that national agreements affecting hundreds of thousands of workers perpetuate, without thought, inequalities of gender and race. A case in point is the 1988 regrading of NHS clinical nursing staff which included very many black women (see also Chapter 12). Eight unions, including NUPE, were party to this regrading. NUPE for example had in post a National Woman's Officer (white) and a National Equal Rights Officer (black). Yet there was no women on their national bargaining team for nurses. The situation in the other unions was the same. In consequence issues of race and gender were not considered; the scheme which emerged was racially highly discriminatory, as demonstrated in a CRE report entitled *Clinical Nurse Grading: the Cost of a 'Colour-blind' Approach* (CRE, 1992). NUPE has since supported redressive action by taking individual complaints through the industrial tribunal system. But many nurses failed to appeal until it was too late. Had women, black and white, been part of the top table bargaining team, the problem of racial discrimination would have been addressed early on and there would have been a different outcome.

Women in the blue collar unions are now making their way into the higher structures of mainstream decision making, but much more slowly than in the white collar unions. By 1991 although NUPE had one women leading the national bargaining for the ambulance workers and one on the local authority team, there were none on the national teams for NHS nurses or ancillary staff. In the same year NUPE's National Woman's and National Equal Rights Officers were appointed to the national committee which plans bargaining strategy. This move brought them nearer to the point where decisions are actually taken, but they were still absent from the top table. Bargaining is still, for the most part, between men and men.

Conclusions

This chapter has discussed the impact of the values and practices of the culture of femininity on trade union negotiation, beginning with its contribution to a new and wider negotiating agenda. This has emerged through the introduction of a range of women's issues, some new, others important themes in early trade unionism, and by the changing of priorities. The changes in the agenda have improved the representation of women and have thus been of direct benefit to them. More have been drawn into active involvement thus strengthening the movement as a whole. And this suggests that if women's issues were accorded an equal place on the agenda with men's, the full resources of women members' energies and enthusiasms might become available to the movement. In the words of a woman officer change could be managed 'creatively and effectively, using all resources regardless of gender' (Cameron, 1989:36).

However the actual practice of negotiation is carried out by a paid officer workforce which is still overwhelmingly male. Women's interests and issues will be far better represented when more paid officers are women, but this require a radical change in the culture of masculinity that rules the paid officer workforce. A redefinition of the paid officer's job is needed, cutting down on excessive hours and making it more accessible to women, and a change from sexist attitudes and behaviour. An increase in women paid officers would bring not only new values, but new styles of negotiating. Women's sharing and non-confrontational approach would make the negotiating process more democratic and more flexible and enhance its ability to deal with current problems

The nineteen-nineties are proving a harsh environment for trade unionism, with problems of economic recession and restructuring in context of a free market and continuing government hostility. To tackle these problems the movement badly needs a new vision and a new defence. The reassertion of basic themes, the priority of fairness and justice over sectional gain, the importance of community life, themes which can appeal to men as well as women, may point one way forward.

CONCLUSION

14 Feminization: New priorities, old themes

This book has shown at both local and national level a discrepancy within the trade union movement between what is publicly stated and what actually happens. Thus in Part 1 we saw how, at branch level, despite the existence of formal democratic structures and procedures women could not get their voices heard. On the contrary, they were excluded from debate, their opinions were blocked and their protests and challenges suppressed.

In Parts 2 and 3, looking at the movement from a wider perspective, we noted the frequent failure of trade unions to implement fully, or with energy and enthusiasm, policies addressed to women's interests. One example is union practice in respect of equal pay. They give public support. Yet twenty years after the Equal Pay Act provided a method for seeking legal redress, women still earn only two-thirds of what men earn. The tribunal system is cumbersome and costly, but it can be used effectively especially after its amendment in 1983. Nevertheless, until recently, the unions put little effort and resources into using it.

Improving women's pay through revaluing their work and formally regrading traditional 'women's jobs' is a recent and important initiative in the union fight for equal pay. It does not, however, sufficiently address the question of extra payments which are usually attached to men's, but rarely to women's, jobs. Further, regrading is not high on the movement's bargaining agenda and so its impact on women's pay is small. Increasing casualization, temporary contracts and part-time working pose a big threat to all workers' pay, but particularly to women's. The unions have made policy and run campaigns about these forms of working, but put relatively little effort and few resources into combatting and controlling them.

A wide gap exists between what the unions claim for women and what they deliver, but more to the point, between what they claim and what they *attempt* to deliver. What is the reason for this? We have argued that a bias against women and their interests runs throughout the union movement, that from its inception it has been a movement to defend the interests of the white working class male, against all comers. It is suffused with a culture of white working-class masculinity which is antithetical to women. It is basically, in Bea Campbell's words, a 'men's movement'. The case studies in Part 1 have provided ample evidence of the way in which this culture works to stereotype women and to define them as out of place in the union movement. At the same time it is used to define men as primary breadwinners and to justify privileging men in job evaluation and wage negotiation. The case studies show how in the setting of the trade union movement, masculine culture is closely bound up with male power and control over women. Moreover, since men are dominant in the society, masculinity dominates the culture and so imposes its values. Women tend to see themselves as they are seen by men and to accept trade unionism as of little relevance to them. The case studies date from the late seventies and early eighties. Recent research carried out by Cynthia Cockburn shows that the culture of masculinity within the unions is still a very powerful force. Men's power and their hostility to women who challenge it appear to be still as strong as ever (Cockburn, 1991).

Despite the formidable alliance of male power and masculine culture reported in the case studies, Part 1 has some positive messages for women. We noted examples of male power being used to support women's personal development as trade unionists. This is the typically feminine way of using power, to facilitate rather than to dominate: power as 'capacity' (Haraway, 1988; Cockburn, 1991:241). This suggests that some of the links between male power and masculine culture can be broken.

The studies also indicated that women were on the move. We reported changes in trade union consciousness among women, the dawning of gender consciousness in relation to trade unionism, and deliberate attempts to throw off the yoke of male control. In the Introduction we suggested that women have access to an alternative culture, that of femininity, derived from the particularity of their lives as women and their experience of caring and subordination. In Chapter 6 we saw women in the hospital disputes and the miners' strike drawing on this culture of femininity and acting, in defiance of their union in the former case, to defend public health care and working class communities.

Chapter 7 at the end of Part 1 sounds a strikingly optimistic note. It reports from a union branch in N. Ireland where the women, who predominate, have recreated their branch to reflect their own culture of femininity. They have done this, with the leadership of women paid officers, through a deliberate strategy of empowering workers at the grass-roots. The culture is one where hierarchy and unnecessary confrontation are eschewed and informality and inclusiveness fostered. The branch has tried to break the link between office-holding and power. Traditional offices have been split and shared and the time in office limited. These practices have begun to work their way upward. Women from this branch who are elected to higher office do not stay long. They feel a responsibility to encourage other women to follow after them, so that power is shared. We see this branch as a strong challenge to the culture of masculinity, a model for organizational change that other branches could follow.

In the next two parts we sought to see how far union policies were facilitating the emergence of fair representation for women, bringing their issues into the negotiating arena and furthering their participation in negotiation. We began Part 2 by examining union policies which have been designed to encourage women, but which fall short of ensuring them a part in decision making.

We next discussed policies of structural empowerment, which aim to give women a formal role in the governing bodies of the unions. Proportionality is currently among the most popular of these policies. The goal of proportionality is the representation of women in all agenda-setting and decision-making bodies in proportion to their numbers in the membership. The means of achieving this are the use of targets, monitoring, quotas and other measures of positive affirmation. Proportionality has been incorporated into the constitution of the new union UNISON, but only in respect of women. Some unions are considering adopting it also in connection with minority interests, while others are planning to use monitoring and targeting, but without a full commitment to proportionality. Proportionality has considerable power to improve women's position. Yet in our view, because it does nothing to curb the power men exert through office-holding and informal networks, or the culture of masculinity that underpins both, it cannot guarantee fair representation.

UNISON has adopted a less popular method of empowerment, that of reserving seats on the NEC and other committees for women only. UNISON has also reserved seats on regional committees for low-paid women, thus ensuring them a voice in union government. We see this particular measure as a significant step towards achieving fair representation for grass-roots women workers.

A different means of helping women achieve power, lies in transforming the system of women's advisory structures set up after the TUC 1979 Charter into what we term a 'corporate voice'. This transformation can be achieved by firstly ensuring the election rather than appointment of all members and delegates, and secondly granting the committees and conferences which comprise the structures the right to a voice and a vote in the unions' main policy-making bodies. Such a corporate voice would give the collective voice of women independent representation alongside the voices of individual members. It would help offset the systematic disadvantages of women in the unions and hence in the labour market. Several unions, NALGO, NUCPS and UNISON for example, have gone along this path. NALGO and UNISON have, additionally, given the status of corporate voices to three other groups: black, disabled, and lesbian and gay workers.

This raises another question we looked at, how far unions have been able to represent the interests of the diverse groups of women found within the collectivity. Unions first had the task of identifying groups which could be considered in need of special representation. By the early 1990s most unions recognised women as having such a need and had created special structures for their representation. They had also come to recognise the representational needs of workers from subordinated minorities, generally black, disabled, and lesbians and gay workers. At least one union, MSF, had formally recognised also the special needs of young workers (TUC, 1991c). But the distinctive needs of women in these minority groups were not considered to require separate representation. However, some unions have developed procedures to ensure that women are adequately represented on the minority group national committees. UNISON's provision for the representation of low-paid women gives structural recognition, for the first time, to a subordinated group defined by its position in the labour market.

The concern about the representation of women, black people and other subordinate groups which surfaced in the seventies and eighties was part of a more general worry about the state of democracy within the movement. In this context the notion of self-organization emerged as a means of democratically representing subordinated minorities, enabling them to define their own needs, free from the control of dominant majorities. Unions such as NALGO and UNISON have written into their rules a degree of self-organization for both women and subordinate minority groups. Self-organization has also been recommended as a means of assisting recruitment in these categories. However, the women from subordinated minorities have no gender-specific structure of representation. They may be able to express their views through either the women's or the minority groups' special structures. In the case of black women there is some evidence that more attention is paid to their interests by black workers' than by the women's groups.

In Part 3 we looked at trade union negotiation and the cultures of masculinity and femininity. We explored three areas: how far recent union initiatives, in furthering women's issues, have offered a challenge to the culture of masculinity; how union negotiation has been responding to the needs of different groups of women and thus reflecting the value which women's culture puts on diversity; and what are the implications of feminizing the negotiating agenda and practice.

We began by showing just how badly men in unions - in their struggle to maintain superior status and earnings - can treat women during negotiation. Walby has provided a historical analysis of the unions' exclusion and subordination of women (Walby, 1986); our analysis detailed some of the social processes and cultural practices which support it. We pointed to the crucial importance of negotiation and the need for women to participate in it. Next we turned to the unions' own challenges to the culture of masculinity, trying to see how far they have been able to negotiate equality for women in the labour market. We looked at agreements dealing with matters of pay, training and promotion, sexism and sexual harassment, maternity and childcare and - of great importance in the recessionary nineties - women's right to work.

Much union negotiation has failed women because it is based on the traditional model of the full-time male. One of the greatest benefits union negotiators could achieve would be to establish, throughout industry, patterns of working which are compatible with the reality of women's domestic responsibilities: work 'fit for women'. Such work patterns could also change men's lives, enabling them to spend more time with their families.

Encumbered by a traditional male negotiating model the unions face problems of a weakened and fragmented labour force. The diversity coming from ethnic and cultural sources is matched by a diversity of interest created by the labour market.

Recession has increased competition among employers. They have forced down wages, worsened conditions, diminished benefits. They have extended part-time working, temporary contracts and are casualizing work. Women are the weakest section of the workforce: their need for flexible working patterns makes them peculiarly vulnerable to exploitation by employers. The living standards of the working class are threatened and the credibility of the union movement to act in their defence is undermined. If unions acknowledged and negotiated around a new model of a flexible worker, they would be better able to deal with this increasingly fragmented labour force, to defend and even advance their interests and those of their class.

We took examples of union efforts to recruit and negotiate among marginalized groups, including part-timers, homeworkers, black and ethnic women. It is not a record of great achievement, but there are signs that unions are beginning to respond to these groups. Some have made persistent attempts to seek the views of workers at the grass-roots and to identify and address issues of black women. At a local level several unions have worked closely with community groups on behalf of minorities. These examples show that in some parts of the movement, for example at the level of equal rights officers and at the grass-roots, there is firm commitment to minorities including minority women. Whether or not the movement as a whole is yet willing to commit its energies and resources to these marginalized groups is unclear.

The men in the union movement have traditionally claimed a wide agenda, professing concern for all workers, women as well as men, for union and socialist struggles outside the UK as well as within. But this has been largely on the level of rhetoric. The reality has been different: there has always been an emphasis on sectional gain for men, especially in those occupations and those unions that were strongly organized. There are, of course, other strands in the men's movement. Under the leadership of Jack Jones for example, the TGWU, and on occasions much of the union movement, has supported the cause of pensioners. But such are not part of the mainstream of men's concerns.

Women's perspective is different. Because their lives are grounded in community as well as in paid work, in caring for others as well as in working on their own account, their trade union agenda has always been wider than men's. In the final chapter we discussed the way in which women's issues had changed the negotiating agenda. Important new issues have been brought onto the movement's agenda, such as health and the quality of community life, childcare and the responsibilities of a multicultural society. But their most significant contribution may be in changing the priorities assigned to existing issues and in breathing new life into traditional goals of equality and social justice which are too easily forgotten. Women's priorities perhaps could be summed up as including, on a par with their own particular interests, those of children, carers and community. Their concern with mutual responsibility goes beyond the value of solidarity expressed in picketing support during industrial action. The miners' wives did go out onto the picket lines, but most of their energies were put into trying to save their communities. Women's concern with mutual responsibility extends into the daily life of the community with issues such as standards of health care, nutrition of children, care of the elderly, housing and homelessness, domestic violence and child abuse. This can be interpreted as a return to the old values of the union movement, to redistribution in its widest sense, to the notion of the union as a sword of justice. By helping women, unions are in fact helping themselves.

The premise underlying this book is that an understanding of the structural and cultural practices underpinning women's subordination will help in efforts to improve their position. How have previous chapters clarified our understanding? What do they indicate about ways of moving women's interests forward? Part 1 has established the profound importance of cultural practices, both in maintaining the status quo (as in the reigning culture of masculinity), and as an engine of social change (in challenging men's power). The supportive behaviour of male paid officers shows that changed cultural practice can operate within old structures. The women of N. Ireland show how changes in cultural practice can lead to structural change. Both indicate ways forward for women.

In Part 2 we argued strongly for changes in both structure and cultural practice. 'Policies of empowerment', which changed power relations between women and men, were preferred to those 'policies of encouragement' which left men's power intact. But structural empowerment has limitations. Men's networks of informal power and the cultural practices which support them remain untouched. However, there is one policy of encouragement - women-only education - that stands out. It gives women the confidence and resources to challenge the cultural practices by which men subordinate them.

Part 3 shows how women's values, embedded in the culture of femininity, have shaped recent negotiations, making the unions more responsive to women's needs. The feminization of negotiation, with its less confrontational and more democratic style, would sustain and accelerate these gains. The cultural changes which women themselves bring to the movement seem to hold most hope for the future.

APPENDICES

APPENDICES

Appendix 1 - 1979 TUC Charter for Equality for Women within Trade Unions

1. The National Executive Committee of the union should publicly declare to all its members the commitment of the union to involving women members in the activities of the union at all levels.

2. The structure of the union should be examined to see whether it prevents women from reaching the decision-making bodies.

3. Where there are large women's memberships but no women on the decision-making bodies, special provision should be made to ensure that women's views are represented, either through the creation of additional seats or by co-option.

4. The National Executive Committee of each union should consider the desirability of setting up advisory committees within its constitutional machinery to ensure that the special interests of its women members are protected.

5. Similar committees at regional, divisional and district level could also assist by encouraging the active involvement of women in the general activities of the union.

6. Efforts should be made to include in collective agreements provision for time off without loss of pay to attend branch meetings during working hours where that is practicable.

7. Where it is not practicable to hold meetings during working hours, every effort should be made to provide child-care facilities for use by either parent.

8. Child-care facilities, for use by either parent, should be provided at all district, divisional and regional meetings and particularly at the union's annual conference, and for training courses organised by the union.

9. Although it may be open to any members of either sex to go to union training courses, special encouragement should be given to women to attend.

10 The content of journals and other union publications should be represented in non-sexist terms.

The 1979 Charter was updated in 1990 to include the following paragraph:

> Unions should aim to have women represented on decision-making bodies in proportion to their numbers in membership. Targets should be set, with a timetable for achievement. Failure to meet targets should mean that quotas are adopted.

Appendix 2 - Summary of cases and action referred to in text

Case 1 - Chapter 1
Theme   Mechanisms of male control
Focus   Trade union branch
Jobs involved   Nursing and ancillary hospital work
Location   Hospital
Union   COHSE
Source   Observation: branch meetings, Oct 1977 to Nov 1978; three weeks' participant observation in hospital kitchen.

Case 2 - Chapter 2
Theme   Women's challenge in collective bargaining
Focus   Trade union branch
Jobs involved   Manufacturing and cleaning
Location   Factory
Union   TGWU
Source   Interviews

Case 3 - Chapter 3
Theme   Political ideology and consciousness
Focus   Trade union branch
Jobs involved   Teaching
Location   City
Union   NUT
Source   Observation: local association meetings from 1978 to 1980; interviews

Case 4 - Chapter 4
Theme   Effect of industrial action and paid officer support on trade union and gender consciousness
Focus   Workplace
Jobs involved   Cooking and kitchen work
Location   School kitchen, union meetings and union action
Union   NUPE
Source   Three months' participant observation in 1978 in a school kitchen; interviews

Case 5 - Chapter 4
Theme   Effects of industrial action on gender consciousness
Focus   Branch meetings and union action
Jobs involved   Nursing and ancillary hospital work
Location   Hospital, union meetings and action
Union   NUPE
Source   Observation: branch meetings between 1978 and 1980; interviews; public meetings.

Case 6 - Chapter 5
Theme   Failure of women's bid for control
Focus   Trade union branch
Jobs involved   Cooking and kitchen work
Location   City
Union   GMWU
Source   Interviews; observation of women's committee of trades council; informal contacts

Case 7 - Chapter 5
Theme   Success of women's challenge
Focus   Trade union branch
Jobs involved   Cooking and kitchen work
Location   City
Union   NUPE
Source   As Case 4

Case 8 - Chapter 7
Theme   Creating a member-led and woman-led branch
Focus   Trade union branch
Jobs involved   Nursing and ancillary hospital work
Location   Belfast Hospital
Union   NUPE
Source   Published material

Case 9 - Chapter 10
Theme   Union fails women in factory negotations
Focus   Workplace
Jobs involved   Sewing machinists
Location   Factory
Union   TGWU
Source   Six months' observation in factory in 1959.

Action referred to in Chapter 6
Theme   Women-initiated industrial action
Focus   A variety of industrial action
Jobs involved   Manufacturing and public service
People involved Workers, workers' wives, people in community
Location   Various places in UK
Unions   COHSE, GMWU, NUPE, TGWU, NUM and others.
Source   Publications

Appendix 3 - Numbers and proportion of women in the movement in 1985 and 1990

	TGWU	GMB	NALGO	AEU	MSF	NUPE	USDAW	UCATT	COHSE	UCW	NUT	BIFU	SOGAT	NCU	NGA	CPSA	NAS/UWT	RMT	NUCPS
Total membership																			
1990	1,249,573	870,000	750,462	741,647	653,000	603,000	407,247	258,000	210,000	203,000	185,661	170,481	167,777	149,351	131,186	128,214	118,000	117,000	112,812
Women in membership																			
1990	210,758	267,89—	398,660	105,022	140,000	430,000	251,371	4,000	165,900	59,205	133,675	94,446	47,426	31,074	8,791	90,742	51,564	6,000	41,147
Women in membership (%)																			
1990	16.9	30.8	53.1	14.2	21.4	71.3	61.7	1.5	79.0	29.2	72.0	55.4	28.3	20.8	6.7	70.8	43.7	5.1	36.5
1985	16.2	30.4	na	na	na	na	60.7	0.8	80.0	25.0	65.9	52.0	29.8	20.3	6.0	71.2	41.9	4.6	na
Women on national executive (%)																			
1990	7.7	29.4	42.0	0	21.6	46.1	31.3	0	50.0	14.3	28.6	18.8	5.6	0	0	35.7	17.9	0	17.5
1985	2.6	2.6	30.1	0	na	na	12.5	0	11.5	14.3	16.7	14.6	5.6	0	0	42.9	5.1	0	19.2
Women at union conference (%)																			
1990	na	17.4	na	11.8	18.4	33.3	27.1	0	34.3	28.3	na	na	16.1	12.0	4.1	38.0	27.2	5.9	23.1
1985	na	13.3	na	6.5	na	na	23.3	0	30.0	25.0	na	na	9.1	12.0	2.2	na	na	0	na
Women on TUC delegation (%)																			
1990	20.6	19.8	41.7	7.4	25.5	36.1	26.9	0	31.6	13.3	40.0	15.4	5.6	5.0	3.6	33.3	14.3	5.6	26.3
1985	na	3.6	29.2	0	na	na	30.8	4.0	na	7.1	19.4	25.9	15.0	10.0	0	48.3	na	0	25.9
Women full-time national officers (%)																			
1990	3.4	11.8	31.6	0.6	21.4	38.5	20.0	0	54.2	23.1	42.9	23.8	12.5	25.0	7.7	12.5	26.7	0	24.0
1985	na	7.7	25.7	0.6	na	0	11.1	0	na	15.4	18.2	23.7	10.0	18.5	6.7	18.8	na	0	18.8
Women regional full-time officers (%)																			
1990	na	3.6	13.4	0	4.8	11.0	18.6	0	22.6	na	20.0	30.0	3.2	na	0	na	6.7	0	0
1985	na	2.0	8.6	0	na	6.7	13.1	0	12.5	na	8.0	26.3	3.9	na	0	na	0	0	0

	IPMS	NATFHE	FBU	EIS	EMA	MU	ISTC	BFAWU	AUT	ACTT	NUJ	STE	ASLEF	FDA	NAPO	BALPA	NULMW	NACO
Total membership																		
1990	89,429	79,404	47,000	45,000	41,900	40,528	40,000	34,379	31,807	29,976	29,774	28,181	18,713	9,483 [3]	6,714	5,394	5,161	4,427
Women in membership																		
1990	11,013	28,590	1,000	30,000	488	7,461	2,700	na	4,771	na	8,761	3,445	87	1,953 [3]	3,289	77	2,648	623
Women in membership (%)																		
1990	12.3	36.0	2.1	66.7	1.2	18.4	6.8	na	15.0	na	29.4	12.2	0.5	20.6 [3]	49.0	1.4	51.3	14.1
1985	10.0	29.2	2.1	na [5]	0.7	15.3	6.9	na	15.0	na	29.2	na	0.1	na	45.0	0.3	na	7.9
Women on national executive (%)																		
1990	16.0	33.3	5.9	33.3	7.7	4.5	0	20.0	15.4	na	10.6	15.4	0	20.0	33.3	0	31.6	4.5
1985	16.0	27.8	5.9	na	0	0	0	20.0	11.5	na	21.2	18.8	0	27.3	36.8	0	26.3	0
Women at union conference (%)																		
1990	8.2	32.8	3.0	46.3	0	8.0	2.5	na	18.8	na	na	9.9	2.2	na	na	0	na	8.6
1985	9.8	28.7	3.0	na	na	8.6	2.2	na	na	na	na	na	0	17.0 [4]	na	0	na	0
Women on TUC delegation (%)																		
1990	22.2	40.0	0	22.2	0	16.7	0	na	28.6	na	28.6	0.0	0	33.3	50.0	0	50.0	0
1985	26.3	40.0	0	22.2	0	0	0	na	28.6	na	0.0	33.3	0	0	0	0	0	0
Women full-time national officers (%)																		
1990	25.0	30.8	0	16.7	27.3	14.3	0	0	40.0	66.7	45.5	28.6	0	50.0	33.3	14.3	0.0	25.0
1985	28.6	36.4	0	16.7	8.3	12.5	0	0	50.0	na	50.0	41.7	0	50.0 [6]	0	0	50.0	0
Women regional full-time officers (%)																		
1990	25.0	16.7	na [1]	33.3	9.1	12.5	0	20.0	0	na	33.3	25.0	0	na	33.3	na	na	0
1985	na	16.7	na [1]	33.3	0	0	0	20.0	0	na	33.3	na	0	na	na	na	na	0

Note: From figures supplied by unions.
1. 1985 information is for NUR only. 2. 1985 information is for SCPS plus CSU. 3. 1989 figure. 4. 1986 figure. 5. Figure not thought to have changed. 6. Including female general secretary.

Source - L R D 1991

Appendix 4 - Postal Questionnaires 1990

1 Representation of women

Eighteen unions were contacted: ten with the largest number of women members (AEU, BIFU, COHSE, GMB, MSF, NALGO, NUPE, NUT, TGWU and USDAW); four with a high proportion of women members (CPSA, HVA, NUHKW, and NUTGW); and ACTT, IRSF, NAS/UWT and RMT.

Unions were asked the number and percentage of women in different parts of their organizations in 1976, 1986 and 1990. They were asked about the membership; the NEC; delegations to annual conferences; delegations to TUC conferences; and the paid officer workforce. Insufficiency in the data received for early years made a comparative analysis impossible.

2 Women and minorities: progressive measures

Twenty-three unions with National Women's Officers or National Officers for Equal Rights were contacted assuming that they would have progressive policies towards women, black and disabled people. They were: AEU, ACTT, AUT, BETA, BIFU, CCSU, COHSE, FBU, GMB, MSF, NALGO, NAS/UWT, NATFHE, NCU, NGA, NUCPS, NUPE, NUT, NUTGW, TGWU, TSSA, UCATT, USDAW. The questionnaire covered three categories of respondents:

Trade union members were asked about:
   Targeting and monitoring the ratio of women, black and disabled people
      represented on national and regional committees and at national and
      TUC Conference
   Education and training provision for women
   Implementation of the 1979 TUC Charter for Women
   Measures to encourage the representation of women's views at
      workplace and branch level.

Trade union employees were asked about:
   Targeting and monitoring ratios of women, black and disabled employees
   Measures to improve equal opportunities in union employment.

Women's and Equal Rights Officers were asked about:
   Position and influence in the union
   Problems encountered in carrying out this role.

Appendix 5 - Abbreviations

Trade Unions

ACTT	Association of Cinematograph, Television and Allied Technicians (amalgamated with BETA to form BECTU in 1991)
AEEU	Amalgamated Engineering and Electrical Union
AEF	Association of Engineering and Foundry Workers
AEU	Amalgamated Engineering Union (amalgamated with EETPU to form AEEU in 1992)
APEX	Association of Professional, Clerical and Computer Staff, white collar union associated with GMWU (amalgamated with GMBATU to form GMB in 1989)
ASBSBSW	Amalgamated Society of Boilermakers, Shipwrights, Blacksmiths and Structural Workers (amalgamated with GMWU to form GMBATU in 1982)
ASLEF	Associated Society of Locomotive Engineers and Firemen
ASTMS	Association of Scientific, Technical and Managerial Staffs (amalgamated with TASS to form MSF in 1988)
AUEW	Amalgamated Union of Engineering Workers
AUT	Association of University Teachers
BALPA	British Air Line Pilots Association
BECTU	Broadcasting, Entertainment, and Cinematograph Technicians' Union
BETA	Broadcasting and Entertainment Trades Alliance (amalgamated with ACTT to form BECTU in 1991)
BFAWU	Bakers, Food and Allied Workers' Union
BIFU	Banking, Insurance and Finance Union
CCSU	Council of Civil Service Unions
C/N/N	COHSE/NALGO/NUPE (three unions which amalgamated in 1993 to form UNISON)
COHSE	Confederation of Health Service Employees
CPSA	Civil and Public Services Association
CSU	Civil Service Union (amalgamated with SCPS in 1988 to form NUCPS)
EETPU	Electrical, Electronic, Telecommunications and Plumbing Union (amalgamated with AEU to form AEEU in 1992)
EIS	Educational Institute of Scotland
EMA	Engineers' and Managers' Association

FBU	Fire Brigades Union
FDA	Association of First Division Civil Servants
GMB	GMB - Britain's General Union
GMBATU	General and Municipal Workers' and Boilermakers' and Allied Trades Union (amalgamated with APEX to form GMB in 1989)
GMWU	General and Municipal Workers' Union (amalgamated with ASBSBSW to form GMBATU in 1982)
GNCTU	Grand National Consolidated Trade Union
GPMU	Graphical, Paper and Media Union
HVA	Health Visitors Association
IPMS	Institute of Professionals, Managers and Specialists
IRSF	Inland Revenue Staff Federation
ISTC	Iron and Steel Trades Confederation
MSF	Manufacturing Science Finance
MU	Musicians' Union
NACO	National Association of Co-operative Officials
NALGO	National and Local Government Officers' Association
NAPO	National Association of Probation Officers
NAS	National Association of Schoolmasters
NAS/UWT	National Association of Schoolmasters/Union of Women Teachers
NATFHE	National Association of Teachers in Further and Higher Education
NCU	National Communications Union
NFWW	National Federation of Women Workers (amalgamated with the National Union of General Workers in 1921)
NGA	National Graphical Association (amalgamated with SOGAT to form GPMU in 1992)
NUAAW	National Union of Agricultural and Allied Workers (amalgamated with TGWU in 1982)
NUCPS	National Union of Civil and Public Servants
NUGW	National Union of General Workers (amalgamated with two other unions in 1924 to form GMWU)
NUHKW	National Union of Hosiery and Knitwear Workers (amalgamated with the National Union of Footwear and Allied Trades to form NUKFAT in 1991)
NUJ	National Union of Journalists
NUKFAT	National Union of Knitwear, Footwear and Apparel Trades
NULMW	National Union of Lock and Metal Workers
NUM	National Union of Mineworkers

NUPE	National Union of Public Employees
NUR	National Union of Railwaymen
NUS	National Union of Seamen
NUT	National Union of Teachers
NUTGW	National Union of Tailors and Garment Workers' (amalgamated with GMB in 1991)
NUWT	National Union of Women Teachers
RCN	Royal College of Nursing
RMT	National Union of Rail, Maritime and Transport Workers
SCPS	Society of Civil and Public Servants
SOGAT	Society of Graphical and Allied Trades (amalgamated with NGA to form GPMU in 1992)
STE	Society of Telecom Executives
TASS	Technical, Administrative and Supervisory Staffs (amalgamated with ASTMS to form MSF in 1988)
TGWU	Transport and General Workers' Union
TSSA	Transport Salaried Staffs' Association
TWU	Tobacco Workers' Union
UCATT	Union of Construction, Allied Trades and Technicians
UCW	Union of Communication Workers
UDM	Union of Democratic Miners
UNISON	UNISON (created in 1993 by amalgamation of COHSE, NALGO and NUPE)
USDAW	Union of Shop, Distributive and Allied Workers
UWT	Union of Women Teachers

Trade union organizations

CUCW	Conference of Unions Catering for Women (now WTUC)
NWAC	National Women's Advisory Committee
SERTUC	South East Regional Trade Union Congress
TUC	Trades Union Congress
TUCWC	Trades Union Congress Women's Committee
WTUC	Women's Trade Union Congress

Other Organisations

CLCLC	Central London Community Law Centre
CP	Community Programme
CRE	Commission for Racial Equality
CRER	Centre for Research on Ethnic Relations
CREW	Centre for Research on European Women
EC	European Community
EOC	Equal Opportunities Commission
EOR	Equal Opportunities Review
EWL	European Women's Lobby
GEC	General Electrical Company
ICI	Imperial Chemical Industries
ILO	International Labour Organisation
ILP	Independent Labour Party
IMF	International Monetary Fund
IRS	Industrial Relations Services
LRD	Labour Research Department
NCCL	National Council of Civil Liberties (now Liberty)
NHS	National Health Service
NPEC	National Pay Equity Campaign
PSA	*Public Service Action*
SEWA	Self-Employed Women's Association (India)
SCAT	Services to Community Action and Trade Unions
STA	Socialist Teachers' Alliance
STUEAS	Southall Trade Union and Employment Advisory Service
TEC	Training and Enterprise Council
WAPC	Women Against Pit Closures
WEA	Workers' Educational Association
WRRC	Women's Research and Resource Centre
WWW	Women Working Worldwide
YOP	Youth Opportunities Programme
YTS	Youth Training Scheme

References

Adams, Mary Louise (1989) 'There's no place like home: on the place of identity in feminist politics', *Feminist Review,* No.31.

Alberti, Johnson (1989) *Beyond Suffrage: Feminists in War and Peace 1914-28* (London: Macmillan).

Alexander, Sally (1974) 'The night cleaners: an assessment of the campaign' in Allen, Sandra, L. Saunders and J. Wallis (eds) *Conditions of Illusion* (Leeds: Feminist Books).

Allen, Sheila and Carol Wolkowitz (1987) *Homeworking, Myths and Realities* (London: Macmillan).

Allen, Sheila and Fiona Measham (1991) 'In defence of home and hearth? Families, friendships and feminism in mining communities', paper presented to Coal, Culture and Community Conference, Sheffield City Polytechnic. Also in *Journal of Gender Studies* (forthcoming).

Amos Valerie and Pratibha Parmar (1984) 'Challenging imperial feminism', *Feminist Review*, No. 17.

Anderson, Bridget (1993) *Britain's Secret Slaves: an Investigation into the Plight of Overseas Domestic Workers,* No. 5 in ASI's Human Rights Series (London: Anti-Slavery International).

Anthias, Floya and Nira Yuval-Davis (1983) 'Contextualizing feminism: gender, ethnic and class divisions', *Feminist Review*, No. 15.

Ardener, Edwin (1975) 'Belief and the problem of women' and 'The problem revisited' in S. Ardener (ed.) *Perceiving Women* (London: Dent).

Banks, Olive (1981) *Faces of Feminism* (Oxford: Martin Robertson).

Barrett, Michèle (1987) 'The concept of difference', *Feminist Review*, No. 26.

Barrett, Michèle and Mary McIntosh (1982) *The Antisocial Family* (London: Verso).
Barrett, Michèle and Mary McIntosh (1985) 'Ethnocentrism and socialist-feminist theory', *Feminist Review*, No. 20.
BBC Radio 4 (1988a) 'Women and the struggle for equal pay', *File on Four*, June 1.
BBC Radio 4 (1988b) *Woman's Hour,* November 2.
BBC Radio 4 (1990) *Today,* September 6.
Beale, Jenny (1982) *Getting it Together* (London: Pluto Press).
Beechey, Veronica (1978a) 'Some notes on female wage labour and capitalist production', *Capital and Class*, Vol. 3.
Beechey, Veronica (1978b) 'Women and production: a critical analysis of some sociological theories of women's work' in Kuhn and Wolpe (eds).
Beechey, Veronica and Tessa Perkins (1987) *A Matter of Hours: Women, Part-time Work and the Labour Market* (Cambridge: Polity Press).
Benton, Sarah (1975) *Patterns of Discrimination against Women in the Film and Television Industries* (London: ACTT).
Boston, Sarah (1980) *Women Workers and the Trade Unions* (London: Davis-Poynter).
Braverman, H. (1974) *Labour and Monopoly Capitalism* (New York and London: Monthly Review Press).
Briskin, Linda (1990) 'Identity politics and the hierarchy of oppression: a comment', *Feminist Review,* No. 35.
Bruegel, Irene (1979) 'Women as a reserve army of labour: a note on recent British experience', *Feminist Review,* No. 3.
Bryan, Beverley, Stella Dadzie and Susanne Scafe (1985) *The Heart of the Race* (London: Virago).
Cadbury, Edward, M. Cécile Matheson and George Shann (c. 1907) *Women's Work and Wages* (London: T. Fisher Unwin).
Caldwell, Lesley (1983) 'Courses for women: the example of the 150 hours in Italy', *Feminist Review*, Vol. 14.
Cameron, Ivy (1989) *Equal Opportunities for Women: a Challenge for the Finance Industry and BIFU*, unpublished.
Campbell, Beatrix (1980) 'Work to rule: wages and the family', *Red Rag* (London: Publications Co-operative).
Campbell, Beatrix (1986b) 'Value added', *Guardian*, August 4.
Campbell, Beatrix (1989) 'Bargain women', *New Statesman*, December 1.
Campbell, Beatrix (1990) 'Trading places', *Guardian*, October 10.
Carter, April (1988) *The Politics of Women's Rights* (Harlow: Longmans).
Cavendish, Ruth (1982) *Women on the Line* (London: Routledge and Kegan Paul).

Chambers, Gerald and Christine Horton (1990) *Promoting Sex Equality: the Role of Industrial Tribunals* (London: Policy Studies Institute).

Channel 4 (1988) 'Union made', *Women Working*, August 17 (London: Cinecontact).

Channel 4 (1989) 'If we were asked', feature by Red Flannel, December 18.

Chapman, Rowena and Jonathan Rutherford (eds) (1988) *Male Order: Unwrapping Masculinity* (London: Lawrence and Wishart).

Charles, Nicola (1983) 'Women and trade unions in the workplace', *Feminist Review*, No. 15.

Chodorow, Nancy (1978) *The Reproduction of Mothering* (Berkley: University of California Press).

CLCLC (Central London Community Law Centre) (1985/6) *Organising as Women Trade Unionists* (London: CLCLC).

Clegg, H.A, A.Killick and R.Adams (1961) *Trade Union Officers* (Oxford: Basil Blackwell).

C/N/N (COHSE, NALGO, NUPE) (1990) *The Challenge of a New Union: Reports of the COHSE, NALGO and NUPE Executives to the 1990 Annual Conferences* (London: C/N/N).

Cockburn, Cynthia (1981) 'The material of male power', *Feminist Review*, No. 9.

Cockburn, Cynthia (1983) *Brothers* (London: Pluto).

Cockburn, Cynthia (1985) *Machinery of Dominance: Women, Men and Technical Knowhow* (London: Pluto Press).

Cockburn, Cynthia (1988) 'Masculinity, the left and feminism' in Chapman and Rutherford (eds).

Cockburn, Cynthia (1991) *In the Way of Women: Men's Resistance to Sex Equality in Organisations* (London: Macmillan).

COHSE (1979) *Report: the Position of Women within COHSE* (London: COHSE).

Colling, Trevor and Linda Dickens (1989) *Equality Bargaining: Why Not?* (London: HMSO).

Commission for the European Communities (1990) *Childcare in the European Communities 1985-90* (Brussels: Commission for the European Communities).

Community Action (1986) No. 72 (London: Community Action).

Connell, R.W.(1987) *Gender and Power* (Cambridge: Polity Press).

Coote, Anna and Beatrix Campbell (1982) *Sweet Freedom: a Struggle for Women's Liberation* (London: Pan).

Coulson, Margaret, Branka Magas and Hilary Wainwright (1975) 'The housewife and her labour under capitalism - a critique', *New Left Review*, No. 89.

Coyle, Angela (1985) 'Going private: the implications of privatization for women's work', *Feminist Review*, No. 21.
Coyle, Angela (1986) *Dirty Business: Women's Work and Trade Union Organization in Contract Cleaning* (London: Low Pay Unit).
Coyle, Angela (1988) 'Introduction: continuity and change: women in paid work' in Coyle and Skinner (eds).
Coyle, Angela (1989) 'Women in management: a suitable case for treatment', *Feminist Review*, No. 31.
Coyle, Angela and Jane Skinner (eds) (1988) *Women and Work: Positive Action for Change* (London: Macmillan).
Crawley, Christine (1991) 'British women beckoned in from the cold', *Guardian*, December 8.
CRE (Commission for Racial Equality) (1992) *Clinical Nurse Grading: the Cost of a 'Colour Blind' Approach* (London: CRE).
Creighton, Colin (1985) 'The family and capitalism in marxist theory' in Martin Shaw (ed.) *Marxist Sociology Revisited* (London: Macmillan).
CREW (Centre for Research on European Women) (1990a) 'Equality: EC women's lobby takes off', *CREW Reports,* Vol. 10, No. 2.
CREW (1990b) 'Equality: women visible in trade union list for single market', *CREW Reports,* Vol. 10, No. 3/4.
Crompton, Rosemary and Nicola Le Feuve (1992) 'Gender and bureaucracy: women in finance in Britain and France' in Savage and Witz (eds).
Cunnison, Sheila (1983a) 'Participation in local union organisation. School meals staff: a case study' in Gamarnikow et al.(eds) *Gender, Class and Work* (London: Heinemann).
Cunnison, Sheila (1983b) 'The Manchester factory studies ....' in Ronald Frankenberg (ed.) *Custom and Conflict in British Society* (Manchester: Manchester University Press).
Cunnison, Sheila (1986) 'Gender, consent and exploitation among sheltered housing wardens' in Purcell et al.(eds) *The Changing Experience of Employment* (London: Macmillan).
Cunnison, Sheila (1987) 'Women's working lives and trade union participation' in Allat et al.(eds) *Women and the Life Cycle* (London: Macmillan).
Cunnison, Sheila (1988) 'Move over brother, we want some more of the action', *Newsletter* (Hull: Centre for Gender Studies).
Cunnison, Sheila (1989) 'Trade unions: the case of gender consciousness' in R. Burgess (ed.) *Investigating Society* (London: Longmans).
Cunnison, Sheila (1991) 'Equal value legislation and the trade unions: a case study in the UK', *Journal of Gender Studies*, Vol. 1, No. 1.

Cunnison, Sheila (forthcoming) 'Women teachers: career identity and perceptions of family constraints - changes over a recent decade', *Research Papers in Education* (Exeter: University of Exeter).

Dalla Costa, Mariarosa and Selma Jones (1973) *The Power of Women and the Subversion of the Community* (Bristol: Falling Wall Press).

Davies, Celia and J. Rosser (1986) 'Gendered jobs in the health service: a problem for a labour process analysis' in David Knights et al. (eds) *Gender and the Labour Process* (Aldershot: Gower).

de Lyon, Hilary and Frances Migniuolo (eds) (1989) *Women Teachers - Issues and Experiences* (Milton Keynes: Open University Press).

Dickens, Linda, Barbara Townley and David Winchester (1988) *Tackling Sex Discrimination through Collective Bargaining: the Impact of Section 6 of the Sex Discrimination Act 1986* (London: HMSO).

Dinnerstein, Dorothy (1978) *The Rocking of the Cradle* (London: Souvenir).

Donovan, Lord (1968) *Report of the Royal Commission on Trade Unions and Employers' Associations* (London: HMSO).

Downs, Roger (1988) *Behind the Fringe* (Saffron Walden: Monks Partnership).

Drake, Peter et al. (1980) *Which Way Forward? An Interim Review of Issues for the SCPS* (London: SCPS).

Edholm, Felicity, Olivia Harris and Kate Young (1977) 'Conceptualising women', *Critique of Anthropology*, Vol. 3, No. 9/10.

Eisenstein, Zillah (ed.) (1979) *Capitalist Patriarchy and the Case for Socialist Feminism* (New York: Monthly Review Press).

Elias, Patrick (1990) 'Law and union democracy: the changing shape' in Fosh and Heery (eds).

Elliot, Ruth (1982) 'Something is stirring - women and TUC education', *The Industrial Tutor*, Vol. 3, No. 6.

Elliot, Ruth (1984) 'How far have we come? Women's organization in the unions in the United Kingdom', *Feminist Review*, No. 16.

Ellis, Valerie (1987) 'Current trade union attempts to remove occupational segregation in the employment of women' in Walby (ed.).

EOC (1990) *Equal Pay for Men and Women: Strengthening the Acts* (Manchester: EOC).

EOC (1992) *Pregnant Women at Work: a Response to the EC's Proposed Directive* (Manchester: EOC).

EOR (from 1980) *Equal Opportunities Review* (London: Eclipse).

EOR (1987) 'Equal value: the trade union response', *Equal Opportunities Review*, No. 11.

EOR (1993) 'Equal opportunities and the Trade Union Reform and Employment Rights Bill', *Equal Opportunities Review*, No. 47.
Everywoman (1992) May.
Fairbrother, Peter (1988) *Flexibility at Work: the Challenge for the Unions* (London: WEA).
Feminist Review (1984) *Many Voices, One Chant: Black Feminist Perspectives*, No. 17.
Filby, M. (1991) '"The figures, the personality and the bums": service work and sexuality', *Work, Employment and Society*, Vol. 6, No. 1.
Finch, Janet and Dulcie Groves (1980) 'Community care and the family: a case for equal opportunities?', *Journal of Social Policy*, Vol. 9, No. 4.
Fine, Gary (1987) 'One of the boys: women in a male-dominated setting' in Kimmel (ed.).
Fisher, Alan and Bernard Dix (1974) *Low Pay and How to Fight it* (London: Pitman).
Flanders, Allan (1970) *Management and Unions* (London: Faber and Faber).
Fosh, Patricia and Sheila Cohen (1990) 'Local trade unionists in action: patterns of union democracy' in Fosh and Heery (eds).
Fosh, Patricia and Edmund Heery (eds) (1990) *Trade Unions and their Members: Studies in Union Democracy and Organization* (London: Macmillan).
Friedman, Henry and Sander Meredeen (1980) *The Dynamics of Industrial Conflict* (London: Croom Helm).
Fryer, R. H., Andy Fairclough and Tom Manson (1974) *Organization and Change in the National Union of Public Employees* (Warwick: University of Warwick).
Gardiner, Jean (1975) 'Women's domestic labour', *New Left Review*, No. 89.
Gilligan, Carol (1982) *In a Different Voice: Psychological Theory and Women's Development* (London: Harvard University Press).
Glendinning, Caroline (1990) 'Dependency and interdependency: the incomes of informal carers', *Journal of Social Policy*, Vol. 19, No. 4.
GMB (1987) *Winning a Fair Deal for Women: a GMB Policy for Equality* (London: GMB).
GMB (c. 1987) *Voices: a GMB Policy for Equality* (London: GMB).
GMB (1992a) *Negotiators' Guide to Equal Opportunities Policies* (GMB: London).
GMB (1992b) *Who Cares for Kids?* (London: GMB).
GMB (1992c) *Ability 2000: Equality at Work for People with Disabilities* (London: GMB).

GMB (1992d) *Negotiators' Guide to Flexible Working* (London: GMB).
Gregory, Jeanne (1987) *Sex, Race and the Law* (London: Sage).
Gregory, Jeanne (1992) 'Equal pay for work of equal value: the strengths and weaknesses of legislation', *Work, Employment and Society*, Vol. 6, No. 3.
Gribbin, Jim (1992) *Municipal Review and AMA News*, April.
Griffin, Susan (1982) *Made from the Earth* (London: Women's Press).
Grimshaw, Jean (1986) *Masculinity, Femininity and Mothering*, Occ. Paper No. 3 (Hull: Centre for Gender Studies).
Grimshaw, Jean (1989) *Feminist Philosophers: Perspectives on Philosophical Traditions* (Brighton: Wheatsheaf Books).
Haraway, Donna (1988) 'Situated knowledges: the science question in feminism and the privilege of partial perspective', *Feminist Studies*, Vol. 14, No. 3.
Harper, Keith (1987) 'Work bias "costs women" £15 bn a year', *Guardian*, May 19.
Harper, Keith (1992) 'COHSE settles sex bother claim', *Guardian*, July 2.
Harrison, Marjorie (n.d.) *Women in ASTMS*, unpublished, School of Industrial and Business Studies, University of Warwick.
Hartmann, Heidi (1981) 'The unhappy marriage of marxism and patriarchy: towards a more progressive union' in L. Sargeant (ed.) *Women and Revolution: a Discussion of the Unhappy Marriage of Marxism* (USA: Southend Press).
Hearn, Jeff (1987) *The Gender of Oppression: Men, Masculinity and the Critique of Marxism* (Brighton: Wheatsheaf).
Hearn, Jeff and David Morgan (eds) (1990) *Men, Masculinities and Social Theory* (London: Unwin Hyman).
Heery, Edmund and John Kelly (1988a) *Union Women*, mimeo (London: London School of Economics).
Heery, Edmund and John Kelly (1988b) 'Do women female representatives make a difference? Women full-time officials and trade union work', *Work, Employment and Society*, Vol. 2, No. 4.
Heery, Edmund and John Kelly (1990) 'Full-time officers and the shop steward network: patterns of co-operation and interdependence' in Fosh and Heery (eds).
Heffer, Simon (1990) 'Hard words on bad language', *Daily Telegraph*, September 6.
Hobbs, May (1976) *Born to Struggle* (Vermont: Daughters Publishing Inc.)
Hoel, Barbro (1982) 'Contemporary clothing "sweatshops", Asian female labour and collective organization' in West (ed.).

Hoskyns, Catherine (1991) 'The European women's lobby', *Feminist Review*, No. 38.
Humphries, Jane (1977) 'Class struggle and the persistence of the working class family', *Cambridge Journal of Economics*, Vol. 1, No. 3.
Hunt, Judith (1976) *Organising Women Workers* (London: WEA).
Hunt, Judith (1982) 'A woman's place is in her union', in West (ed.).
Hunt, Pauline (1980) *Gender and Class Consciousness* (London: Macmillan).
Hurstfield, Jennifer (1978) *The Part Time Trap* (London: Low Pay Unit).
Huws, Ursula (1982) *Your Job in the Eighties* (London: Pluto).
Huws, Ursula (1984) *The New Homeworkers; New Technology and the Changing Location of White Collar Work*, Pamphlet No. 28 (London: Low Pay Unit).
Huws, Ursula (1989) *Negotiating Equality* (London: WEA).
IRS (Industrial Relations Services) (1991) *Pay and Gender in Britain* (London: HMSO).
IRSF (1987) *Best Practice and Realistic Expectations: the Role of Women in the IRSF* (London: IRSF).
ITV Yorkshire (1988) *Redundant Women,* August 1.
James, Selma (1976) *Women, the Unions and Work: What is Not to be Done*, Notting Hill Women's Liberation Group, London (first published 1972) (Bristol: Falling Wall Press).
Jenson, Jane, Elisabeth Hagen and Ceilaigh Reddy (eds) (1988) *Feminization of the Labour Force* (Cambridge: Polity).
Kimmel, Michael (ed.)(1987) *Changing Men* (California: Sage).
Kuhn, Annette and AnnMarie Wolpe (eds) (1978) *Feminism and Materialism* (London: Routledge and Kegan Paul).
Land, Hilary (1975) 'The myth of the male breadwinner', *New Society*, No. 679.
Ledwith, Sue (1991) *Sweet Talk, Soft Deals? Gender and Workplace Industrial Relations*, Working Papers in Economics, Business and Management, No. 35 (London: Polytechnic of North London).
Ledwith, Sue, Mike Hayes, Paul Joyce and Anita Gulati (1985) *Women in SOGAT '82* (Hadleigh, Essex: SOGAT).
Ledwith, Sue, Fiona Colgan, Mike Hayes and Paul Joyce (1990) *The Social Construction of Women's Trade Union Activism,* Working Papers in Economics, Business and Management, No. 33 (London: Polytechnic of North London).
Lee, Gloria (1987) 'Black members and their unions' in Lee and Loveridge (eds) *The Manufacture of Disadvantage: Stigma and Social Closure* (Milton Keynes: Open University Press).

Leonard, Alice, (1987) *Pyrrhic Victories: Winning Sex Discrimination and Equal Pay Cases in the Industrial Tribunals: 1980-1984* (London: HMSO).

Leonard, Avril (1991) 'Women in struggle: a case study in a Kent mining community' in Redclift and Sinclair (eds).

Lewenhak, Sheila (1977) *Women and Trade Unions: an Outline History of Women in the British Trade Union Movement* (London: Ernest Benn).

Liddington, Jill and Jill Norris (1978) *One Hand Tied Behind Us: the Rise of the Women's Suffrage Movement* (London: Virago).

Littlewood, Margaret (1989) 'The "wise married woman" and the teaching unions' in de Lyon and Migniuolo (eds).

London Bridge (1987) *Equal Opportunities for Local Authority Workers: the Trade Union Experience in Seven London Labour Boroughs* (London: Empirica).

LRD (Labour Research Department) (1986) 'Women in multinationals - the common cause', *Labour Research,* Vol. 75, No. 8.

LRD (1988a) 'Working for equality in the unions', *Labour Research*, Vol. 77, No. 3.

LRD (1988b) 'Are unions working for black members?', *Labour Research* Vol. 77, No. 7.

LRD (1989) *Bargaining Report*, February.

LRD (1990a) *The Law at Work* (London: LRD).

LRD (1990b) *Bargaining Report*, May.

LRD (1991) *Women in Trade Unions: Action for Equality* (London: LRD).

LRD (1992a) *Out at Work* (London: LRD).

LRD (1992b) *Bargaining Report*, October.

Lyon, Joy (1991) 'Money and power: evaluating income generating projects for women' in Redclift and Sinclair (eds).

McDonough, Roisin and Rachel Harrison (1978) 'Patriarchy and the relations of production' in Kuhn and Wolpe (eds).

McGwire, Scarlett (1986) 'Betrayed from Within', *Guardian*, March 18.

McIlroy, J. (1988) 'Sexism and trade union education', *Trade Union Studies Journal,* No. 5.

MacInnes, John (1990) 'The future of this great movement of ours' in Fosh and Heery (eds).

Martin, Jean and Ceridwen Roberts (1984) *Women and Employment* (London: OPCS).

Meade-King, Maggie (1986) 'Why reserved seats for men will mean women have succeeded', *Guardian*, May 3.

Meyer, Mrs Carl and Clementina Black (1909) *Makers of Our Clothes* (London: Duckworth and Co.)

Mills, C.Wright (1970, first published 1959) *The Sociological Imagination* (Harmondsworth: Penguin).

Milward N. and M.Stevens (1986) *British Workplace Industrial Relations 1980-84* (Aldershot: Gower).

Mitchell, Juliet (1974) *Psychoanalysis and Feminism* (London: Allen Lane).

Monthly Film Bulletin (1987) Review of film *Business as Usual*, Vol.54, Part 644.

Moore, Robert (1975) *Racism and Black Resistance in Britain* (London: Pluto).

Moreno, Clara, Carmen Pedrosa, Jenny Stiles and Anne Lamming (1982) 'Resident domestics campaign', in Ann Curneo et al. (eds) *Women in Collective Action* (London: Association of Community Workers).

Morris, Jenny (1991) *Pride Against Prejudice* (London: Women's Press).

Munro, Anne (1990) *Women in Trade Unions: a Study of Hospital Ancillary Workers* (Warwick: PhD Thesis, University of Warwick).

NALGO (1991) *Childcare and Mothercare: Provision for the 1990s* (London: NALGO).

NALGO National Women's Committee (1992a) *Stop Sexual Harassment in the Workplace: Guidelines for NALGO Branches* (London: NALGO).

NALGO National Women's Committee (1992b) *You Are Not Alone: Domestic Violence is a Trade Union Issue* (London: NALGO).

NATFHE (1991) 'Women's TUC Blackpool' *Natfhe Journal*, No. 2.

NCCL (National Council for Civil Liberties) (1989) *Equal Rights for Women*, Vol. 4 No. 1.

Nelson, Jayne (1977/8) *Women in Trade Unions: the Use of Special Women's Officers, Committees and Groups, their Influence and Effectiveness*, mimeo (London: WRRC Feminist Library).

Norfolk, Bob and Jim Stirton (1985) *A Preliminary Report on Stress* (London: NUPE).

North Yorkshire Women Against Pit Closures (1985) *Strike 84-5*, People's History of Yorkshire IX (Leeds: North Yorkshire WAPC).

NPEC (National Pay Equity Campaign) (1992a) *Revaluing Women's Work, Winning Pay Equality*, Report of 1991 NPEC Conference (London: NPEC).

NPEC (1992b) 'Campaigning for pay equality: lessons from home and abroad' in NPEC (1992a).

NUCPS (1988) *Union Matters: Advisory Structures* (London: NUCPS).

NUPE (1966-76, 1988) *Public Employees* (London: NUPE).

NUPE (1984) *Women's Working Party Report* (London: NUPE).

NUPE (1992) *Indirect discrimination: how to spot hidden race discrimination, a guide for negotiators,* NUPE Guidelines (London: NUPE).
NUPE (c. 1992a) *Dealing with cases of racial harassment,* NUPE Guidelines (London: NUPE).
NUPE (c. 1992b) *Working for Just Immigration Laws* (London:NUPE).
NUPE N. Ireland Women's Committee, (1992) *Women's Voices: an Oral History of Northern Irish Women's Health* (Dublin: Attic Press).
NUT (1980) *Promotion and the Woman Teacher* (London:NUT).
Oakley, Anne (1974) *The Sociology of Housework* (Oxford: Martin Robertson).
Oakley, Anne (1981) *Subject Women* (Oxford: Martin Robertson).
Olsen, Tillie (1980) *Silences* (London: Virago).
Parmar, Pratibha (1982) 'Gender, class and race: Asian women in resistance' in (ed.) Centre for Cultural Studies, University of Birmingham *The Empire Strikes Back: Race and Racism in the 1970s* (London: Hutchinson).
Pateman, Trevor (1975) *Language, Truth and Politics* (Sidmouth: Jean Stroud and Pateman).
Phillips, Angela (1991) 'Jobs for the girls', *Guardian*, Nov.12.
Phillips, Anne (1987) *Divided Loyalties* (London: Virago).
Phillips, Anne and Barbara Taylor (1980) 'Sex and skill: notes towards a feminist economics', *Feminist Review*, No. 6.
Phizacklea, Annie (1983) (ed.) *One-Way Ticket, Migration and Female Labour* (London: Routledge and Kegan Paul).
Pollert, Anna (1981) *Girls, Wives, Factory Lives* (London: Macmillan).
Porter, Marilyn (1982) 'Standing on the edge: working class housewives and the world of work' in West (ed.).
Pringle, Rosemary (1988) *Secretaries Talk: Sexuality, Power and Work* (London: Allen and Unwin).
PSA (Public Service Action) (1983) Nos 4 & 5 (London: SCAT Publications).
PSA (1984) No. 8 (London: SCAT Publications).
PSA (1985) No. 13 (London: SCAT Publications).
PSA (1988) No. 38 (London: SCAT Publications).
PSA (1989) No. 41 (London: SCAT Publications).
Purcell, Kate (1979) 'Militancy and acquiescence amongst women workers' in Sandra Burman (ed.) *Fit Work for Women* (London: Croom Helm).
Purcell, Kate (1982) 'Female manual workers: fatalism and the reinforcement of inequalities' in D. Robbins et al. (eds) *Re-thinking Social Inequality* (London: Gower).

Purcell, Kate (1986) *Gender and Experience at Work: an Ethnographic Study of Work and Social Interaction in a Manufacturing Workshop* (PhD Thesis, University of Manchester).

Purcell, Kate (1989) 'Gender and the experience of employment' in Duncan Gallie (ed.) *Employment in Britain* (London: Basil Blackwell).

Redclift, Nanneke and M. Thea Sinclair (eds) (1991) *Working Women: International Perspectives on Labour and Gender Ideology* (London and New York: Routledge).

Rees, Teresa (1990) 'Gender, power and trade union democracy' in Fosh and Heery (eds).

Riley, Denise (1983) *War in the Nursery: Theories of the Child and Mother* (London: Virago).

Robbins, Diana (1986) *Wanted: Railman* (London: HMSO).

Robertson, N. and K. Sams (eds) (1976) 'The role of the full-time officer', *Economic and Social Review*, Vol. 18, No. 1.

Roche, Jim (1970) 'The Leeds clothing strike', *Trade Union Register*.

Roundtable (1988) 'Mending the broken heart of socialism', in Chapman and Rutherford (eds).

Rowbotham, Sheila (1989a) *The Past is Before Us* (Harmondsworth: Penguin).

Rowbotham, Sheila (1989b) 'Making way for homeworkers', *Guardian*, November 5.

Rowbotham, Sheila, Lynne Segal and Hilary Wainwright (1979) *Beyond the Fragments* (London: Merlin).

Savage, Mike (1992) 'Women's expertise, men's authority: gendered organization and the contemporary middle class' in Savage and Witz (eds).

Savage, Mike and Anne Witz (1992) 'The gendering of organizations' in Savage and Witz (eds).

Savage, Mike and Anne Witz (eds) (1992) *Gender and Bureaucracy* (London: Blackwells).

Saville, John (1988) *The Labour Movement in Britain* (London: Faber & Faber).

Seccombe, Wally (1974) 'The housewife and her labour under capitalism', *New Left Review*, No. 83.

Segal, Lynne (1990) *Slow Motion: Changing Men* (London: Virago).

SERTUC (South East Regional Trades Union Council) (1987) *Moving Towards Equality* (London: Greater London Trade Union Resource Unit).

SERTUC (1989) *Still Moving Towards Equality* (London: Greater London Trade Union Resource Unit).

Shaw, Marion (1984) 'The 53rd women's TUC conference' in Joy Holland (ed.) *Feminist Action* (London: Battle Axe Books).
Simmons, Michael (1989) 'Some perspectives on how to make equal opportunity training effective', *Journal of European Industrial Training*.
Simpson, Bill (1973) *Labour: The Unions and the Party* (London: Allen and Unwin).
Sinclair, M. Thea (1991) 'Women, work and skill: economic theories and feminist perspectives' in Redclift and Sinclair (eds).
Social Trends (1991) (London: HMSO).
Sociology (1989) 'The concept of patriarchy' Vol. 23, No. 2.
Somerton, Michael, Keith Forrester and Jonathan Fry (1988) *Trade Union Action on Low Pay* (Batley: West Yorkshire Low Pay Unit).
Spender, Dale (1982) *Invisible Women* (London: Writers and Readers Publishing Cooperative).
Stageman, Jane (1980) *Women in Trade Unions* (Hull: Industrial Studies Unit, University of Hull).
Stead, Jean (1987) *Never the Same Again: Women and the Miner's Strike* (London: Women's Press).
Stone, Karen (1983) 'Motherhood and waged work: West Indian, Asian and White mothers compared' in A. Phizacklea (ed.).
Stoneman, Patsy (1988) *Maternal Thinking*, Occasional paper No. 7 (Hull: Hull Centre for Gender Studies).
Sulaiman, Sandy (1991) 'Tipping the scales of injustice', *Guardian,* May 23.
Sweet and Maxwell (1991) 'Release 1: 15-ix-91', *Encyclopaedia of Employment Law*.
Tate, Jane (1993) 'Organising homeworkers in Canada', *Yorkshire and Humberside Low Pay Unit Newsletter*, No. 15.
Taylor, Barbara (1983) *Eve and the New Jerusalem* (London: Virago).
TGWU (1988) *Trade Unions in the Community: a TGWU Consultative Link-up Conference* (London: TGWU).
TGWU (1989a) *Forward T&G* (London: TGWU).
TGWU (1989b) *Putting Kids in the Picture* (London: TGWU).
TGWU (1990) *Carers at Work* (London: TGWU).
TGWU (1991a) *Equality Fact Pack* (London: TGWU).
TGWU (1991b) *Equality for All* (London: TGWU).
TGWU (1991c) *Changing Values: Winning Equal Pay for Work of Equal Value* (London: TGWU).
TGWU (1992) *T&G Record* (London: TGWU).
Tolson, Andrew (1977) *The Limits of Masculinity* (London: Tavistock).

Tribune (1986) 17 January.
TUC (1975) *Charter: Twelve Aims for Working Women* (London: TUC).
TUC (1978a) *Trade Union Charter for Facilities for the Under-Fives* (London: TUC).
TUC (1978b) *A Statement on Homeworking* (London: TUC).
TUC (1979a) *Charter for Equality for Women within Trade Unions* (London: TUC).
TUC (1979b) *Congress Report* (London: TUC).
TUC (1981) *Black Workers' Charter* (re-issued 1988) (London: TUC)
TUC (1983) *Working Women* (London: TUC).
TUC (1984) *Images of Inequality: the Portrayal of Women in the Media and Advertising* (London: TUC).
TUC (1985a) *TUC Guide on the Employment of Disabled People* (London: TUC).
TUC (1985b) *Homeworking: a TUC Statement* (London: TUC).
TUC (1986) *The Wider Involvement of Women in the Trade Union Movement* (London: TUC).
TUC (1987) *Black and Ethnic Minority Women in Employment and Trade Unions* (London: TUC).
TUC (1989a) *Equality in Action: a Guide to Removing Sex Bias from Collective Agreements* (London: TUC)
TUC (1989b) *Childcare and Nursery Education - a TUC Charter* (London: TUC).
TUC (1989c) *Black women and Trade Unions: a TUC Checklist* (London: TUC).
TUC (1990a) *Charter for Equality for Women in the Trade Union Movement* (London: TUC).
TUC (1990b) *Charter for Women at Work* (London: TUC).
TUC (1990c) *Trades Union Congress Publications List* (London: TUC).
TUC (1990d) *Racial Harassment at Work* (London: TUC).
TUC (1990e) *Women Across Europe Conference May 2* (London: TUC).
TUC (1990f) *Race Discrimination at Work* (London: TUC).
TUC (1990g) *Childcare Resource Pack* (London: TUC)
TUC (1990h) *Trade Unions Working for Equality: a Resource List of Union Work for Equality of Opportunity* (London: TUC).
TUC (1990i) *Women and Europe: a Trade Union Guide* (London: TUC).
TUC (1990j) *Women's Skills* (London: TUC).
TUC (1990k) *Annual Report to the Women's Conference of the TUC* (London: TUC).
TUC (1991a) *Unions and Europe in the 1990s* (London, TUC).
TUC (1991b) *More than you Bargained for* (TUC: London).

TUC (1991c) *Involvement of Black Workers in Trade Unions* (London: TUC).
TUC (1991d) *Working Women* (London: TUC).
TUC (1991e) *General Congress Report* (London: TUC)
TUC (1992) *Out of School Childcare - a Negotiator's Guide* (London: TUC).
Tuckman, Alan (1985) *Industrial Action and Hegemony: Workplace Occupations in Britain 1971-1981*, PhD thesis, University of Hull.
Turner, A. H. (1962) *Trade Union Growth, Structure and Policy: A Comparative Study of the Cotton Unions* (London: Allen and Unwin).
Turner, Victor W. (1969) *The Ritual Process: Structure and Anti-Structure* (Harmondsworth: Penguin).
UCATT (1989) *Blueprint for Equality* (London: UCATT).
UNISON (1992) *UNISON Rules as at Vesting Day 1993* (London: UNISON).
USDAW (1987) *Getting Involved: Members' Views and Priorities* (Manchester: USDAW).
USDAW (1990) *Women in USDAW: Listening to Part-Time Workers* (Manchester: USDAW).
Virdee, Satnam (1992) *Part of the Union? Trade Union Participation by Ethnic Minority Workers* (London: Commission for Racial Equality).
Virdee, Satnam (1993) *Self-Organization: a Strategy for Tackling Racism* (London: CRE/CRER).
Wajcman, Judy (1983) *Women in Control* (Milton Keynes: Open University Press).
Walby, Sylvia (1986) *Patriarchy at Work* (Cambridge: Polity Press).
Walby, Sylvia (1990) *Theorizing Patriarchy* (London: Basil Blackwell).
Walton, Jenny (1991) 'Women shop stewards in a county branch of NALGO', in Redclift and Sinclair (eds).
Watson, Diane (1988) *Managers of Discontent: Trade Union Officers and Industrial Relations Managers* (London: Routledge).
Weber, Max (1966) *The Theory of Social and Economic Organisation* (New York: Free Press).
Weir, Angela and Mary McIntosh (1982) 'Towards a wages strategy for women', *Feminist Review*, No. 10.
West, Jackie (ed.)(1982) *Work, Women and the Labour Market* (London: Routledge).
West Yorkshire Low Pay Unit (1990) *A Penny a Bag: Campaigning on Homework* (Batley: West Yorkshire Low Pay Unit).
Westwood, Sallie (1984) *All Day Every Day* (London: Pluto).
White, Aidan (1986) 'Cleaning up on equal pay', *Guardian*, March 10.

Wilson, Amrit (1978) *Finding a Voice* (London: Virago).
Wintour, P. (1985) 'Women pledge to sustain fight against pit closures', *Guardian*, August 19.
Wise, Sue and Liz Stanley (1987) *Georgie Porgie: Sexual Harassment in Everyday Life* (London: Pandora).
Wouters, C. (1989) 'The sociology of emotions and flight attendants', *Theory, Culture and Society,* Vol. 6, No. 1.
Wrench, John (1987) 'Unequal comrades: trade unions, equal opportunity and racism' in Richard Jenkins and John Solomons (eds) *Racism and Equal Opportunity Policies in the 1980s* (Cambridge: Cambridge University Press).
WWW (Women Working Worldwide) (1983) *International Conference Report* (Manchester: WWW, Department of Sociology, University of Manchester).
WWW (1992) *The Labour Behind the Label: Resource Pack on Women Working in the Global Textile and Garment Industries* (Manchester: WWW, Dept. of Sociology, University of Manchester).

Index

abortion 10, 30, 64, 65, 221
ACTT 29, 132, 137, 143, 154, 158, 160, 253, 254
adoption leave 197
AEEU 195, 222
AEF 104
AEU 142, 152, 153, 158, 160, 191, 252, 254
agenda, trade union
  feminizing 102, 117-118, 120-121, 124, 138-139, 144, 181, 205, 220-224, 241, 242
  formal 42, 43, 138-139, 171-173, 181-182, 226-227, 242
  informal 42, 43, 45, 144, 172-173, 181
agricultural workers 209
ancillary workers, see hospital workers
APEX 106, 137, 152, 158, 159
apprenticeships 193
Anti-Sweating League 25
Asian women 105-108, 117, 156, 194, see also black women
ASLEF 137, 153, 195, 196
ASTMS 132, 142
asylum seekers 157, 212
attraction, policies of 131-138, 228-229
'atypical' workers 185, 204-205, 210
AUEW 29
AUT 147, 153, 154, 210, 253, 254

BALPA 253

Barking Hospital 109-112
BECTU 216
BETA 254
BFAWU 253
BIFU 154, 159, 189, 216-217, 229, 252, 254
black
  employees 7-8, 18, 43, 154, 155, 254
  union representation of 32, 135, 138, 139, 142, 143, 150, 154, 156-157, 158,162-165, 166, 173, 194, 240
  women 8, 156
  union representation of 32, 106-108, 132, 135, 153, 162-165, 222, 229, 240, 242
  negotiations for 157, 186, 189, 194, 211-214, 232
  see also Asian women
bonus schemes 37, 43, 47, 49, 69
  see also extra payments
Bradford nursery nurses campaign 191, 225
branch
  agenda 42, 43
  feminizing 99-100, 119-127
  men
    and control 43, 47, 51, 52, 53-54, 83, 89-90
    and domination 37-40, 43, 46, 48, 143
    and power 46, 50, 51-52, 78-80, 91
  officers 37, 50, 62, 71-72, 78-79, 83-

275

85, 85-87, 96, 143, 152-153, 172

procedures 49-50, 52-53, 54, 72, 78-79, 90, 121-123
structure 37, 87-89, 96-97
women
 exclusion of 37-40, 41-46, 71-72, 84, 87-88, 237
 challenges of 44-45, 48-50, 54-55, 65-66, 88-91, 97-100, 239
breadwinner, concept of male, see family wage
Bryan, Beverley 108

Cameron, Ivy 14, 229, 234
Campbell, Beatrix 179, 180, 187, 188, 205, 220
Campaign Against Racist Laws 212
cancer screening 143, 221-222
canteen workers 188
career breaks 197-198, 204
carers 132, 139, 196-199, 221, 242
caretakers 82-91
capitalism 4, 8-9, 58, 81
Case 1 36-46, 51, 54, 177, 249
Case 2 47-55, 174, 175, 249
Case 3 56-67, 249
Case 4 69-74, 79-80, 146, 155, 249
Case 5 74-80, 177, 250
Case 6 82-91, 99-100, 177, 250
Case 7 92-100, 250
Case 8 119-127, 173, 227, 250
Case 9 174-178, 185, 250
casual workers 200, 203, 206, 209, 237, 241
Cavendish, Ruth 35, 36, 47, 81
CCSU 254
challenge, see women and challenge
child abuse 221, 242
childcare 22
 provision 122, 193, 198 199
 union support 29, 30, 43, 65, 77, 122, 132, 135, 159, 185, 224, 242
Charles, Nicola 35
Charters, see TUC Charters
civil servants 26, 27, 103, 198
class 40, 55, 56, 57, 103, 104, 112, 113, 145, 163, 188, 241

CLCLC 120, 145, 159, 166, 167

cleaners 38, 39, 48, 49, 52, 103, 108, 220
 school 82-91, 190
cleaning
 contracts 121, 214-215, 220-221
 social value of 120-121
clerical workers 27
Cockburn, Cynthia 4, 9, 13, 14, 16, 17, 22, 119, 120, 122, 123, 173, 181, 182, 189, 203, 211, 223, 224, 225, 230, 231, 238
Cohen, Sheila 150, 152
COHSE 36, 45, 69, 132, 139, 142, 144, 151, 152, 160, 163, 195, 225, 252, 254
 see also Case 1
collective bargaining, see negotiation
Colling, Trevor 136, 143, 152, 172, 173, 174, 179, 184, 186
community
 and union links 102, 108-118, 124, 166, 208, 212-214, 225, 238
 issues 102, 112, 117, 221-222
Connell, R. W. 9, 15
competitive tendering 31, 108, 111, 121, 124, 166, 206-207, 220
consciousness 56, 57, 58, 116
 class 55, 57, 112, 113
 gender 55, 56-57, 59, 62-63, 66-67, 70, 73-74, 76-80, 81, 82, 238
 trade union 36, 56, 66, 70, 73-74, 75-76, 78-80, 81, 238
Conservative Party 30, 132, 139-140
consultation 139-140, 226-227
contractual rights 171
cooks, school 69-70, 71, 87-88
corporate voice 161, 162, 163, 164, 167, 211, 239-240
Coyle, Angela 17, 110, 111, 138, 225, 231
CPSA 29, 152
CRE 194, 212, 233
creche facilities, see childcare
CSU 142, 216
CUCW 27
culture
 local 84-87, 92-95

of femininity 3, 8, 10, 15-18, 46, 117, 125-126, 140, 156, 168, 181, 186, 201-218, 219-234, 238, 241, 243
of masculinity 3, 10, 13-15, 19, 41, 45, 46, 51, 52, 53, 54, 71, 81, 84, 115, 119, 126, 127, 137, 139, 140, 148, 160, 168, 181, 185, 186, 200, 228, 238, 239, 241, 243
trade union 3, 13-15, 51, 53, 136, 140
see also feminizing
Cunnison, Sheila 5, 13, 14, 41, 42, 61, 141, 150, 151-152, 155, 173, 174, 180, 188, 195

democracy
trade union 4, 11, 78-79, 117, 133, 139, 139-140, 149-150, 155, 179, 217-218, 237, 240
deportation 212
Dickens, Linda 136, 143, 152, 172, 173, 174, 179, 184, 186
differences 7, 139
men and women 4, 8, 9-10, 210
ethnic and cultural 7, 8, 18, 210
see also diversity
disabled
employees 8, 43, 207, 254
union representation of 32, 135, 139, 142, 143, 144, 157, 158, 162-165, 240
negotiations for 216-217, 222
women 11, 19, 32, 91, 135, 158, 162-165, 216-217, 222
discrimination 11, 32, 105, 150, 174
direct 180
indirect 180, 212
race 7-8, 105, 180, 212, 223, 233
sex 20, 29, 74, 77, 174, 180, 194, 229
diversity 7-8, 241
of voice 11-12, 150
of women 11, 156, 164-165, 210-217
union representation of 149-150, 155, 156-165, 210-217, 241
domestic responsibilities 4, 5, 6, 9, 12, 187
and trade unions 12, 30, 40-41, 55, 82, 84, 91, 92, 94, 145, 177, 185, 196-199, 202-203, 229, 241
see also reproductive work
domestic violence 65, 221, 222-223, 242

EC 173, 183-185, 187, 191, 198, 225-226
directives 183, 184, 197, 206
TUC 185, 194
Women's Lobby 185, 225
education, trade union 48, 53, 70, 74, 95, 145-147, 228
women-only 48, 53, 78, 82, 146-147, 243
feminizing 70, 146-147
EETPU 133, 191
EIS 253
Elliot, Ruth 74, 139, 140
Elizabeth Garrett Anderson Hospital 109
EMA 153
Employment Act(s) 31
Employment Protection Act 1975 28, 196
empowerment, policies of 157-168, 218, 239, 243
encouragement, policies of 138-145, 243
engineering workers 22
EOC 12, 150, 184, 187, 195
equal opportunities 19, 20, 29, 135, 161, 162, 232
bargaining 180, 185-186, 190-191, 193, 195, 216
employment policies 8, 12, 133, 173, 200, 215
TUC policy 29-30, 147, 247-248
equal pay 20, 21, 22, 60, 61, 86, 117, 132, 180, 186-187, 237
bargaining 188-191
Royal Commission for 28
TUC policy 24, 27-28, 29, 103, 138
women's action for 24, 27-28, 103-108
Equal Pay Act 1970 28, 86, 104-105, 135, 139, 180, 183-184, 237
Equal Pay (Amendment) Regulations 1983 51, 86-87, 174, 180, 184, 187-188, 206
Equal Pay Directive (EC) 183-184
Equal Rights Department (TUC) 144, 157

Equal Rights Officers 141-142, 143, 146, 165, 166, 179, 211, 232, 233, 254
  see also Women's Officers
equality audit 190-191, 206
ethnic identity 7-8, 18, 156
ethnic minorities 18, 138, 150, 157, 242,
  see also Black, Asian Women
extra payments 37, 43, 47, 49, 69, 192-193

Fabian Society 58
Factory Acts, see protective legislation
factory workers 28, 48-50,102, 104, 106-107, 174-178, 189
fair representation, see representation, trade unions
Fakenham, occupation of 35
family
  endowment movement 12, 26-27
  ideology 9, 40-42
  wage 12, 14, 21, 26, 47, 73, 86, 134, 178, 186, 191-192, 237
FBU 132, 153, 162, 196, 253, 254
FDA 143, 152, 153, 154, 216, 228, 253
femininity, concept of 6, 15-18,
  see also culture of femininity
feminism 3, 9, 21, 32, 58, 59, 63, 80, 82
  equal rights 10, 23, 27
  radical 10
  second wave 10-11, 28-29, 62, 102, 185, 205
  socialist 10, 65, 66
  welfare 10, 26-27
feminizing
  agenda 102, 117-118, 120-121, 124, 138-139, 144, 181, 205, 218, 220-224, 241
  branch 99-100, 119-127
  education 70, 146-147
  negotiation 121, 144, 181-182, 185, 224-234, 241, 243
  paid officer 124-125, 126-127, 181, 227-231
First World War 24, 25
flexibility
  work patterns 137, 202-204, 241
  negotiation 217

Ford, sewing machinists' strike 28, 104
Fosh, Patricia 150, 152
Fryer, R. H. 151

gay men 19, 139, 143, 150, 157, 160, 161, 162-165, 173, 216, 240
  see also sexuality
gender 4-6, 16, 60-62, 63-66, 232
  consciousness 50, 55, 62-63, 66-67, 70, 73-74, 76-78, 79-80, 81
  difference 4, 8, 9-10, 210
  identity 11, 16, 81, 150
    see also sex discrimination, women's issues
GMB 133, 135, 136, 137, 142, 143, 153, 154, 159, 160, 162, 179, 189, 190, 192, 193, 194, 197, 200, 204, 208, 212, 216, 222, 223, 224, 252, 254
GMBATU 133, 146
GMWU 69, 84, 100
  see also Case 6
GNCTU 22
GPMU 208
government schemes 210
grading structures 48, 51, 184, 194
  regrading 104, 189-190, 206, 212, 237
grass roots 14, 32, 50, 91, 101-102, 105, 123, 125, 139-140, 167, 185, 226-227, 239, 242
Greenham Common 115
Grunwick 106-108

Haraway, Donna 9, 17, 196, 238
Heery, Edmund 126, 175, 178, 193, 227-228, 229, 231
health
  and safety 132, 144, 207, 209, 222, 226
  women's 20, 132, 143, 185, 221-222, 242
Heathrow Airport 138, 214-215
homeworkers 137, 138, 173, 203, 204, 207-209, 214, 225, 242
homosexuality, see sexuality
homosocial 37-38
hospital workers 36-46, 69, 73, 74-80, 119-127, 132, 188, 190, 191, 212, 232, 233, 238
housing 20, 157, 242

Hunt, Judith 40, 57-58, 121, 132, 142, 160
Huws, Ursula 137, 173, 186, 194

ideology 56, 58, 59, 66-67
　class 40, 58, 59
　family 9, 40, 41
　feminist 57, 58, 59, 60, 62, 63
　left wing 58-59, 60, 62, 63, 73
　trade union 45, 58, 73, 74, 79-80
identity 5-6, 11, 16, 18, 81, 138, 150, 156, 157
ILP 24
image 14, 132-137, 185, 214
immigrant workers 138, 150, 157, 212-214
Immigration Act 1971 211
Indian Workers Association 215
industrial action 64-65, 68-69, 72-74, 75-76, 97-99, 180
　women-initiated 89-91, 101-118, 221, 242
industrial relations, see negotiation
industrial tribunals 105, 184, 187, 195, 207, 209, 233, 237
inequality, see discrimination
Insurance Act 1911 24
International Ladies Garment Workers Union 208
IRSF 138, 152, 158, 162, 254
ISTC 253
IPMS 139, 143, 153, 154, 166, 226, 253

job evaluation schemes 185, 189-190
job segregation
　by sex 5, 6, 13, 38-39, 41, 46, 61, 70, 74, 82, 84, 105, 177, 179, 193
job sharing 127, 193, 204, 229
　see also flexibility
justice, sword of 219, 242, 243

Kelly, John 126, 175, 178, 193, 227-228, 229, 231

Labour Party 24, 58, 69, 73, 77, 104, 150
Labour Representation Committee 1, 24
Lee, Gloria 132, 154
Ledwith, Sue 39, 91, 152, 174, 175, 186

Lady Truckers' Club 193
language 18-19, 213, 214
LRD 132, 137, 142, 143, 144, 152, 153, 154, 162, 166, 172, 188, 192, 206, 207, 214, 216, 226
lay officers 71-72, 85-87, 94-95
　see also branch officers, shop stewards
Leeds clothing workers 104
Leicester Outworkers 138, 208
　see also homeworking
lesbians 11, 19, 43, 156
　union representation 32, 139, 143, 150, 157, 160, 161, 162-165, 240
　negotiations for 173, 215-216, 222
　see also sexuality
local government 191, 193, 194, 195, 200, 206, 212, 233
London Dock Strike 24, 180
low pay 7, 30, 73, 102-103, 117, 133, 134, 135, 137-138, 164, 191-192, 212, 239, 240

men
　and bonding 37-38, 40, 45, 53-54
　and control 15, 36, 41, 43, 47, 50, 51, 52, 53-54, 83, 86, 89-90, 174, 175
　and domination 5, 37-40, 43, 45, 46, 48, 51, 91, 143, 227, 228
　and power 9, 13, 14, 46, 50, 51-52, 78-80, 91, 135, 168, 174, 182, 195, 238, 243
　and violence, see domestic violence
　see also culture of masculinity
management
　women into, 150-151, 186, 193, 230
　manual workers 102-118, 189, 191, 192, 207, 212
　see also Cases 1, 2, 4, 5, 6, 7, 8, 9
masculinity, concept of 6, 13-15
　see also culture of masculinity
Matchgirls' strike 24
maternity 10, 29, 132, 137, 184, 185, 196-197, 224
Maternity Directive (EC) 184, 197
member-led strategies 119, 127, 227
membership, trade union 30, 31
　consultation of 139-140, 226-227
　of women 23-24, 28, 30

Migrant Action Group 213
Miners' Strike 31, 82, 238
Miners' Wives, see WAPC
minimum wage 69, 77, 191-192, 206
 statutory control 25, 31, 207
minorities, see black, disabled, ethnic minorities, lesbians and gay men
minority group structures 210-218, 240, 254
Morris, Jenny 11, 91, 155
monitoring 158, 194, 216, 239
MSF 137-138, 142, 146, 153, 154, 158, 159, 162, 195, 199, 216, 217, 240, 252, 254
multi-national organizations 110
MU 253
Munro, Anne 35, 39, 43, 150, 152, 173

NACO 253
NALGO 29, 132, 137,139, 143, 146, 151, 152, 154, 161, 164, 165, 191, 195, 196, 197, 198, 199, 200, 211, 215, 216, 222, 224, 225, 240, 252, 254
NAPO 154, 159, 160, 253
NAS 61
NAS/UWT 61, 252, 254
NATFHE 152, 153, 154, 159, 200, 210, 228, 232, 253
National Union of Women's Suffrage Societies 25
NCCL 12, 205
NCU 162, 216, 252, 254
NEC 70, 123, 153, 159, 160, 162, 163, 164, 172, 239
negotiation, trade union
 agenda 144, 171, 172, 173, 181
 collective bargaining 172, 174-179
 feminizing 121, 144, 181-182, 185, 219-234, 241, 242, 243
 legal background of 172, 180, 183-185
 men
  and control 47, 50, 51, 86, 174, 175, 240
  challenges to 186-200, 219-234
 structures of 47, 160, 172, 174-175
 women 175, 177, 179, 185-200, 241
networking 102, 127, 166-167, 185, 209, 225-226, 239

NFWW 24, 25, 140, 159
NGA 252, 254
NHS 69, 73, 74, 108-109, 111, 121, 190, 198, 199, 206, 212, 221, 232, 233
Northern Ireland 109, 119-127, 173, 181, 205, 206, 220, 227, 238, 243
NPEC 225
NUAAW 209
NUCPS 136, 142-143, 145, 158, 160, 162, 163, 164, 165, 205, 211, 226, 240, 252, 254
NUGW 140
NUHKW 208, 228, 254
NUJ 29, 137, 143, 144, 154, 158, 253
NULMW 154, 253
NUM 113, 116, 188
NUPE 29, 68, 69, 70, 82, 125, 132, 133-136, 137, 139, 142, 143, 146, 151, 152, 154, 159, 162, 163, 166, 189, 190, 192, 197, 202, 205, 206, 207, 210, 211, 212, 213, 220, 222, 225, 226, 227, 228, 229, 230, 233, 252, 254
 see also Cases 4, 5, 7, 8
NUR 152
nurses 36, 37, 38, 39, 44, 132, 134, 212, 232, 233
NUS 132
NUT 56, 60, 62, 67, 132, 142, 143, 144, 147, 152, 153, 154, 166, 210, 252, 254
 see also Case 3
NUTGW 104, 153, 166, 174, 175, 178, 222, 254
NUWT 61
NWAC, see TUC, Committees

occupational segregation, see job segregation
old people 157, 173, 199, 242
organization, trade union
 international links 110, 114, 225 226
 new forms of 110-111, 116, 119-127, 157
 self 157, 160-161, 162, 163, 167, 240
 separate 23-26
oppression 7, 11, 16, 18, 57, 58, 59, 81, 105, 156, 164-165
 see also subordination

280

organizer, see paid officer, trade union
outworkers, see homeworkers
Owenite movement 21-22

paid officer, trade union
  role of 14, 48, 52-53, 172, 173, 184, 188, 208, 215, 243
  feminizing 124-125, 126-127, 181, 227-231, 239
  in negotiation 177, 224, 234
  men
    attitudes of 70-71, 75, 84-85, 92-94, 243
  women
    under-representation 21, 177-178, 181
    see also Women's Officers
Parmar, Pratibha 106-107
parental leave 64, 185, 197
paternity leave 64, 132, 185, 193, 197
patriarchy 4-6, 8-9, 41, 46
part-time workers 30, 49, 52, 70, 79, 87, 102-103, 117, 133, 136, 138, 139, 184, 190, 200, 203, 204, 205-206, 210, 226, 227, 232, 237, 241, 242
pay 102, 226, 241
  differentials 51, 179, 190
  discrimination 47, 49, 51, 103, 133, 174, 223, 227, 232-233, 237
  extra payments 192-193, 237
  see also equal pay, low pay, value
pensions 144, 185, 242
Phizacklea, Annie 214
policies, trade union
  women
    attraction 131-138
    education of 145-148, 243
    empowerment of 157-168, 239, 243
    encouragement of 138-145, 239, 243,
    see also TUC Charters
Pollert, Anna 5, 35, 36, 41, 51, 57, 81
pornography 195, 221
positive action 30, 31, 239
  targets 158, 194, 239
positive discrimination, see positive action
power 9, 13, 14, 41, 46, 50, 51-52, 78-80, 91, 135, 168, 174, 182, 195, 238, 239

productive work 5, 40
private sector 133, 179, 193, 195
privatization 31, 79, 109-110, 124, 133, 206-207, 225
promotion 64, 67, 180, 186, 193-194, 197-198, 200, 212, 216, 241

proportionality 31, 150, 157-159, 164, 181, 230, 238
protective legislation 22-23, 24
publicity, union 70, 133-135, see also attraction, image
public service workers 11, 70, 103, 108, 179, 206-207, 220
  see also Cases 1, 4, 5, 6, 7
Purcell, Kate 11, 35, 37, 51, 57, 81, 174, 178

race 18, 32, 156, 232
  see also Asian women, black, ethnic minorities
racial discrimination 7-8, 105, 180, 212, 223, 233
Race Relations Act 1976 8, 12, 28, 211
racial harassment 106, 117, 196, 212
racism 7-8, 105-108, 147, 212
RCN 189
Rees, Teresa 14, 39, 91, 139, 150, 152, 177
recruitment, trade union 122, 132, 136, 137-138, 200, 205, 214, 216, 222, 228-229, 240
redundancy 58, 193, 199-200
repetitive strain injury 222
representation, trade union
  men
    numerical domination 37-40, 43, 45, 48, 51, 227-229
  self 155-157
  systems of 38, 149, 181
  women
    numbers, proportions 30, 31, 32, 136, 149, 151-155, 254
    union policies 138-145, 145-148, 157-168, 254
    see also black, disabled, lesbians, gay men, women's advisory structures

281

reproductive work, system of 5, 40, 45, see also domestic responsibilities
research staff, trade union 225, 226, 231-232
reserved seats 26, 30, 31, 70, 133, 134, 153, 159-160, 162, 164, 239
retirement 40, 134, 200
right to work, see work
RMT 138, 153, 154, 252
Rowbotham, Sheila 29, 103, 105, 112, 113, 115, 209, 210

secretarial workers 187, 189
school meals workers 69-74, 92-100, 124, 132, 207
Scottish TUC 27
SCPS 142, 145, 166
Second World War 28, 198
secret ballots 140
Segal, Lynne 15, 16, 196, 200
self-organization 157, 160-161, 162, 163, 167, 240
self-representation 155-157
separate development 23-26
SERTUC 31, 91, 142, 143, 178, 222
SEWA 208
sex discrimination 20, 29, 74, 77, 174, 180, 194, 229
Sex Discrimination Act 1975 12, 28, 135, 174, 180, 184, 195
sexism 61, 67, 85-86, 106, 147, 180, 186, 194-196, 241
 awareness training 147, 186
 union language 132
sexual harassment 32, 50, 132, 143, 167, 185, 194-196, 222, 229, 241
sexuality, 4, 8, 11, 19, 32, 43, 57, 139, 142, 143, 150, 156, 157, 160, 161-165, 173, 185, 215-216, 222, 240
sick pay 203, 206, 207
shop stewards 28, 48, 71, 151-152, 175-177
 men
 attitudes of 85-87, 94-95, 177, 178
 system of representation 38-39, 74
 women
 actions of 48-50, 55, 77-78, 96, 176
 see also branch officers, education, paid officers

Sisterhood of Leicestershire Wool Spinners 21
Six Point Group 27
skill 12, 13, 51, 186, 189-190, 201-202
Social Charter 184
sociological perspectives 3, 4-8
SOGAT 152, 188, 252
Stageman, Jane 30, 41, 51
STE 226, 253
statutory rights 172, 183-185
stress 4, 222, 228, 229
strikes
 anti-privatization 109-110
 miners' 31, 82, 238
 equal pay 104-108,
 see also Winter of Discontent,
structures, trade union, see branch, organization, NEC, Women's Advisory Structures, minority group structures
STUEAS 215
subordination 5, 7, 8, 11, 16, 22, 32, 57, 79, 81, 156, 161, 164, 211, 233, 240, 241, 243

TASS 103, 144, 153
teachers 56-67, 198
technological change 6, 22, 137
temporary workers 184, 203, 204, 207, 237, 241
terminology, see language
TGWU 47, 53, 77, 103, 106, 107, 138, 139, 142, 143, 154, 155, 159, 162, 165, 188, 189, 190, 191, 192, 193, 194, 195, 196, 197, 199, 202, 205, 206, 207, 209, 210, 211, 212, 213, 216, 222, 224, 231, 242, 252, 254,
 Link Up Campaign 206, 209, 214-215
 see also Case 2
Thatcherism, see Conservative Party
trade unions, see individual unions,TUC
 see also agenda, branch, education, membership, negotiation, organization, recruitment, representation, publicity
trade union officers, see branch officers, paid officers, shop stewards, women's officers
Trade Union Act 1984 31

282

Trade Union Reform and Employment Rights Bill 1993 184
training opportunities 180, 186, 193-194, 200, 216, 241
  see also education, trade union
Transfer of Undertakings Regulations 206-207
Trico strike 105
TSSA 137, 254
TUC 22, 23, 26, 28, 29, 32, 47, 53, 103, 132, 135, 138, 144, 146, 147, 151, 154, 159, 160, 165, 185, 191, 195, 299, 211, 215, 216, 240
  Charters
    Black Workers' 157
    Equality for Women within Trade Unions 30, 31, 53, 141, 150, 159, 239, 247-248, 254
    Facilities for the Under-Fives 30, 159
    Twelve Aims for Working Women 30, 157
    Women at work 32
  Committees
    Black Workers' 157
    Equal Rights 157
    Women's Advisory 26, 27, 28, 29, 140-141
  Statements on Homeworking 207-208
  see also education, Scottish TUC, WTUC
TWU 196

UCATT 160, 252, 254
UCW 153, 252
UDM 113
unemployment 26, 28, 30, 31, 157, 173, 203, 210
unfair dismissal 132, 207, 217
unions, see trade unions
union conference delegates 134, 153-154
union recognition 24, 106-108, 179
UNISON 139, 150, 151, 158, 162, 163-164, 165, 190, 239, 240
USDAW 138, 139, 142, 143, 147, 152, 154, 162, 188, 205, 209, 222, 225, 226, 227, 252, 254
UWT 61

value of women's work 52, 54, 103, 117, 120-121, 175, 178, 189-190, 196, 202, 220-221, 237
Virdee, Satnam 126, 161, 165, 196, 209, 214
visual display units 132, 222
voice 6, 8, 10-12, 120-121, 150, 161, 162, 163, 164, 167, 211, 237
vote, right to 23, 24, 25

Wages Act 1986 31
wage bargaining, see negotiation
Wages for Housework 202
Wajcman, Judy 35, 36, 57-58
Walby, Sylvia 22, 26, 59, 173, 241
WAPC 112, 113-117, 242
Westwood, Sallie 5, 35, 47, 51, 53, 57, 174
white collar workers 26, 103, 163, 190, 191, 192, 194, 198, 210
  see also Case 3
Winter of Discontent 30, 68-69, 72-73, 75-77, 78-80, 81-82, 93
women
  and challenge 23, 24, 25, 26-29, 31-32, 44-45, 48-50, 54-55, 65-66, 88-91, 97-100, 101-118, 221, 238, 242, 243
  and inaudibility 6, 8, 10-11, 120-121, 161, 237
  and invisibility 10-11
  and subordination 5, 7, 8, 11, 16, 22, 32, 79, 81, 161, 164, 211, 238, 240, 241, 243
  black 8, 32, 105-108, 117, 132, 135, 153, 156, 157, 162-165, 186, 189, 194, 211-214, 222, 232
  disabled 11, 19, 32, 91, 135, 158, 162-165, 216-217, 222
  lesbian 32, 139, 143, 150, 157, 160, 161, 162-165, 173, 215-216, 222
    see also culture of femininity
  Women's Advisory Structures 53, 140-145, 239, 247
    branch, workplace 143-144, 163, 247
    national 28, 30, 137, 140-143, 146, 162-165, 211, 247, 254
    regional 30, 53, 146, 163, 247, 254
    trades councils 27, 147, 209

see also corporate voice, proportionality, reserved seats
Women's Aid movement 29
Women's Co-operative Guild 25
women's health, see health
Women's Industrial Council 23
women's issues 20, 43, 44, 54, 63-66, 79, 102, 132, 135, 138-139, 144, 147, 220-224, 226, 240
Women's Officers 50, 53, 127, 141-142, 143, 146, 165, 166, 179, 211, 230, 232, 233, 242, 254
WTUC 29, 140, 141, 144, 160
Women's Trade Union League 23, 24, 26
work
  women
    access to 193-194
    insights 12-13
    marriage bar in 26, 61
    men's attitudes to 41-42, 95
    right to 21, 22, 23, 26, 117, 196, 199-200, 241
    value 52, 54, 103, 117, 120-121, 175, 178, 189-190, 196, 202, 220-221, 237
Working Women's Charter Group 29, 64
Wrench, John 105, 154, 196
WWW 166, 208

Yorkshire and Humberside Low Pay Unit 138
young people 157, 240